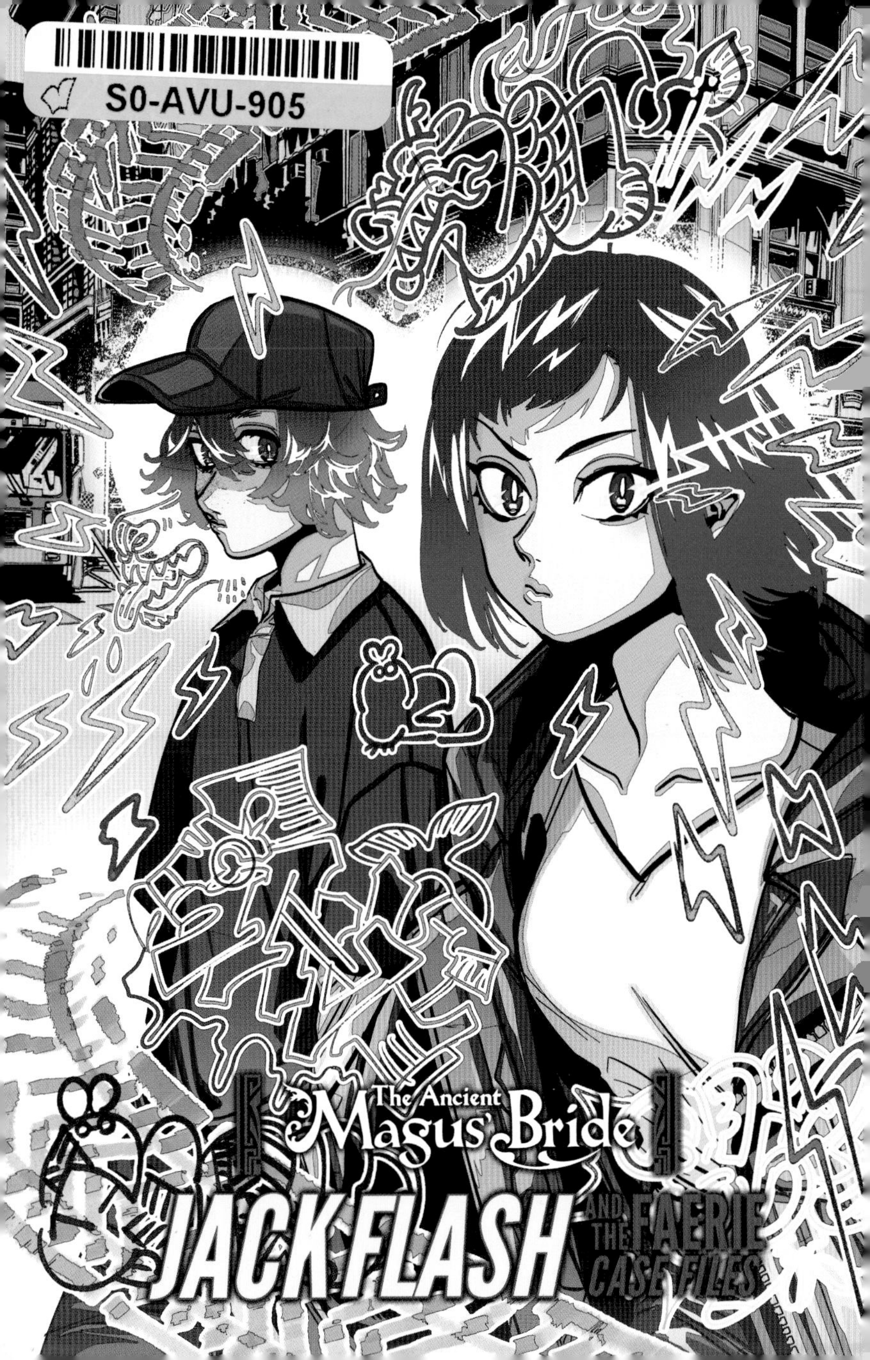
The Ancient
Magus' Bride
JACK FLASH
AND THE FAERIE
CASE FILES

The Ancient Magus' Bride

JACK FLASH AND THE FAERIE CASE FILES

| 3 |

#010 —————— 003

#011 —————— 029

#012 —————— 067

#013 —————— 107

#014 —————— 135

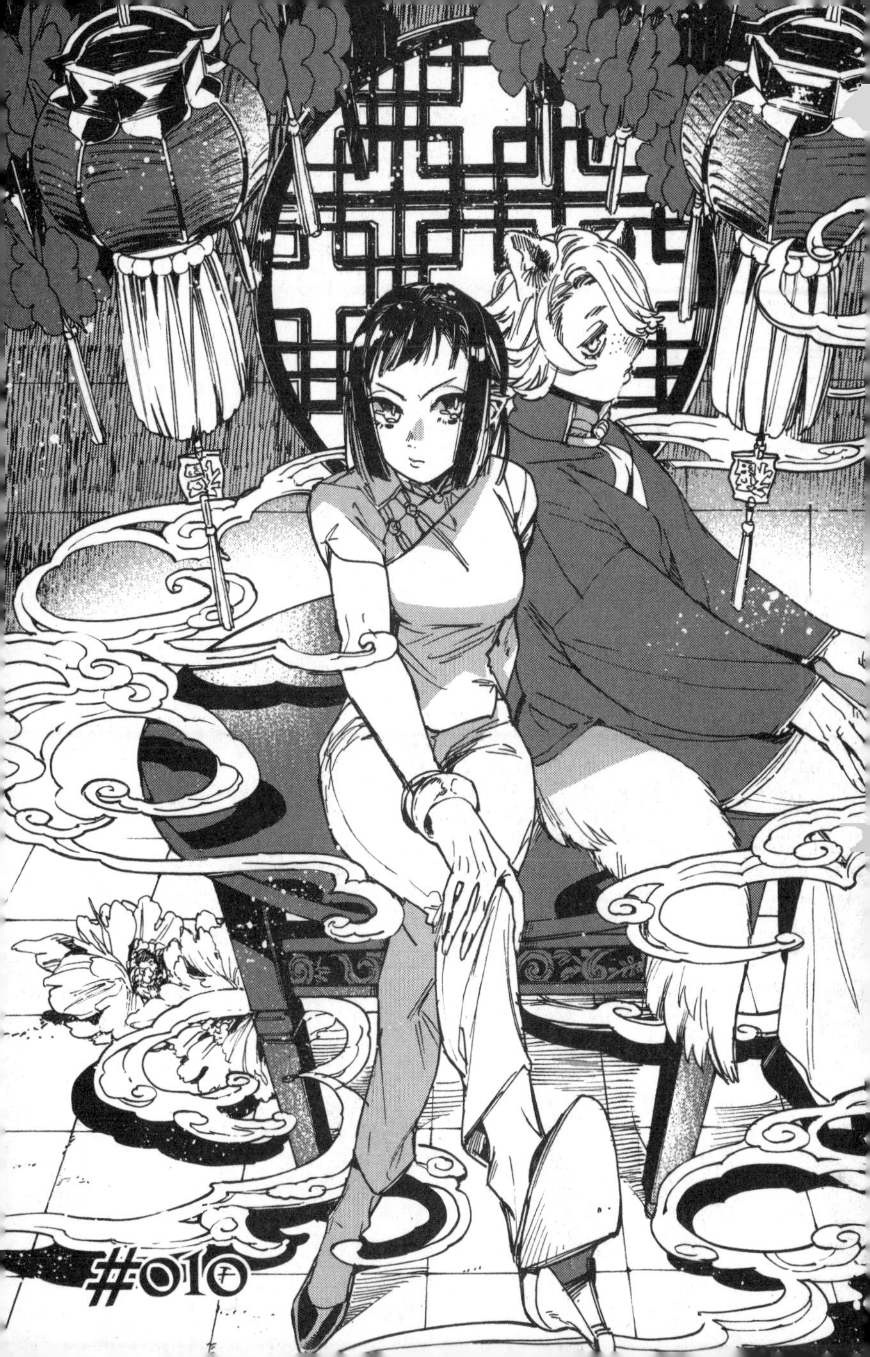
#010

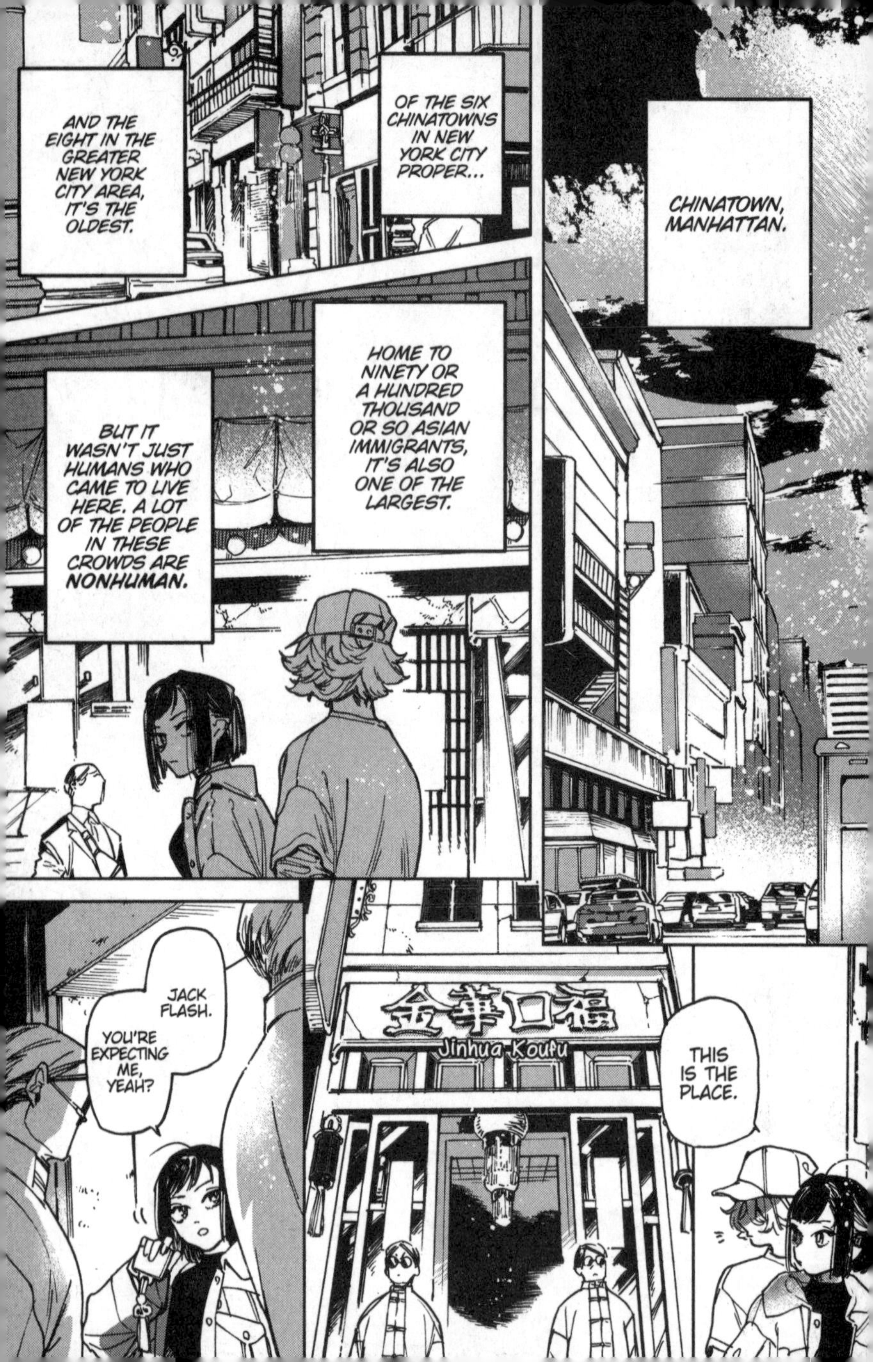

CHINATOWN, MANHATTAN.
OF THE SIX CHINATOWNS IN NEW YORK CITY PROPER...
AND THE EIGHT IN THE GREATER NEW YORK CITY AREA, IT'S THE OLDEST.
HOME TO NINETY OR A HUNDRED THOUSAND OR SO ASIAN IMMIGRANTS, IT'S ALSO ONE OF THE LARGEST.
BUT IT WASN'T JUST HUMANS WHO CAME TO LIVE HERE. A LOT OF THE PEOPLE IN THESE CROWDS ARE **NONHUMAN.**
THIS IS THE PLACE.
金華口福
Jinhua Koufu
JACK FLASH.
YOU'RE EXPECTING ME, YEAH?

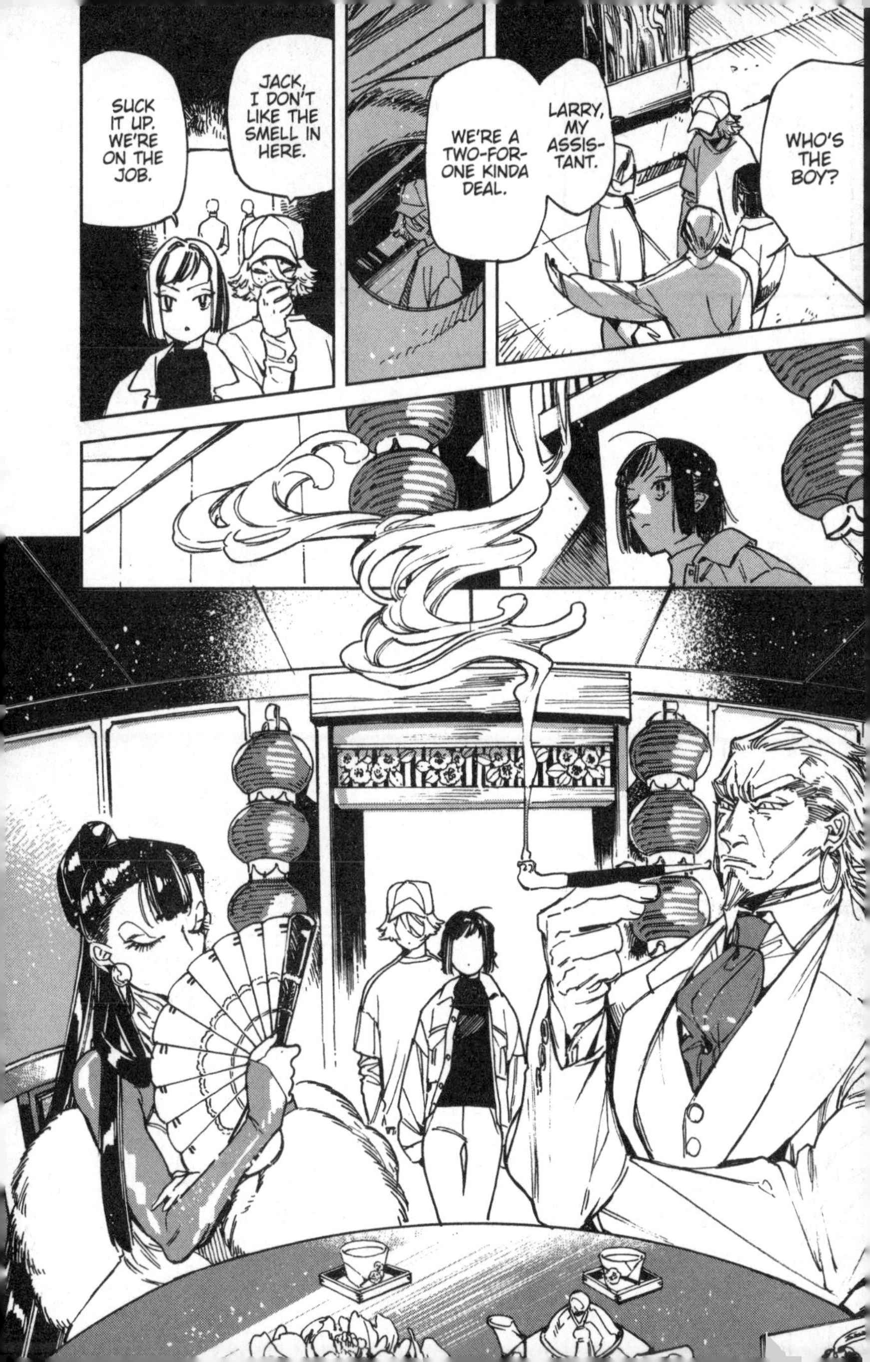
WHO'S THE BOY?
LARRY, MY ASSISTANT.
WE'RE A TWO-FOR-ONE KINDA DEAL.
JACK, I DON'T LIKE THE SMELL IN HERE.
SUCK IT UP. WE'RE ON THE JOB.

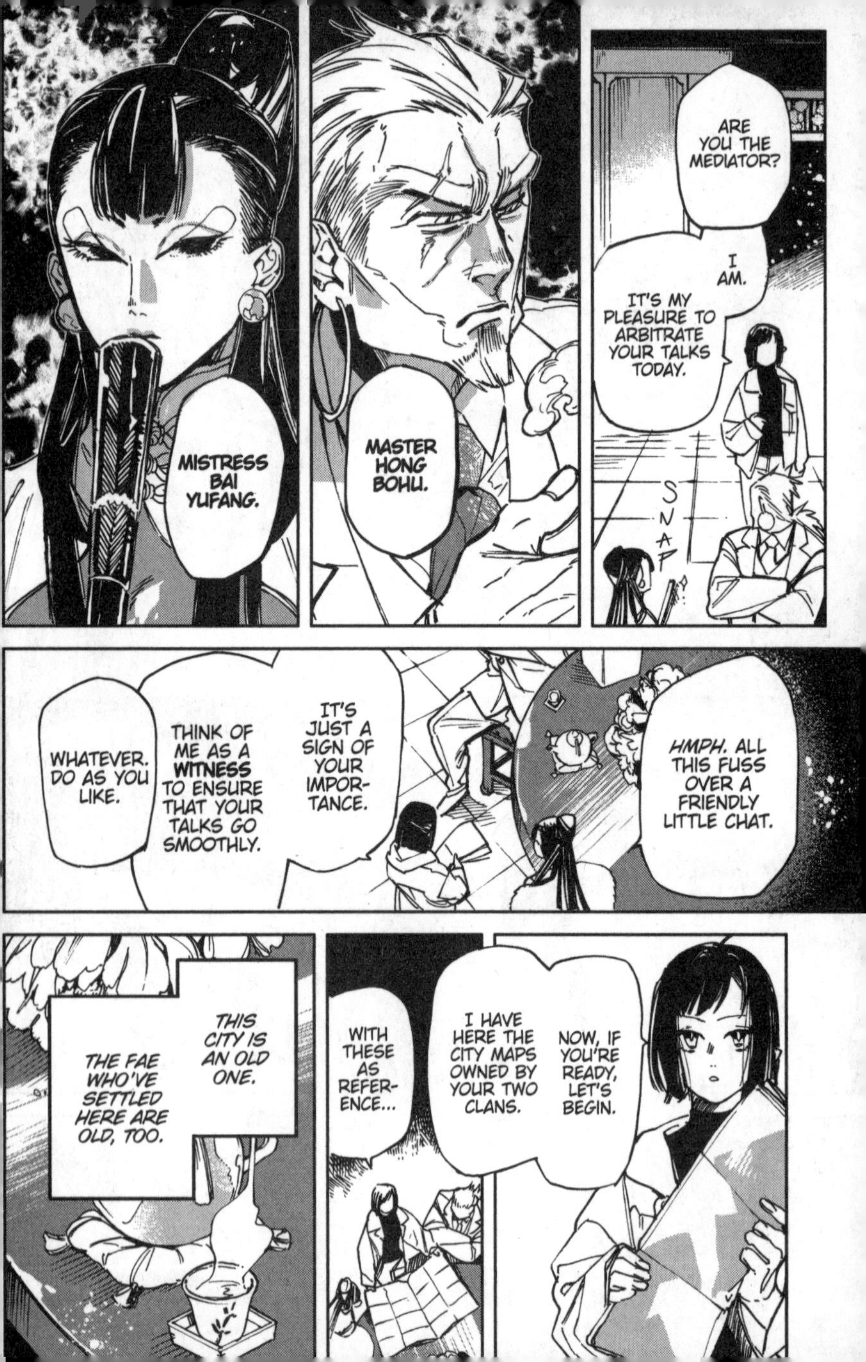
ARE YOU THE MEDIATOR?
I AM.
IT'S MY PLEASURE TO ARBITRATE YOUR TALKS TODAY.
SNAP
MASTER HONG BOHU.
MISTRESS BAI YUFANG.
HMPH. ALL THIS FUSS OVER A FRIENDLY LITTLE CHAT.
IT'S JUST A SIGN OF YOUR IMPORTANCE.
THINK OF ME AS A WITNESS TO ENSURE THAT YOUR TALKS GO SMOOTHLY.
WHATEVER. DO AS YOU LIKE.
NOW, IF YOU'RE READY, LET'S BEGIN.
I HAVE HERE THE CITY MAPS OWNED BY YOUR TWO CLANS.
WITH THESE AS REFERENCE...
THIS CITY IS AN OLD ONE.
THE FAE WHO'VE SETTLED HERE ARE OLD, TOO.

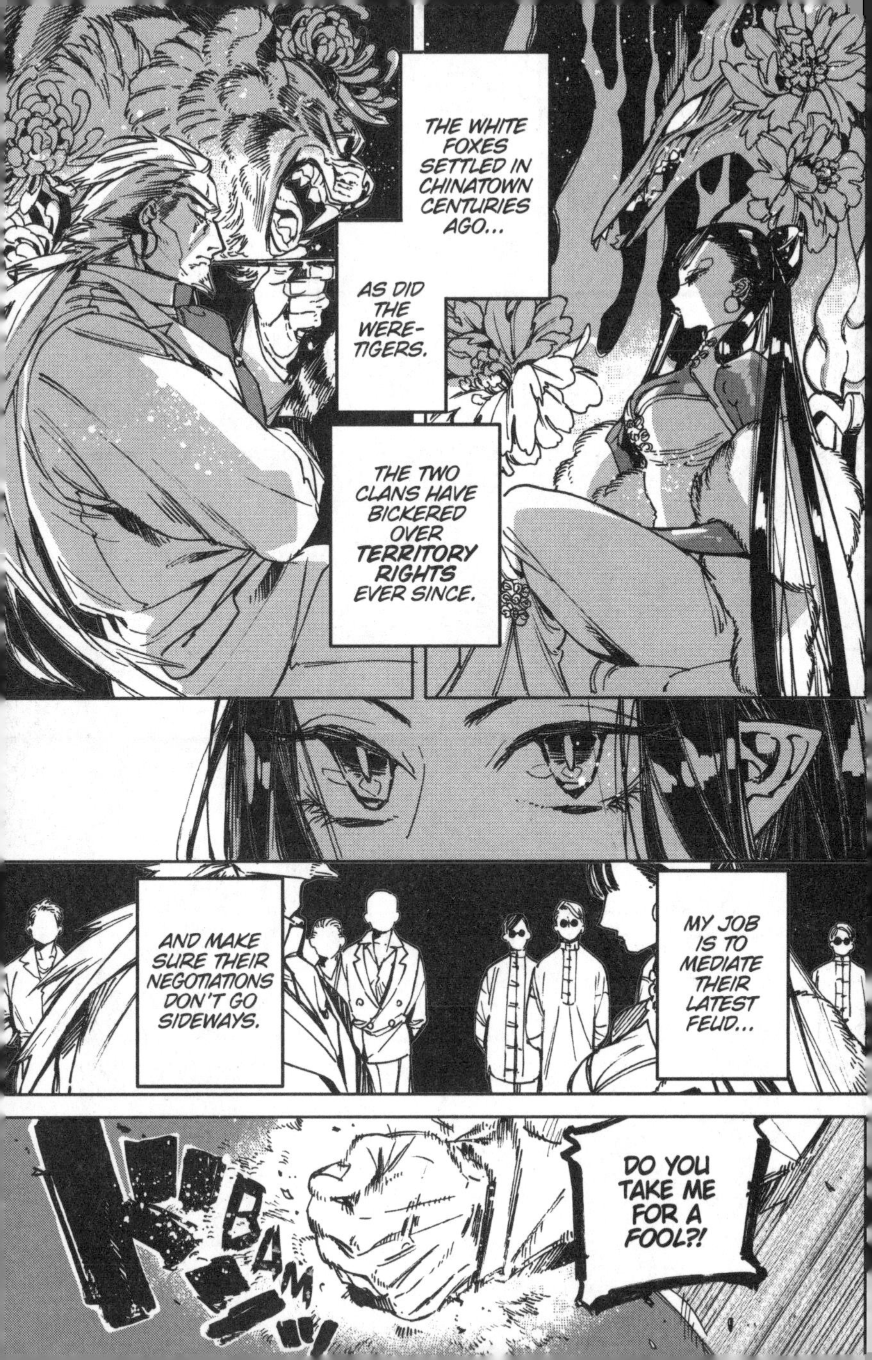
THE WHITE FOXES SETTLED IN CHINATOWN CENTURIES AGO...
AS DID THE WERE-TIGERS.
THE TWO CLANS HAVE BICKERED OVER TERRITORY RIGHTS EVER SINCE.
MY JOB IS TO MEDIATE THEIR LATEST FEUD...
AND MAKE SURE THEIR NEGOTIATIONS DON'T GO SIDEWAYS.
DO YOU TAKE ME FOR A FOOL?!

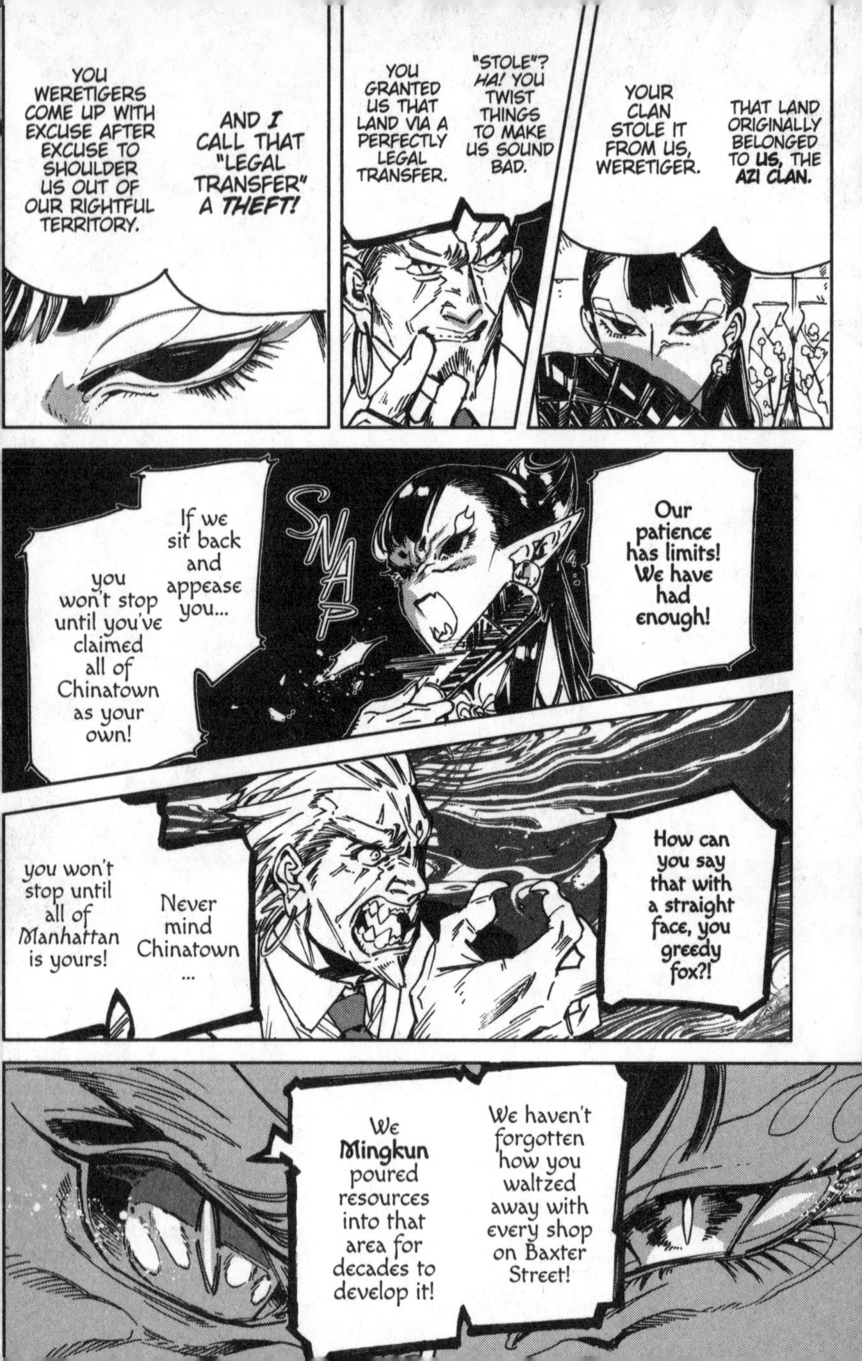
THAT LAND ORIGINALLY BELONGED TO **US**, THE **AZI CLAN.**
YOUR CLAN STOLE IT FROM US, WERETIGER.
"STOLE"? *HA!* YOU TWIST THINGS TO MAKE US SOUND BAD.
YOU GRANTED US THAT LAND VIA A PERFECTLY LEGAL TRANSFER.
AND *I* CALL THAT "LEGAL TRANSFER" A *THEFT!*
YOU WERETIGERS COME UP WITH EXCUSE AFTER EXCUSE TO SHOULDER US OUT OF OUR RIGHTFUL TERRITORY.
Our patience has limits! We have had enough!
SNAP
If we sit back and appease you...
you won't stop until you've claimed all of Chinatown as your own!
How can you say that with a straight face, you greedy fox?!
Never mind Chinatown...
you won't stop until all of Manhattan is yours!
We haven't forgotten how you waltzed away with every shop on Baxter Street!
We **Mingkun** poured resources into that area for decades to develop it!

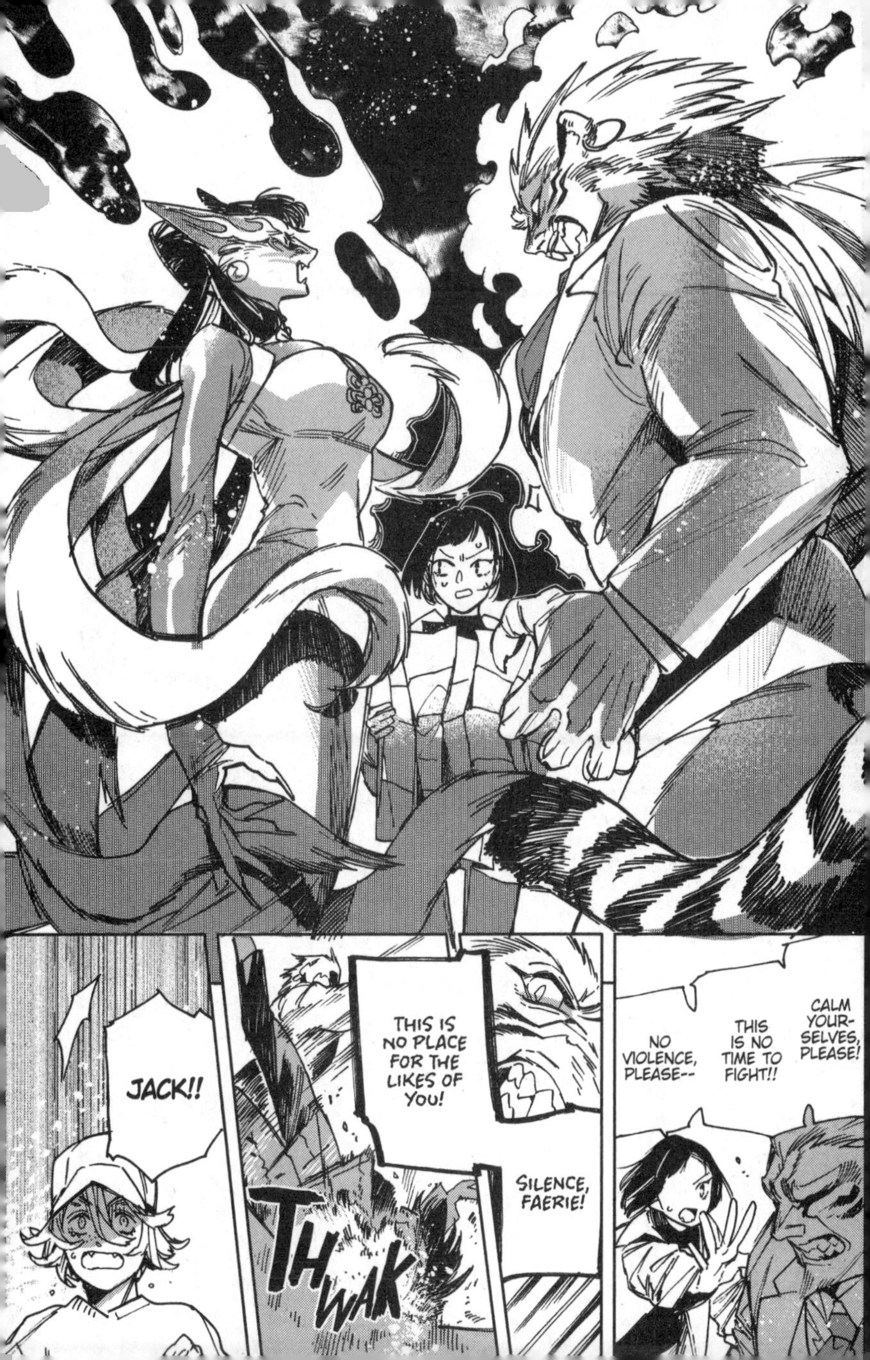
CALM YOUR-SELVES, PLEASE!
THIS IS NO TIME TO FIGHT!!
NO VIOLENCE, PLEASE--
THIS IS NO PLACE FOR THE LIKES OF YOU!
SILENCE, FAERIE!
THWAK
JACK!!

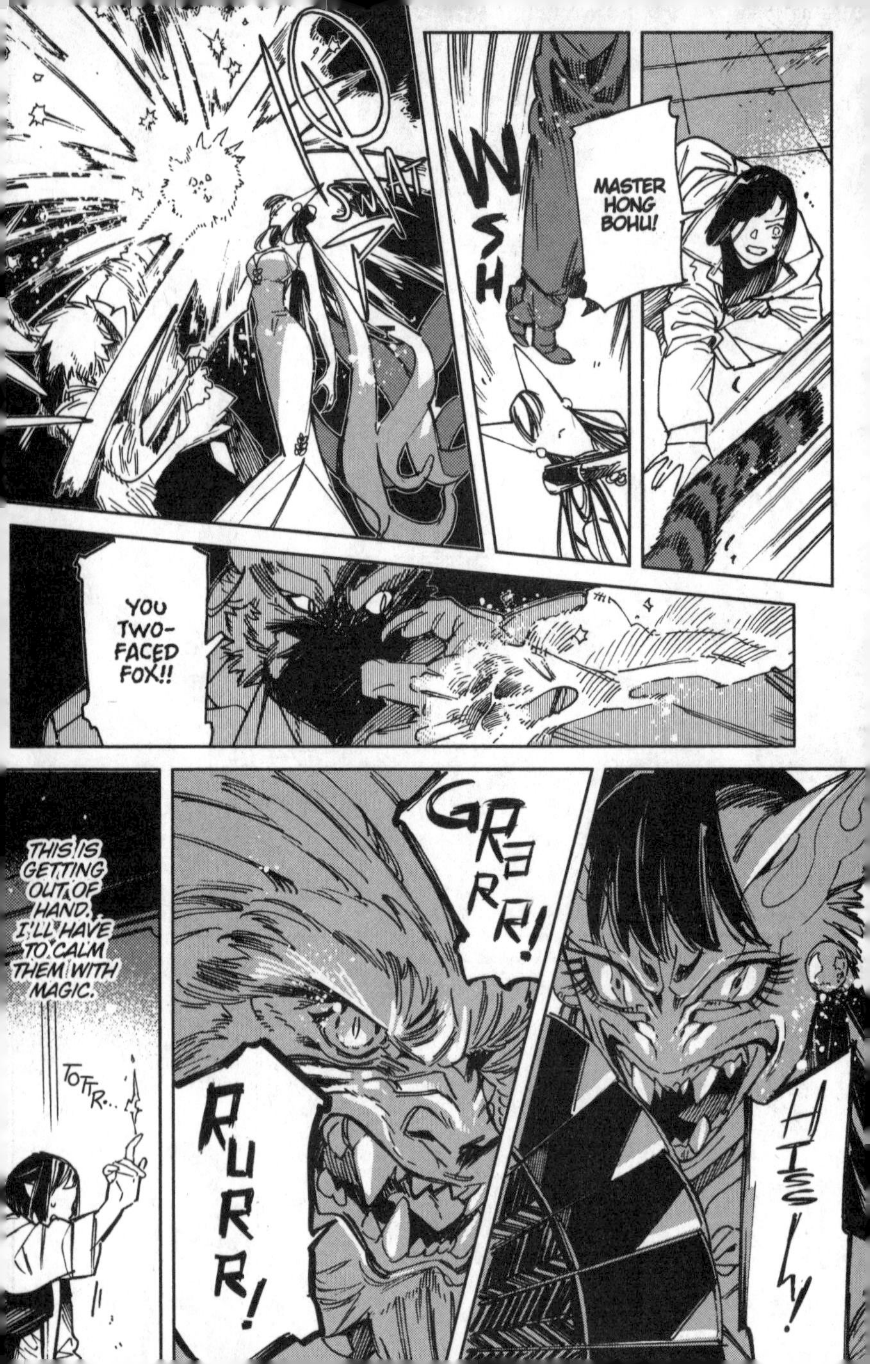
MASTER HONG BOHU!
WSH
SWAT
YOU TWO-FACED FOX!!
HISSS!
GRARRR!
RURR!
THIS IS GETTING OUT OF HAND. I'LL HAVE TO CALM THEM WITH MAGIC.
TOTTR...

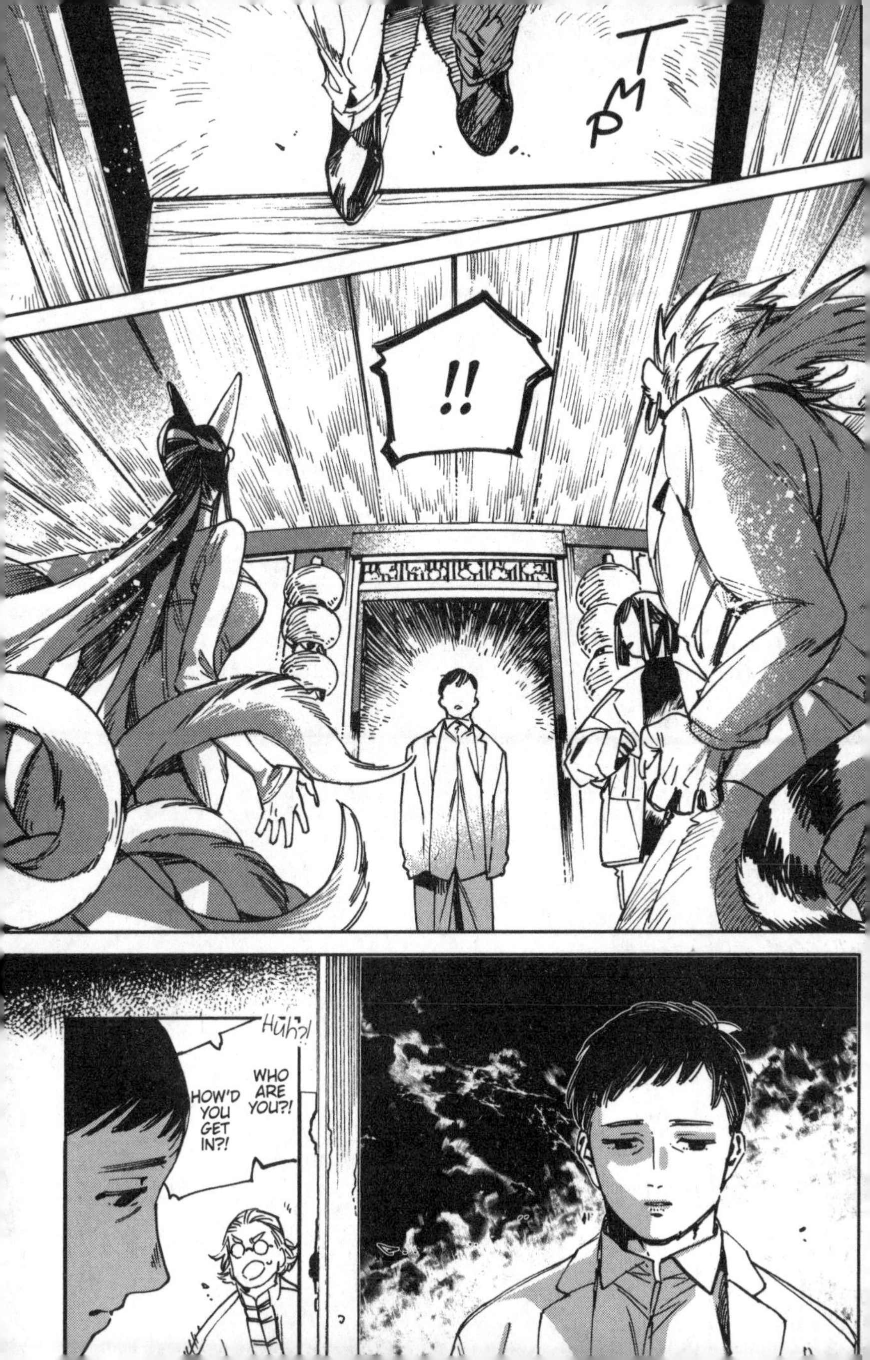
TMP
!!
Huh?!
WHO ARE YOU?!
HOW'D YOU GET IN?!

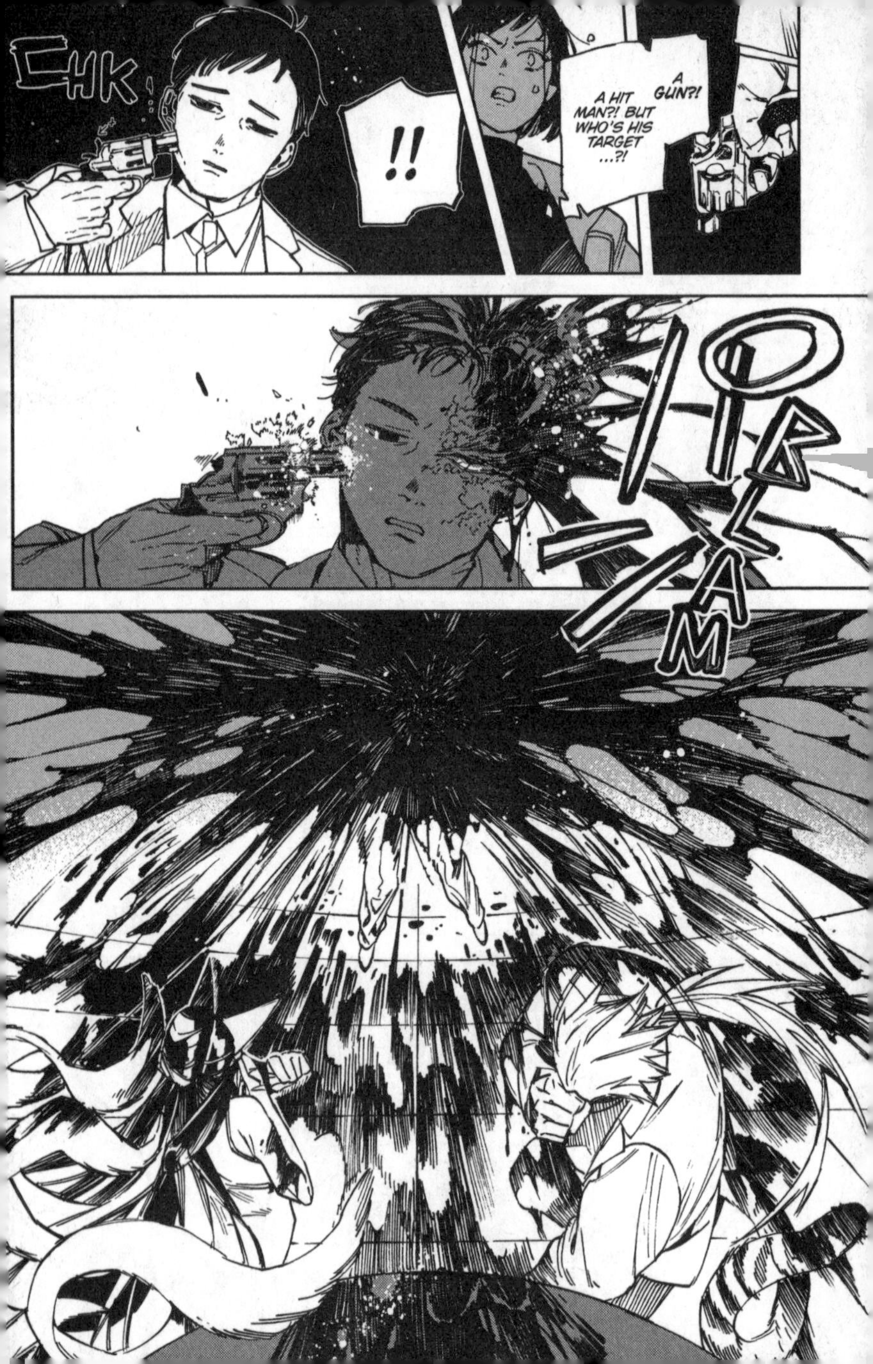
A GUN?!
A HIT MAN?! BUT WHO'S HIS TARGET ...?!
!!
CHK
BLAM

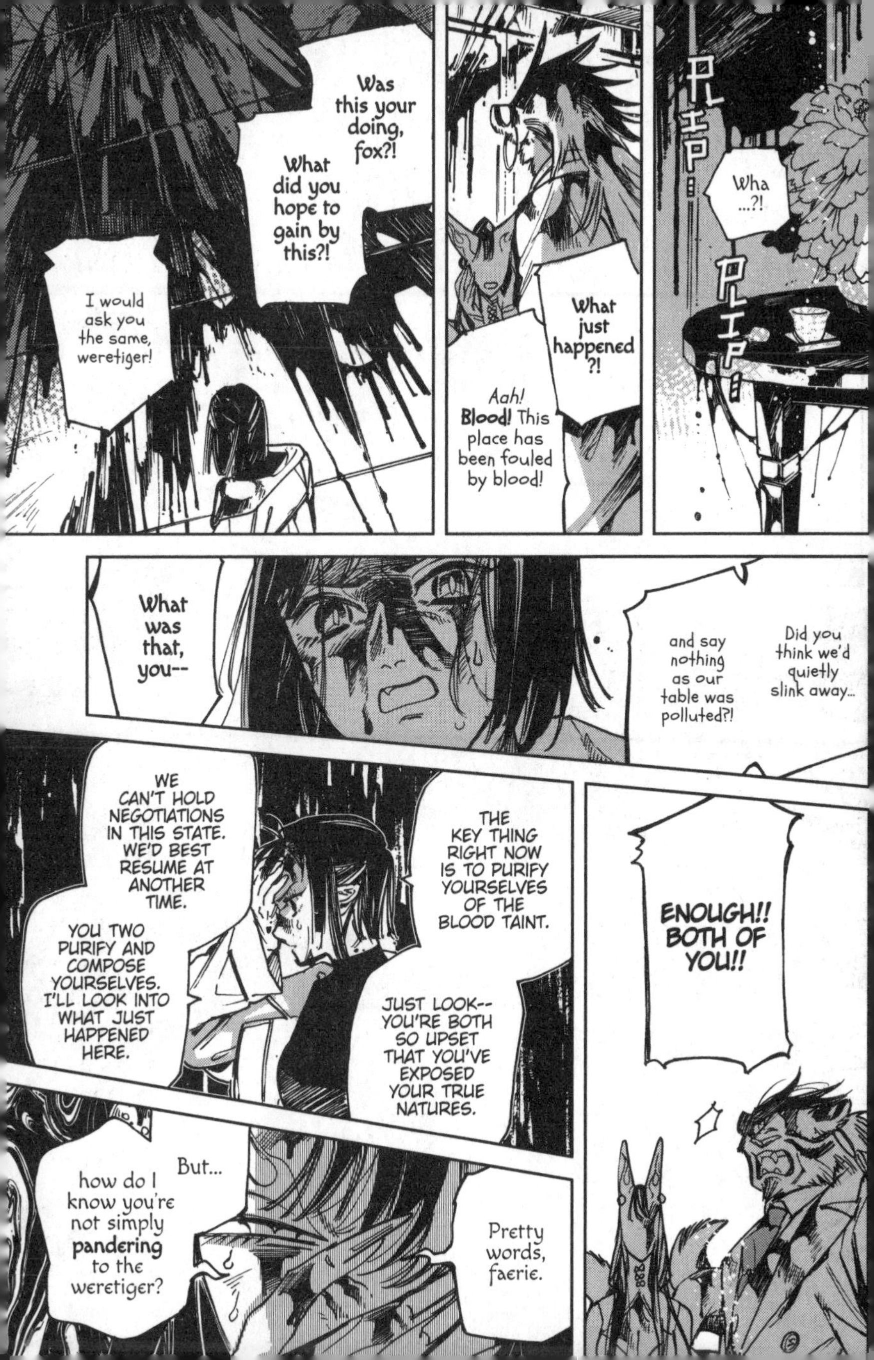
PLIP...
Wha ...?!
PLIP...
What just happened ?!
Aah! **Blood!** This place has been fouled by blood!
Was this your doing, fox?!
What did you hope to gain by this?!
I would ask you the same, weretiger!
Did you think we'd quietly slink away...
and say nothing as our table was polluted?!
What was that, you--
ENOUGH!! BOTH OF YOU!!
THE KEY THING RIGHT NOW IS TO PURIFY YOURSELVES OF THE BLOOD TAINT.
JUST LOOK--YOU'RE BOTH SO UPSET THAT YOU'VE EXPOSED YOUR TRUE NATURES.
WE CAN'T HOLD NEGOTIATIONS IN THIS STATE. WE'D BEST RESUME AT ANOTHER TIME.
YOU TWO PURIFY AND COMPOSE YOURSELVES. I'LL LOOK INTO WHAT JUST HAPPENED HERE.
Pretty words, faerie.
But...
how do I know you're not simply **pandering** to the weretiger?

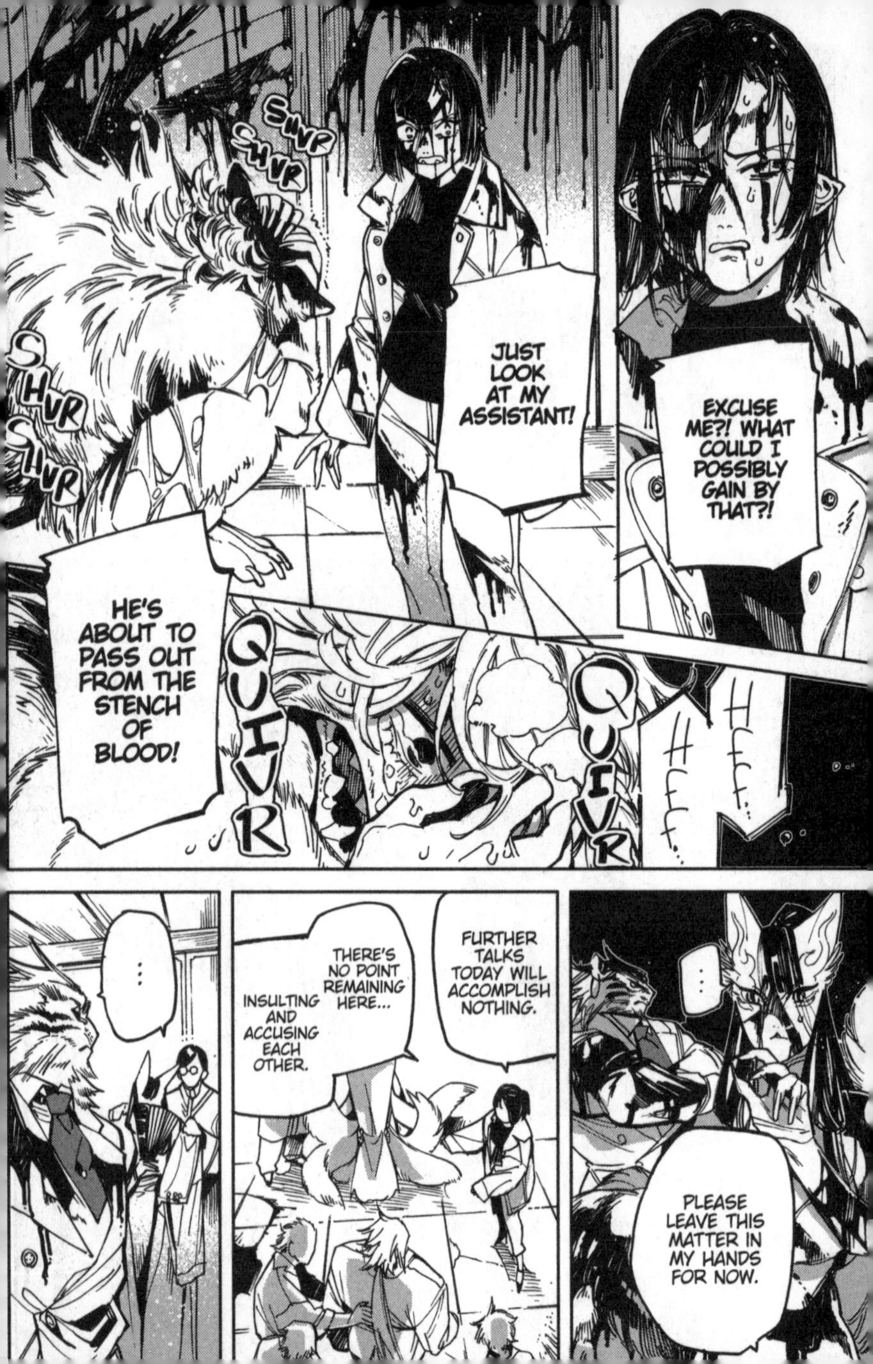
EXCUSE ME?! WHAT COULD I POSSIBLY GAIN BY THAT?!
SHVR SHVR
JUST LOOK AT MY ASSISTANT!
SHVR SHVR
HE'S ABOUT TO PASS OUT FROM THE STENCH OF BLOOD!
QUIVR
QUIVR
HFF...
HFF...
...
PLEASE LEAVE THIS MATTER IN MY HANDS FOR NOW.
FURTHER TALKS TODAY WILL ACCOMPLISH NOTHING.
THERE'S NO POINT REMAINING HERE...
INSULTING AND ACCUSING EACH OTHER.
...

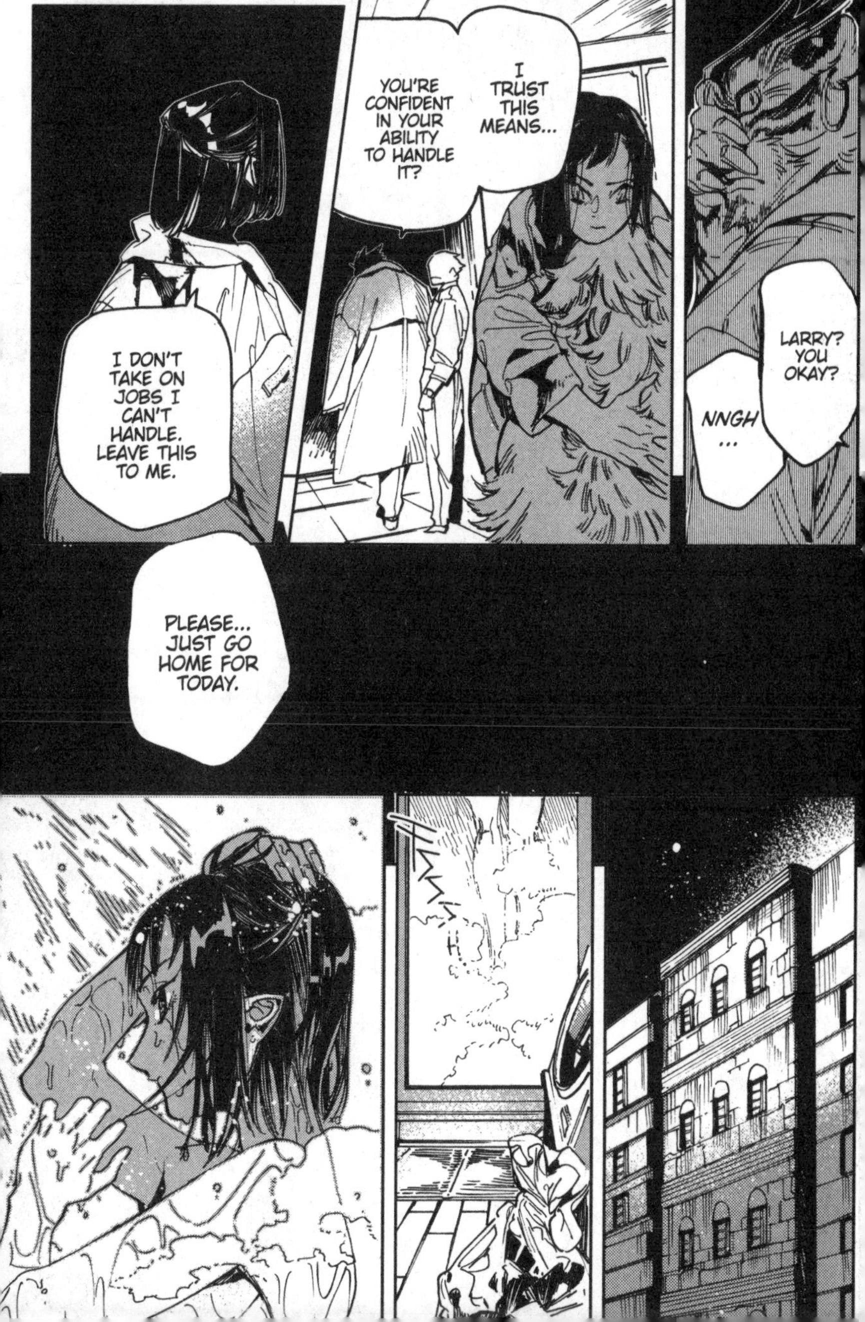
LARRY? YOU OKAY?
NNGH...
I TRUST THIS MEANS...
YOU'RE CONFIDENT IN YOUR ABILITY TO HANDLE IT?
I DON'T TAKE ON JOBS I CAN'T HANDLE. LEAVE THIS TO ME.
PLEASE... JUST GO HOME FOR TODAY.

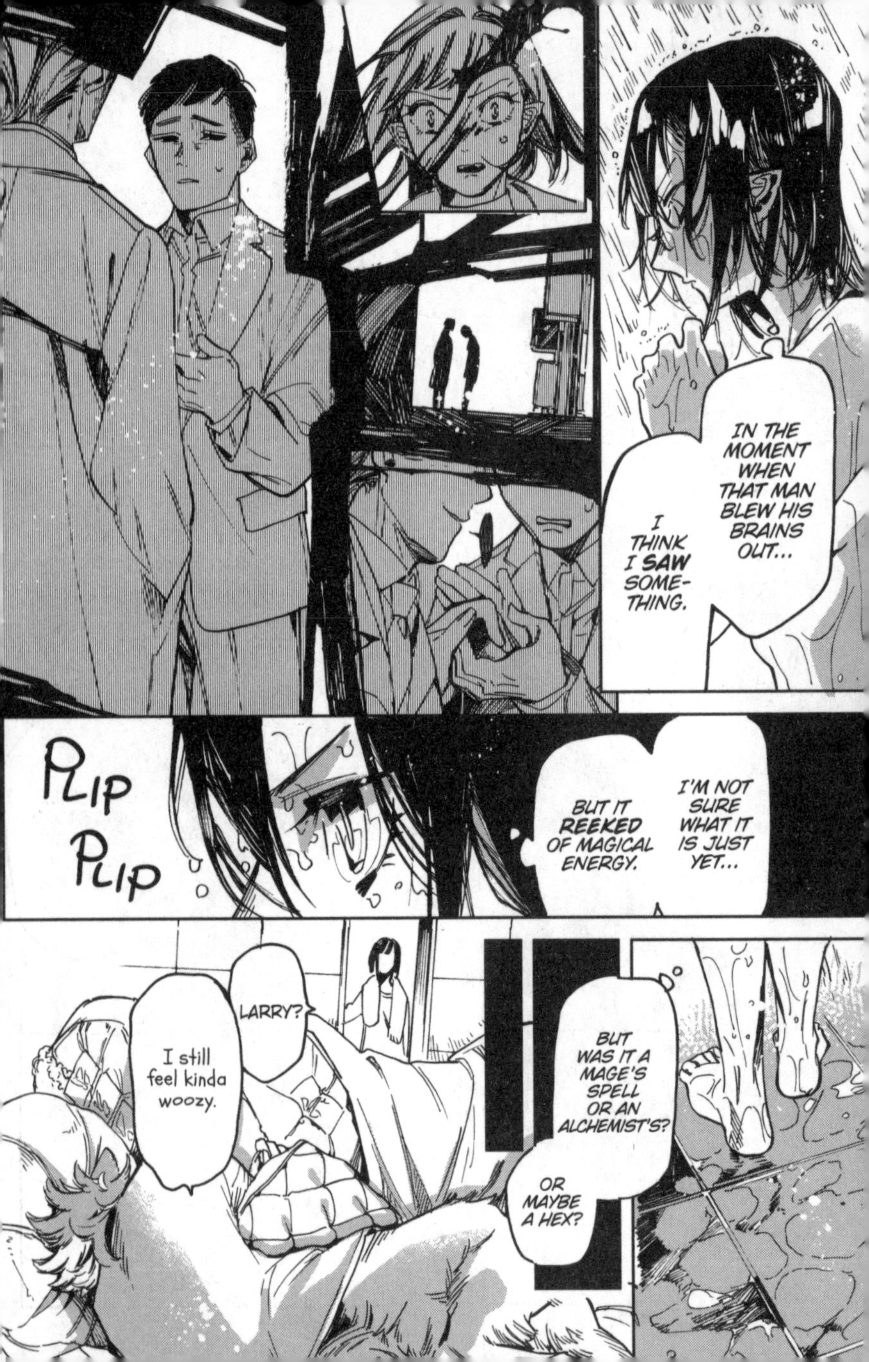
IN THE MOMENT WHEN THAT MAN BLEW HIS BRAINS OUT...
I THINK I SAW SOMETHING.
I'M NOT SURE WHAT IT IS JUST YET...
BUT IT REEKED OF MAGICAL ENERGY.
PLIP PLIP
BUT WAS IT A MAGE'S SPELL OR AN ALCHEMIST'S?
OR MAYBE A HEX?
LARRY?
I still feel kinda woozy.

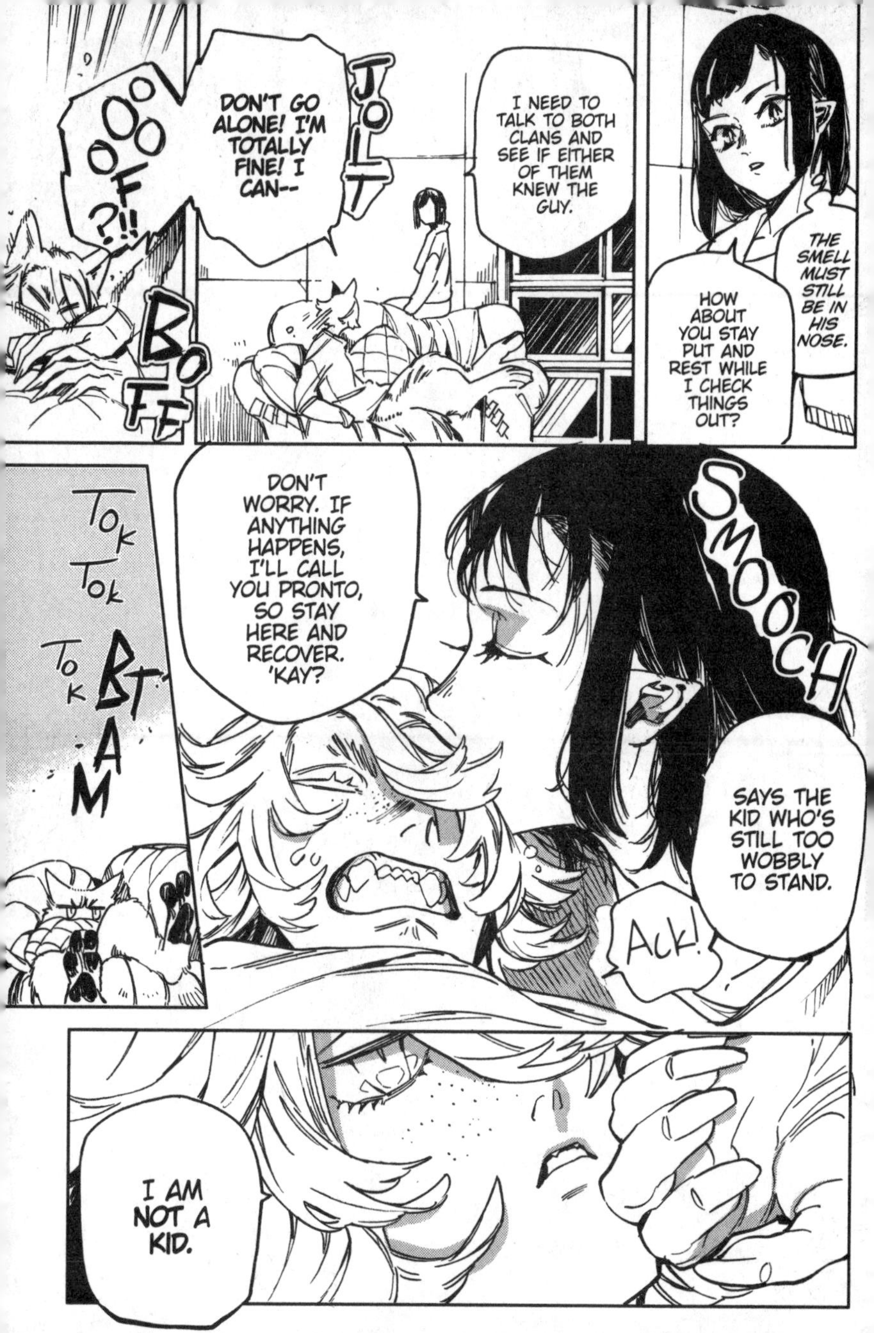
THE SMELL MUST STILL BE IN HIS NOSE.
HOW ABOUT YOU STAY PUT AND REST WHILE I CHECK THINGS OUT?
I NEED TO TALK TO BOTH CLANS AND SEE IF EITHER OF THEM KNEW THE GUY.
JOLT
DON'T GO ALONE! I'M TOTALLY FINE! I CAN--
OOOOOF?!!
BOFF
SMOOOCH
SAYS THE KID WHO'S STILL TOO WOBBLY TO STAND.
ACK!
DON'T WORRY. IF ANYTHING HAPPENS, I'LL CALL YOU PRONTO, SO STAY HERE AND RECOVER. 'KAY?
TOK TOK TOK
BTAM
I AM NOT A KID.

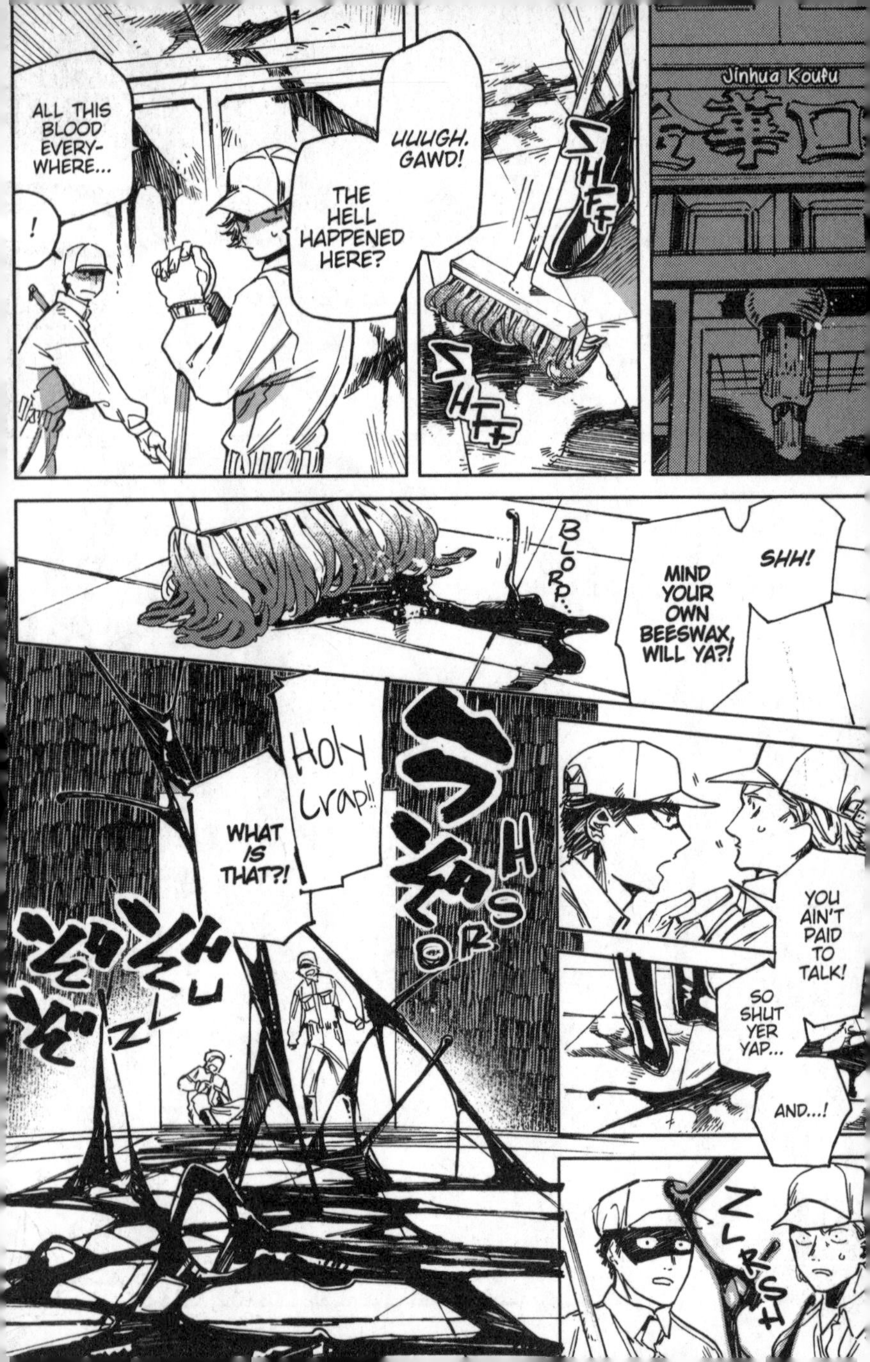
Jinhua Koufu
SHFF
SHFF
UUUGH. GAWD!
THE HELL HAPPENED HERE?
ALL THIS BLOOD EVERY-WHERE...
!
BLORP...
SHH!
MIND YOUR OWN BEESWAX, WILL YA?!
YOU AIN'T PAID TO TALK!
SO SHUT YER YAP...
AND...!
ZLRSH
Holy Crap!!
WHAT IS THAT?!

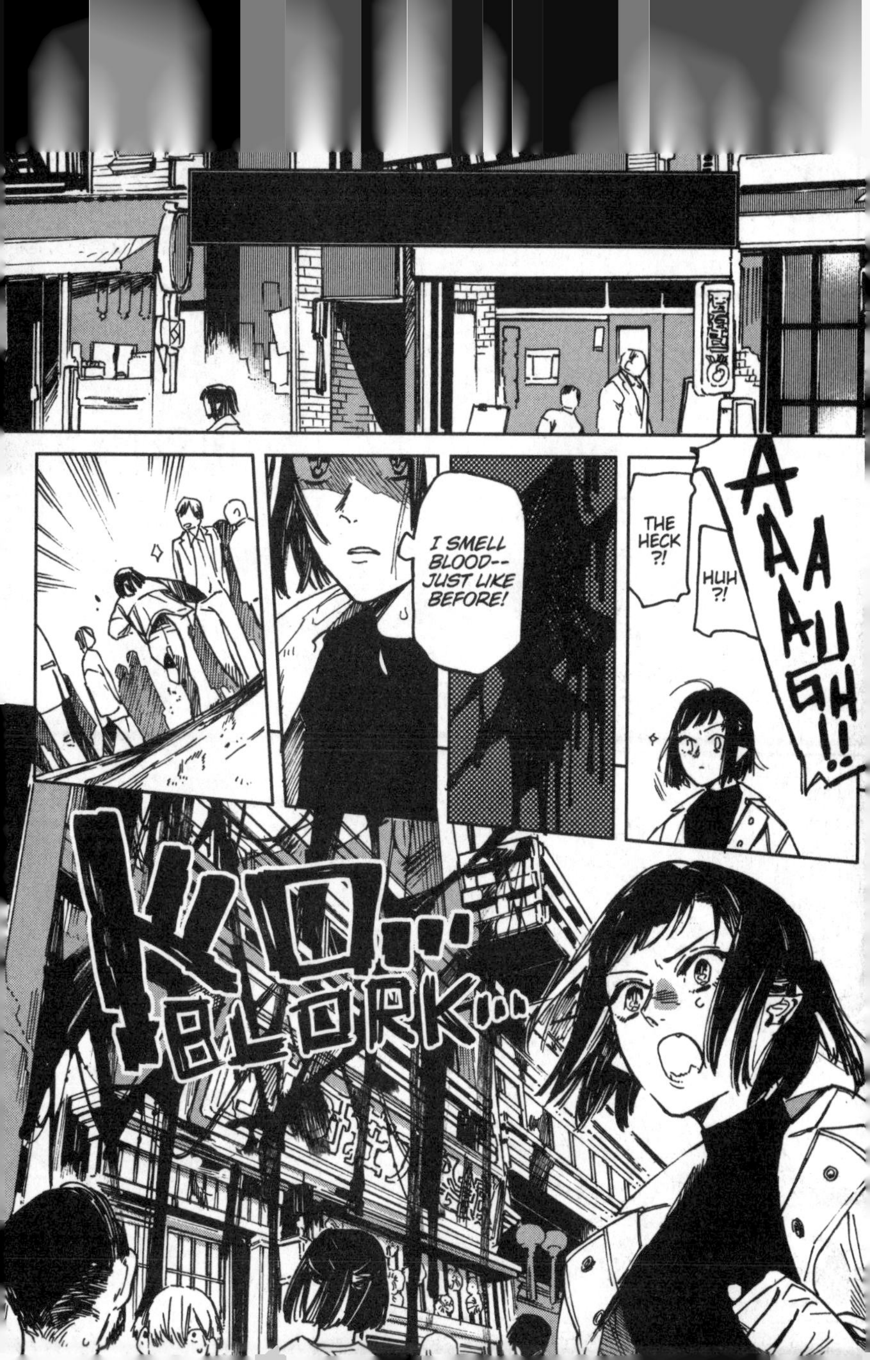
AAAAUGH!!
THE HECK ?!
HUH ?!
I SMELL BLOOD-- JUST LIKE BEFORE!
KLO...
BLORK...

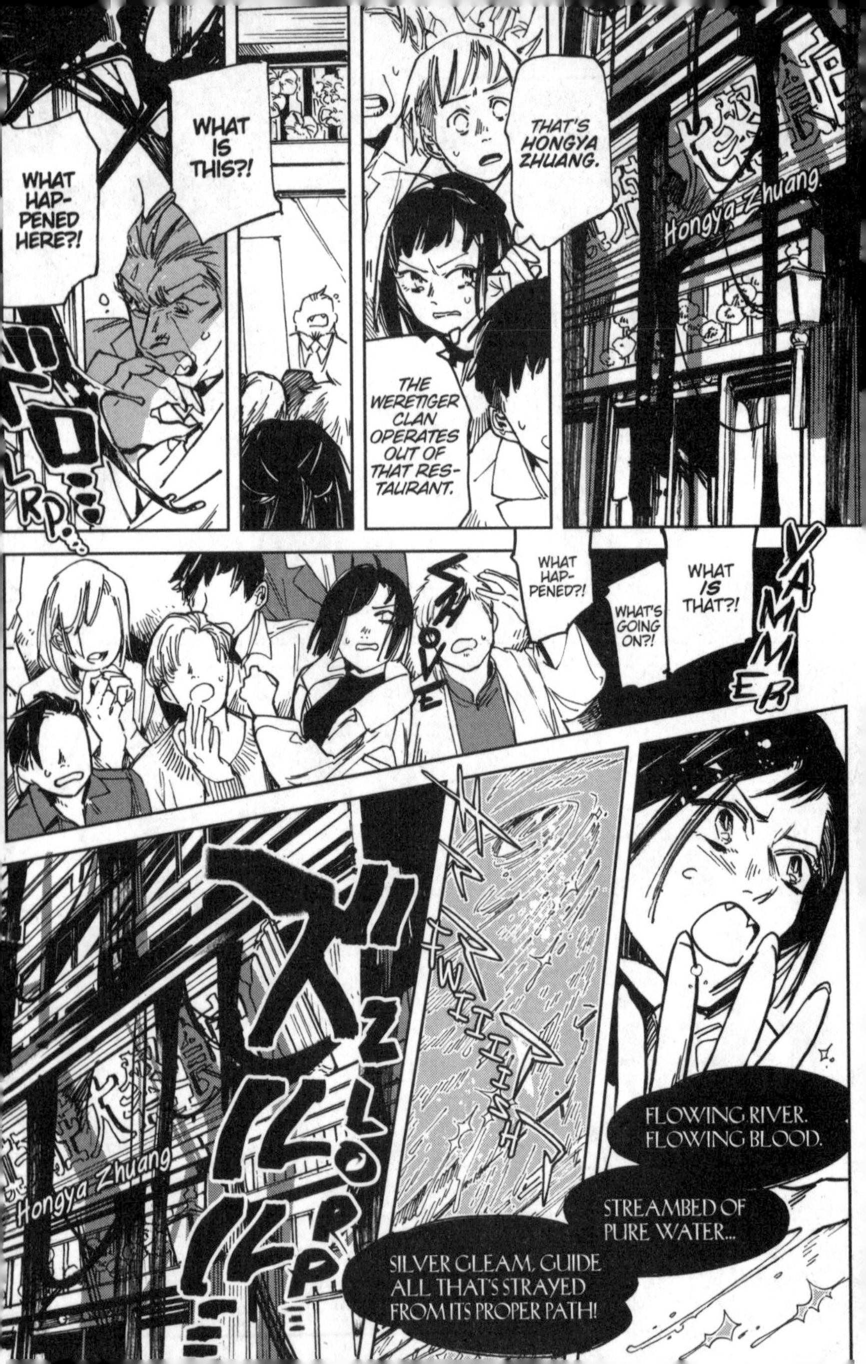
Hongya Zhuang.
THAT'S HONGYA ZHUANG.
THE WERETIGER CLAN OPERATES OUT OF THAT RESTAURANT.
WHAT IS THIS?!
WHAT HAPPENED HERE?!
YAMMER
WHAT IS THAT?!
WHAT'S GOING ON?!
WHAT HAPPENED?!
SHOVE
FLOWING RIVER. FLOWING BLOOD.
STREAMBED OF PURE WATER...
SILVER GLEAM, GUIDE ALL THAT'S STRAYED FROM ITS PROPER PATH!
WHIIIISH
Hongya Zhuang

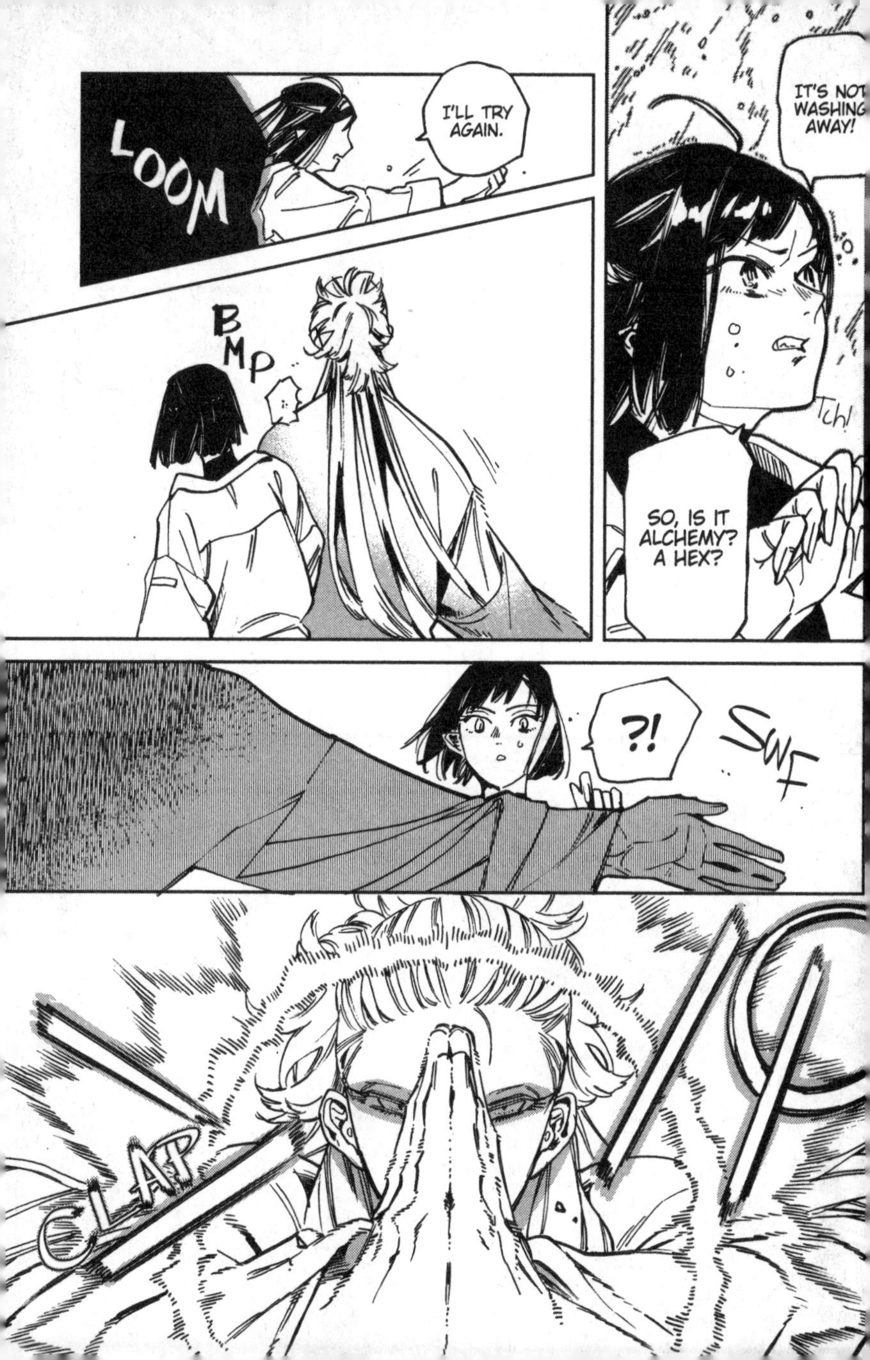
IT'S NOT WASHING AWAY!
Tch!
SO, IS IT ALCHEMY? A HEX?
I'LL TRY AGAIN.
LOOM
BMP
SWF
?!
CLAP

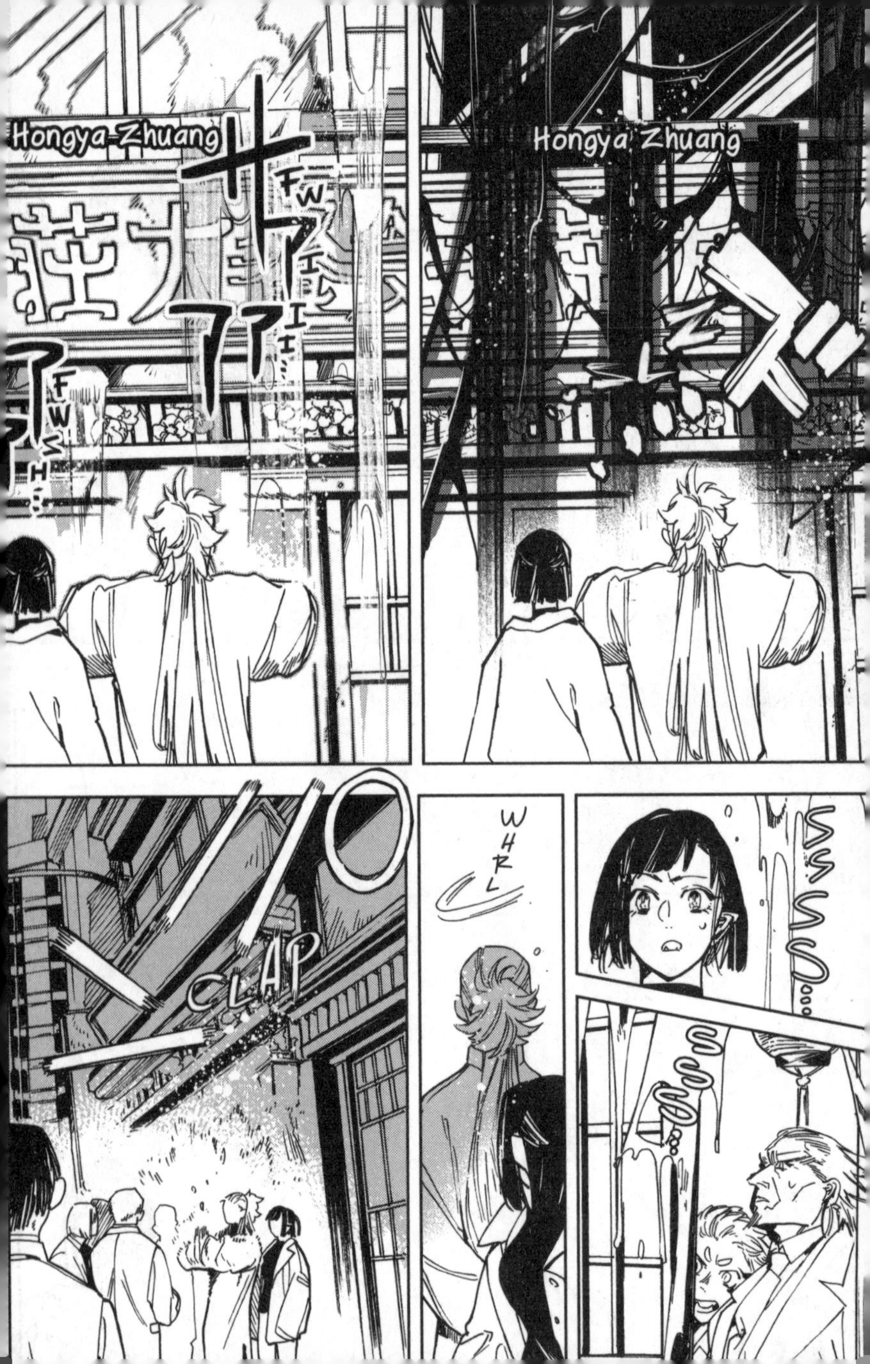
Hongya Zhuang
Hongya Zhuang
FW
FWSH...
SSSS...
SSSS...
WHRL
CLAP

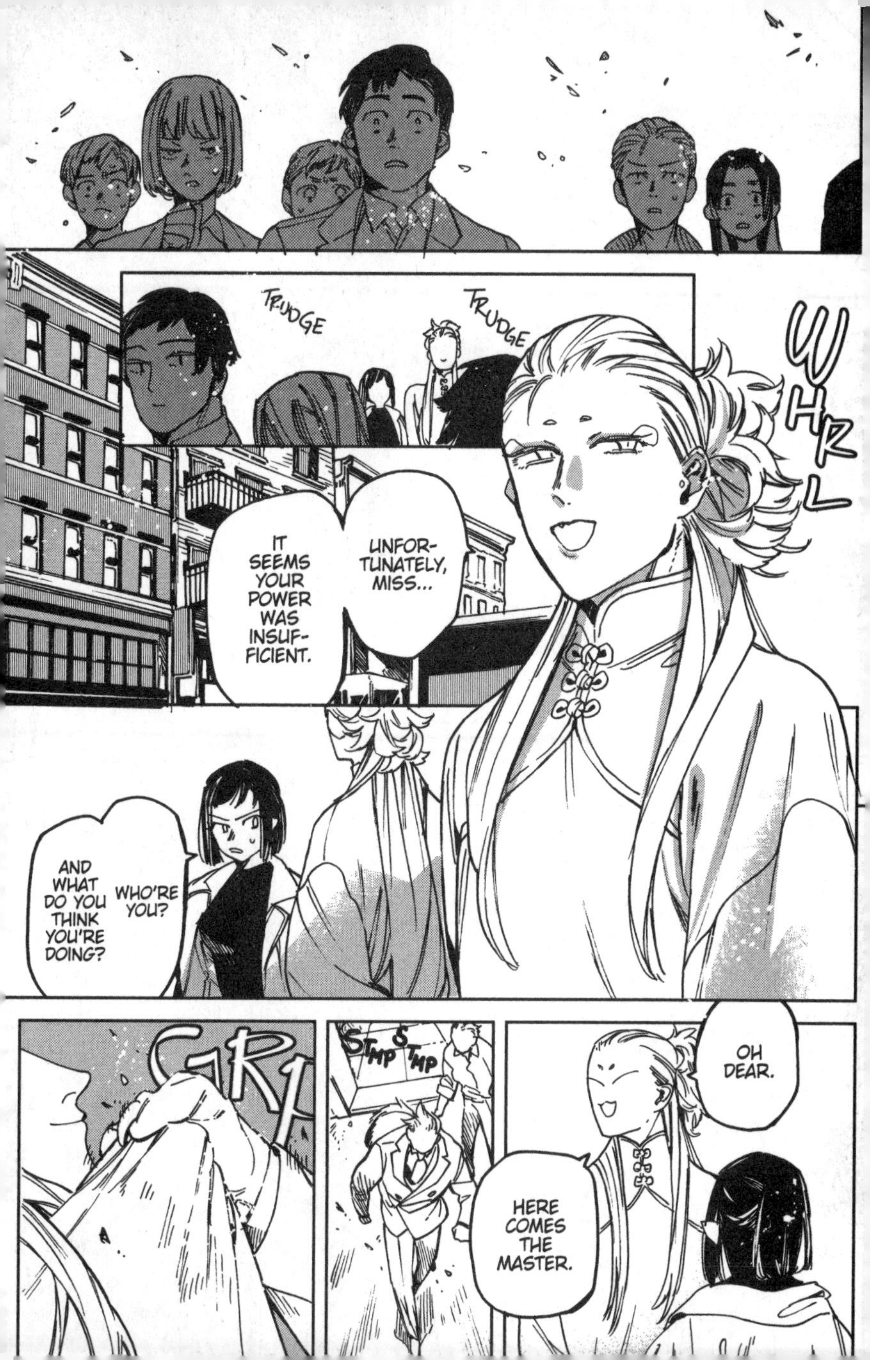
TRUDGE
TRUDGE
WHRL
UNFORTUNATELY, MISS...
IT SEEMS YOUR POWER WAS INSUFFICIENT.
WHO'RE YOU?
AND WHAT DO YOU THINK YOU'RE DOING?
OH DEAR.
HERE COMES THE MASTER.
STMP STMP
GRY

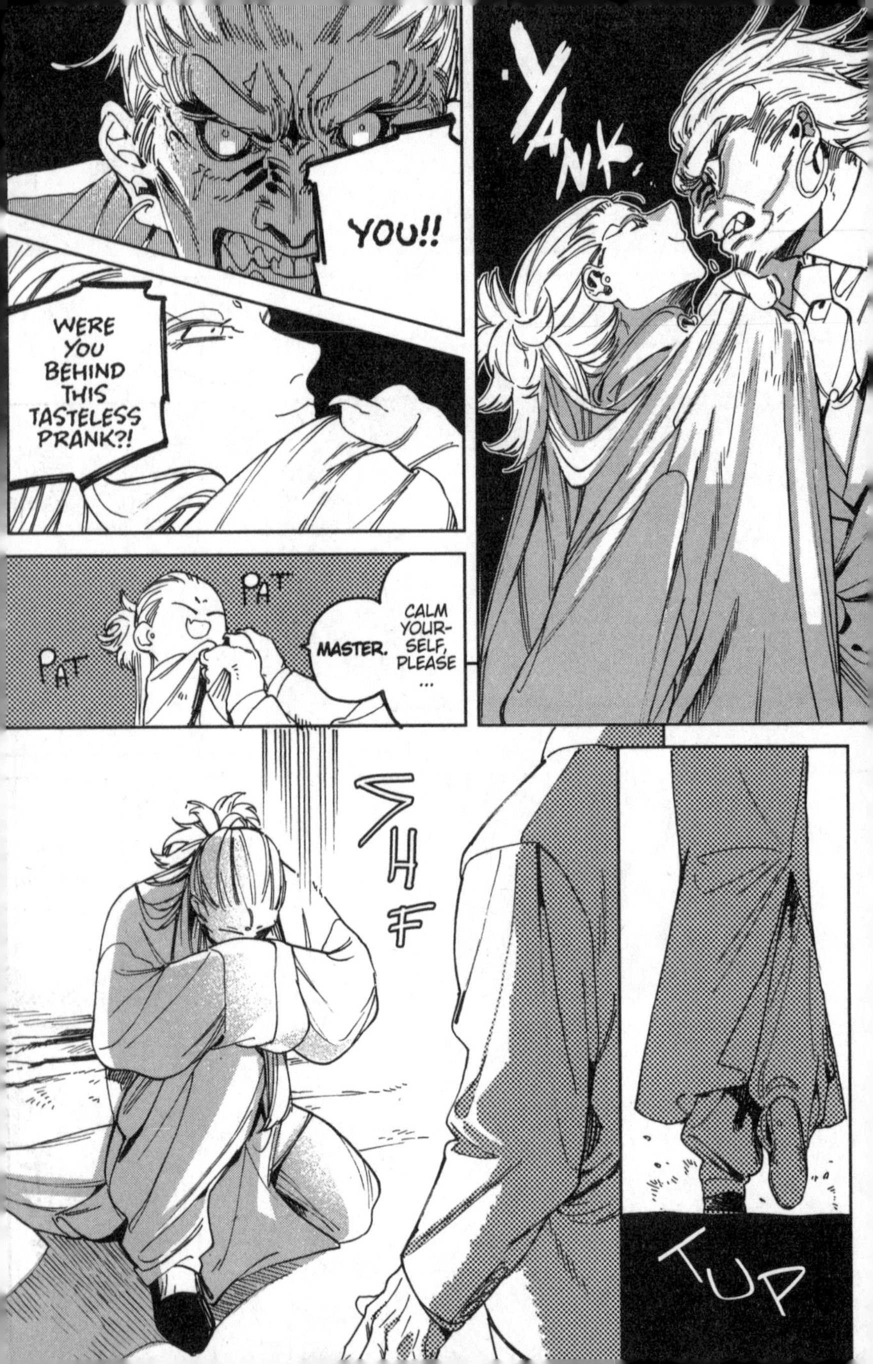
YANK
YOU!!
WERE YOU BEHIND THIS TASTELESS PRANK?!
CALM YOUR-SELF, PLEASE ...
MASTER.
PAT
PAT
TUP
SHF

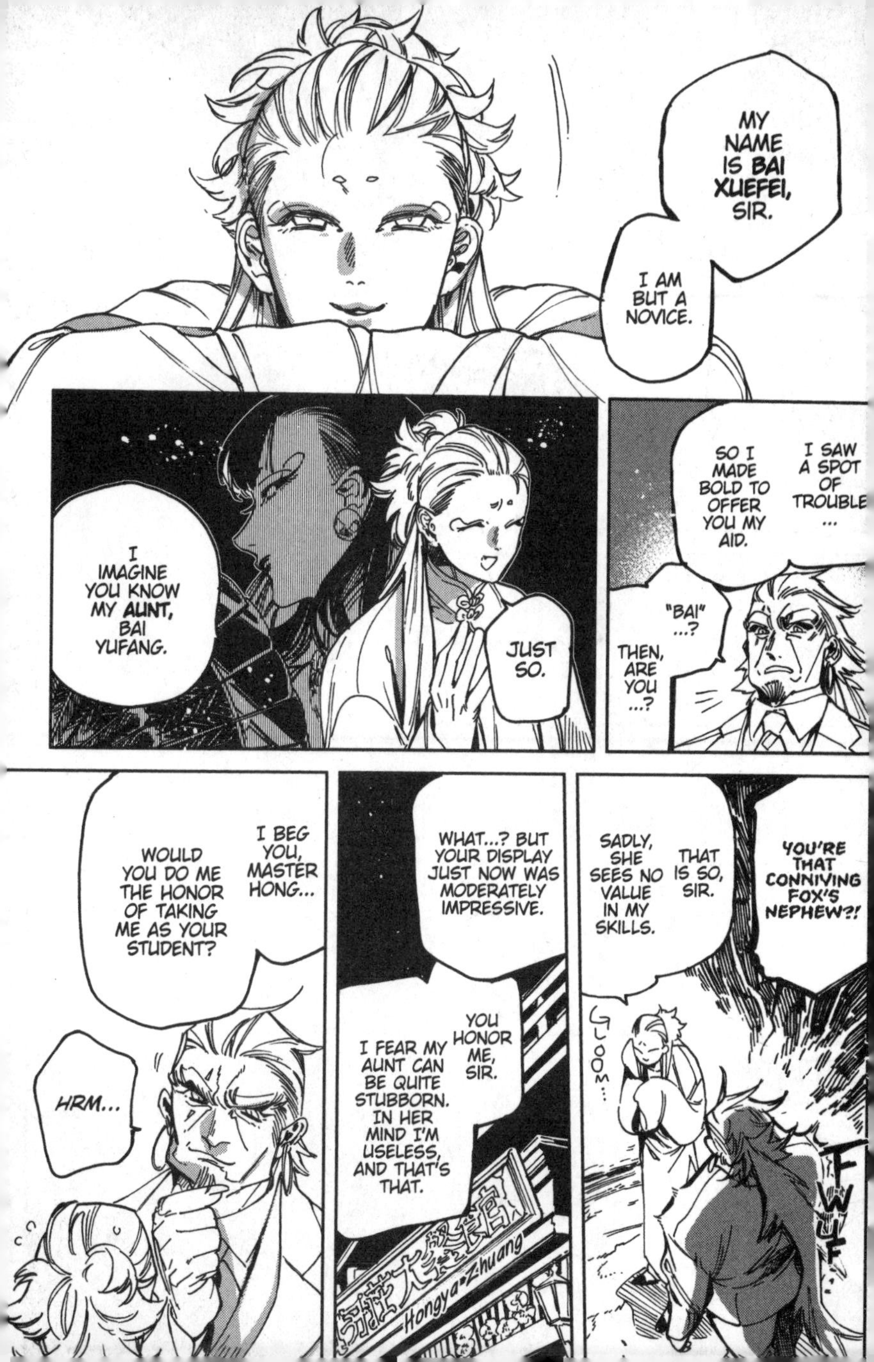

MY NAME IS BAI XUEFEI, SIR.
I AM BUT A NOVICE.
I SAW A SPOT OF TROUBLE ...
SO I MADE BOLD TO OFFER YOU MY AID.
"BAI" ...?
THEN, ARE YOU ...?
JUST SO.
I IMAGINE YOU KNOW MY AUNT, BAI YUFANG.
YOU'RE THAT CONNIVING FOX'S NEPHEW?!
THAT IS SO, SIR.
SADLY, SHE SEES NO VALUE IN MY SKILLS.
GLOOM...
FWUF
WHAT...? BUT YOUR DISPLAY JUST NOW WAS MODERATELY IMPRESSIVE.
YOU HONOR ME, SIR.
I FEAR MY AUNT CAN BE QUITE STUBBORN. IN HER MIND I'M USELESS, AND THAT'S THAT.
Hongya-Zhuang
I BEG YOU, MASTER HONG...
WOULD YOU DO ME THE HONOR OF TAKING ME AS YOUR STUDENT?
HRM...

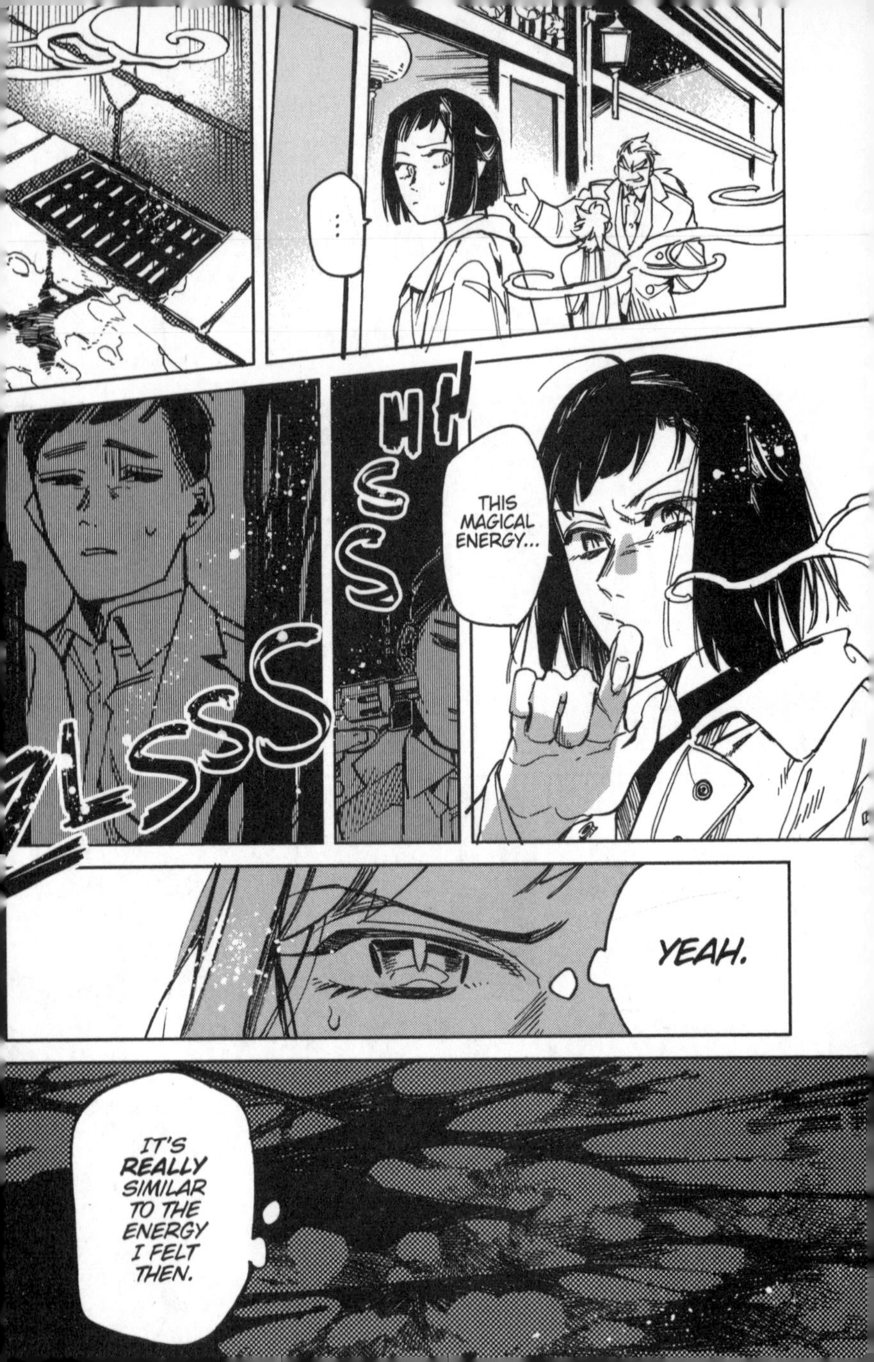
...
THIS MAGICAL ENERGY...
YEAH.
IT'S REALLY SIMILAR TO THE ENERGY I FELT THEN.

The Ancient
Magus' Bride

JACK FLASH AND THE FAERIE CASE FILES

The Ancient Magus' Bride

JACK FLASH AND THE FAERIE CASE FILES

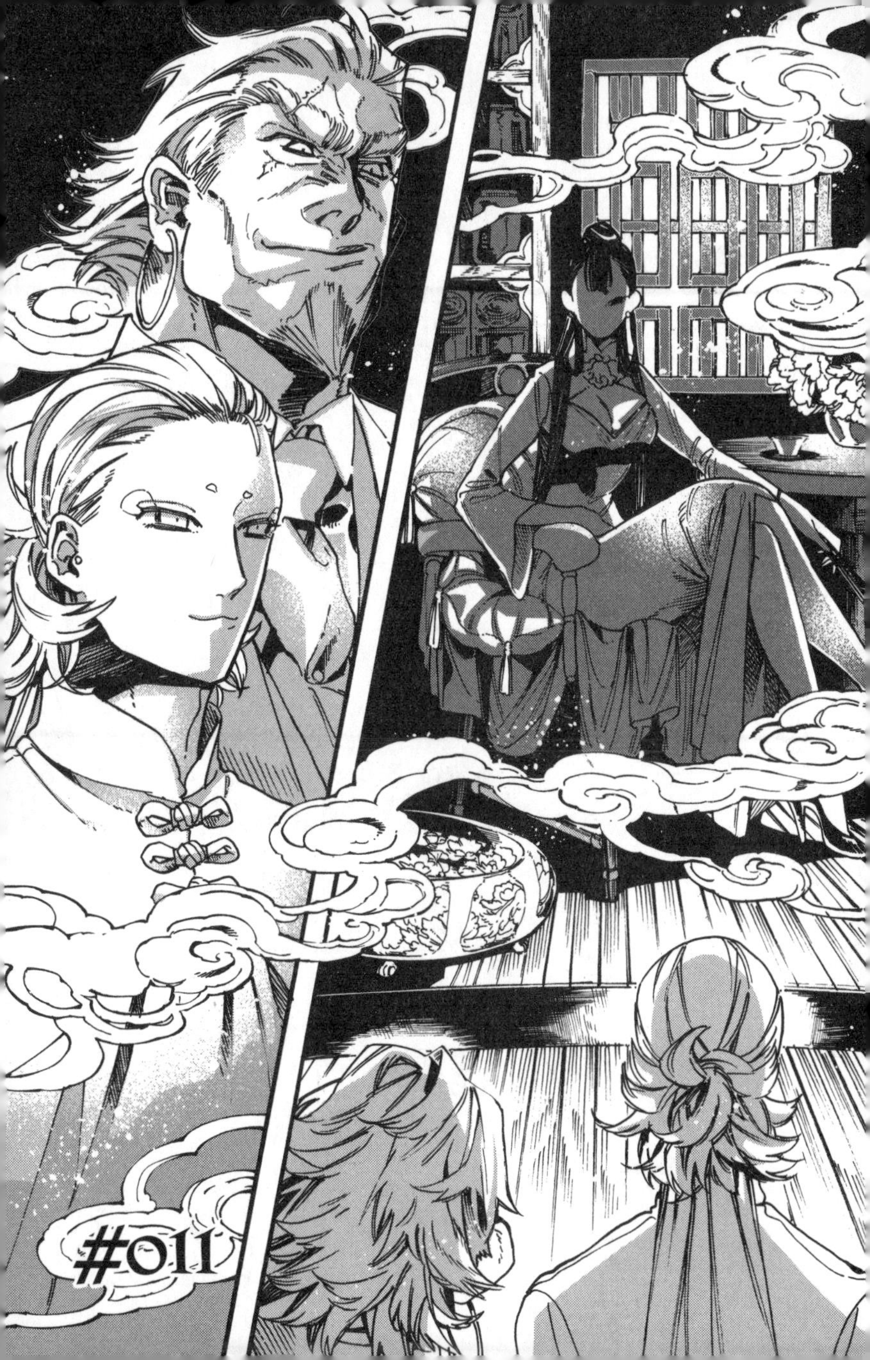
#011

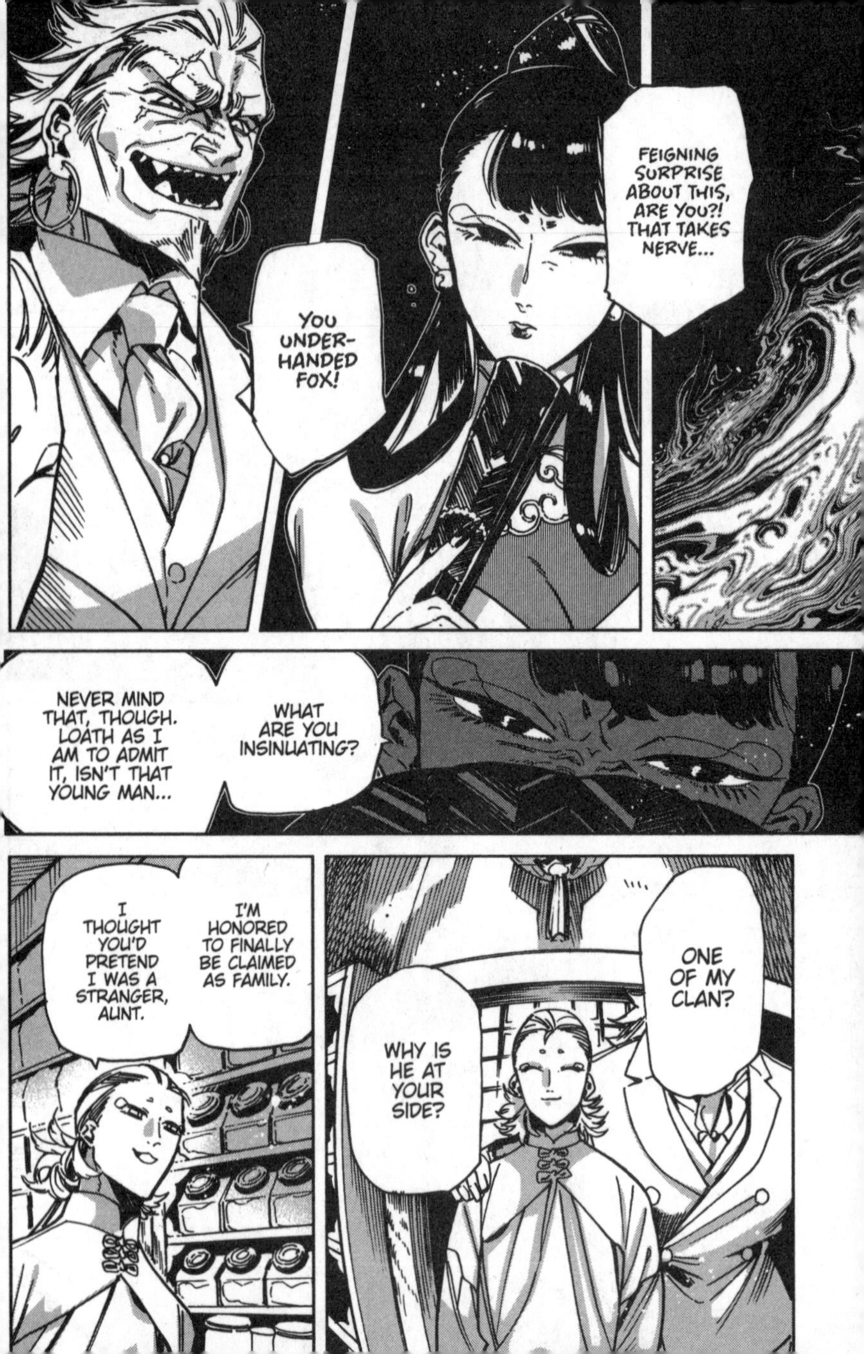
FEIGNING SURPRISE ABOUT THIS, ARE YOU?! THAT TAKES NERVE...
YOU UNDER-HANDED FOX!
WHAT ARE YOU INSINUATING?
NEVER MIND THAT, THOUGH. LOATH AS I AM TO ADMIT IT, ISN'T THAT YOUNG MAN...
...
ONE OF MY CLAN?
WHY IS HE AT YOUR SIDE?
I'M HONORED TO FINALLY BE CLAIMED AS FAMILY.
I THOUGHT YOU'D PRETEND I WAS A STRANGER, AUNT.

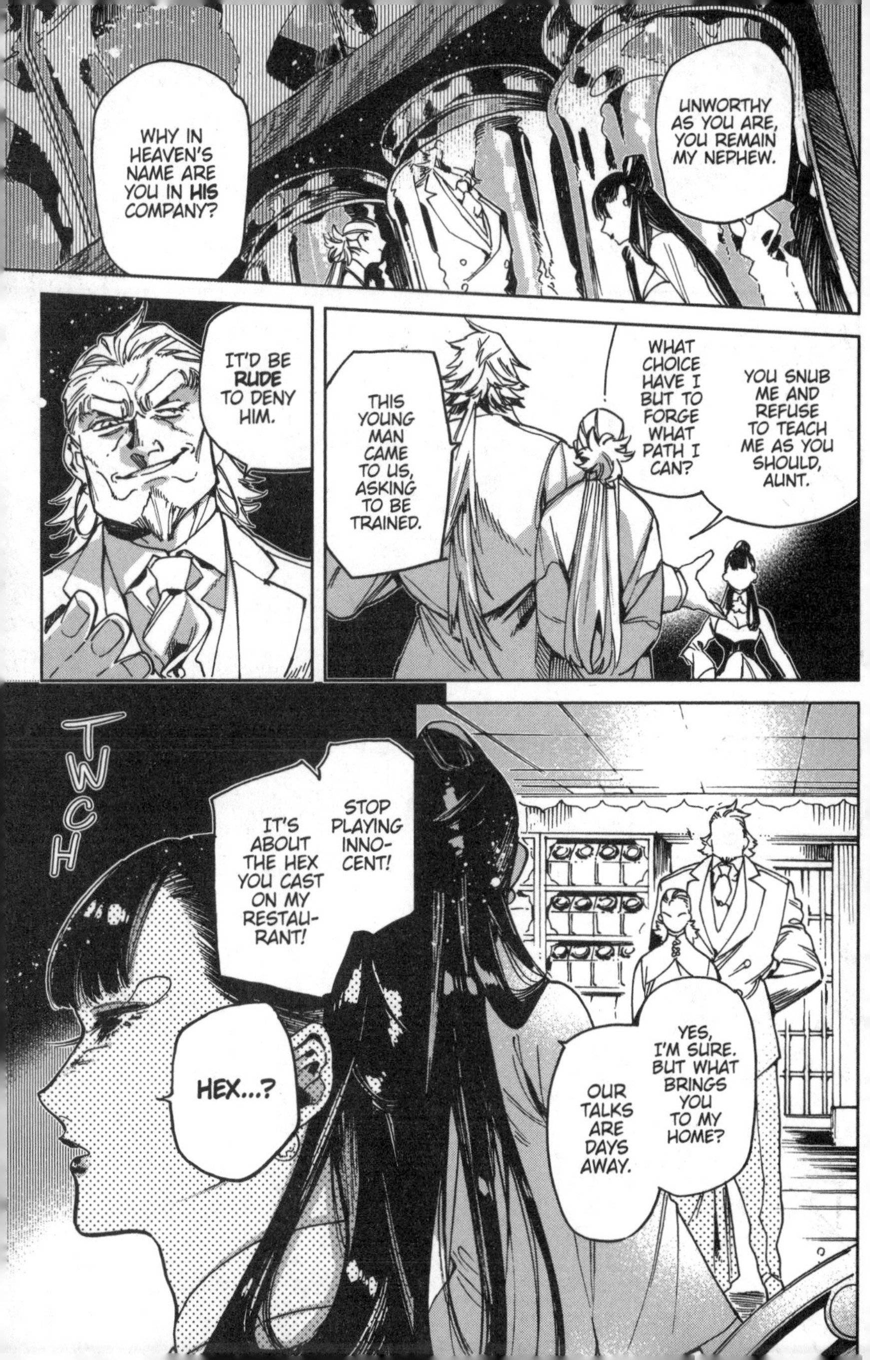
UNWORTHY AS YOU ARE, YOU REMAIN MY NEPHEW.
WHY IN HEAVEN'S NAME ARE YOU IN **HIS** COMPANY?
YOU SNUB ME AND REFUSE TO TEACH ME AS YOU SHOULD, AUNT.
WHAT CHOICE HAVE I BUT TO FORGE WHAT PATH I CAN?
THIS YOUNG MAN CAME TO US, ASKING TO BE TRAINED.
IT'D BE **RUDE** TO DENY HIM.
YES, I'M SURE. BUT WHAT BRINGS YOU TO MY HOME?
OUR TALKS ARE DAYS AWAY.
STOP PLAYING INNO-CENT!
IT'S ABOUT THE HEX YOU CAST ON MY RESTAU-RANT!
TWCH
HEX...?

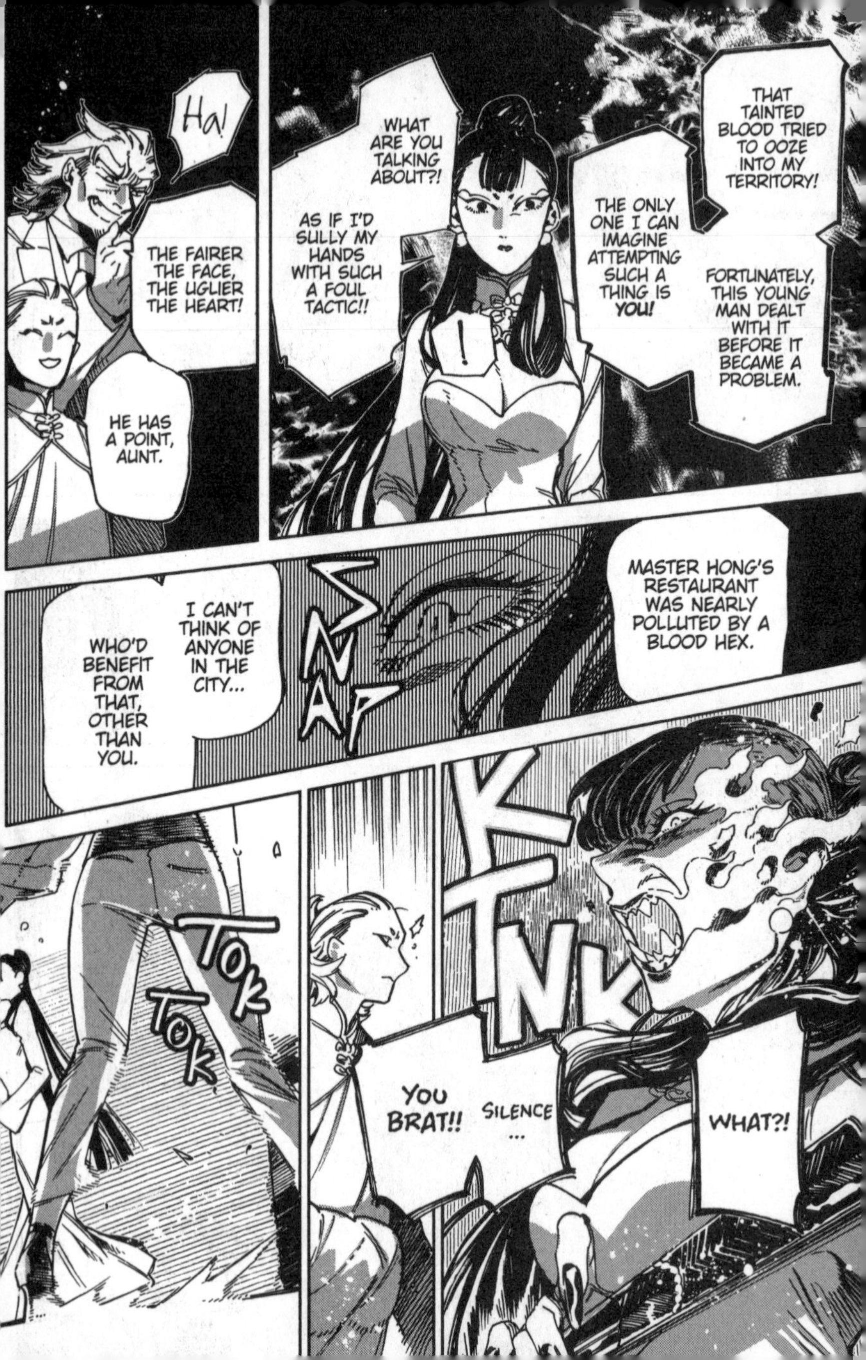
THAT TAINTED BLOOD TRIED TO OOZE INTO MY TERRITORY!
FORTUNATELY, THIS YOUNG MAN DEALT WITH IT BEFORE IT BECAME A PROBLEM.
THE ONLY ONE I CAN IMAGINE ATTEMPTING SUCH A THING IS **YOU!**
WHAT ARE YOU TALKING ABOUT?!
AS IF I'D SULLY MY HANDS WITH SUCH A FOUL TACTIC!!
!
Ha!
THE FAIRER THE FACE, THE UGLIER THE HEART!
HE HAS A POINT, AUNT.
MASTER HONG'S RESTAURANT WAS NEARLY POLLUTED BY A BLOOD HEX.
SNAP
I CAN'T THINK OF ANYONE IN THE CITY...
WHO'D BENEFIT FROM THAT, OTHER THAN YOU.
KTNK
WHAT?!
SILENCE...
YOU BRAT!!
TOK
TOK

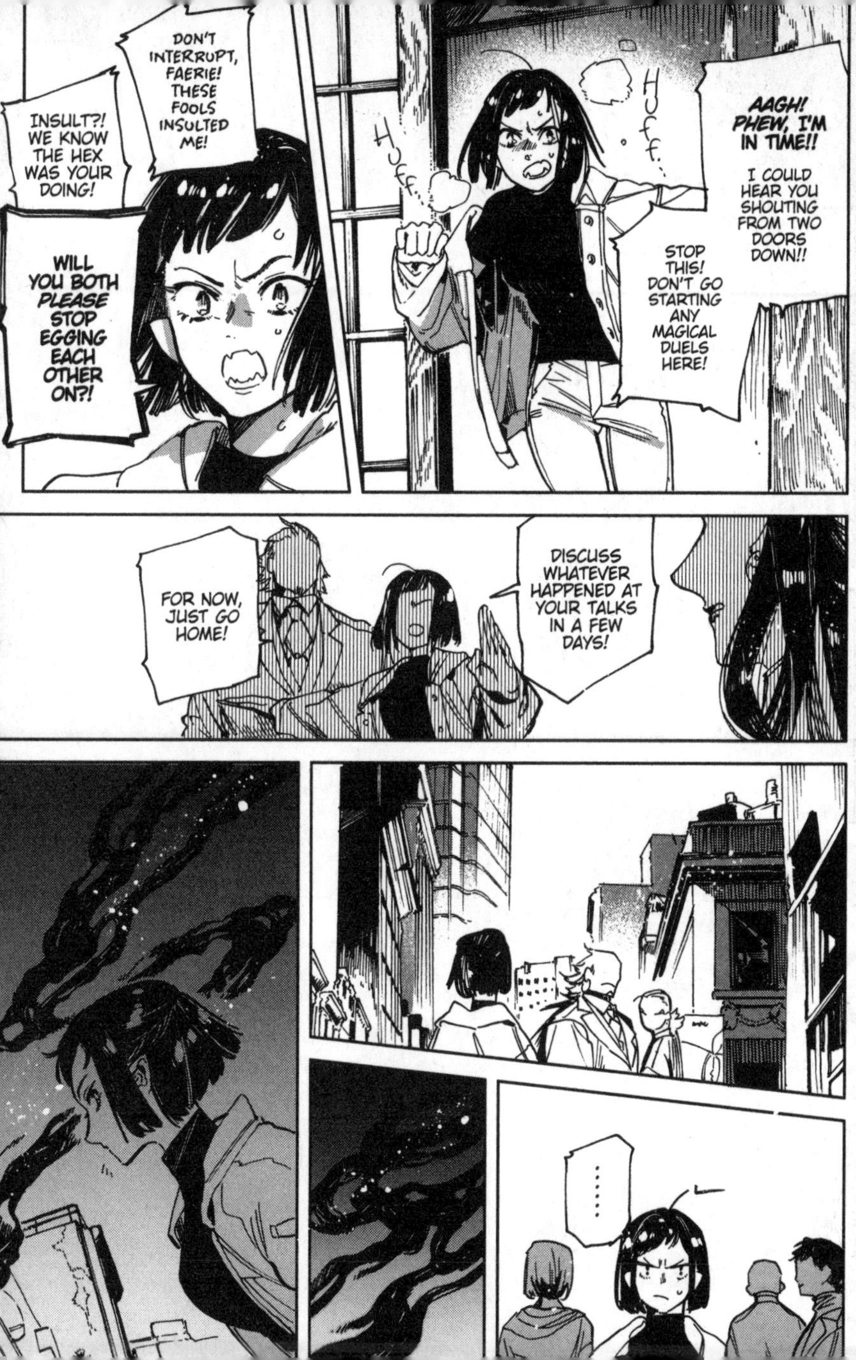
AAGH! PHEW, I'M IN TIME!!
I COULD HEAR YOU SHOUTING FROM TWO DOORS DOWN!!
HUFF... HUFF...
STOP THIS! DON'T GO STARTING ANY MAGICAL DUELS HERE!
DON'T INTERRUPT, FAERIE! THESE FOOLS INSULTED ME!
INSULT?! WE KNOW THE HEX WAS YOUR DOING!
WILL YOU BOTH PLEASE STOP EGGING EACH OTHER ON?!
DISCUSS WHATEVER HAPPENED AT YOUR TALKS IN A FEW DAYS!
FOR NOW, JUST GO HOME!
......

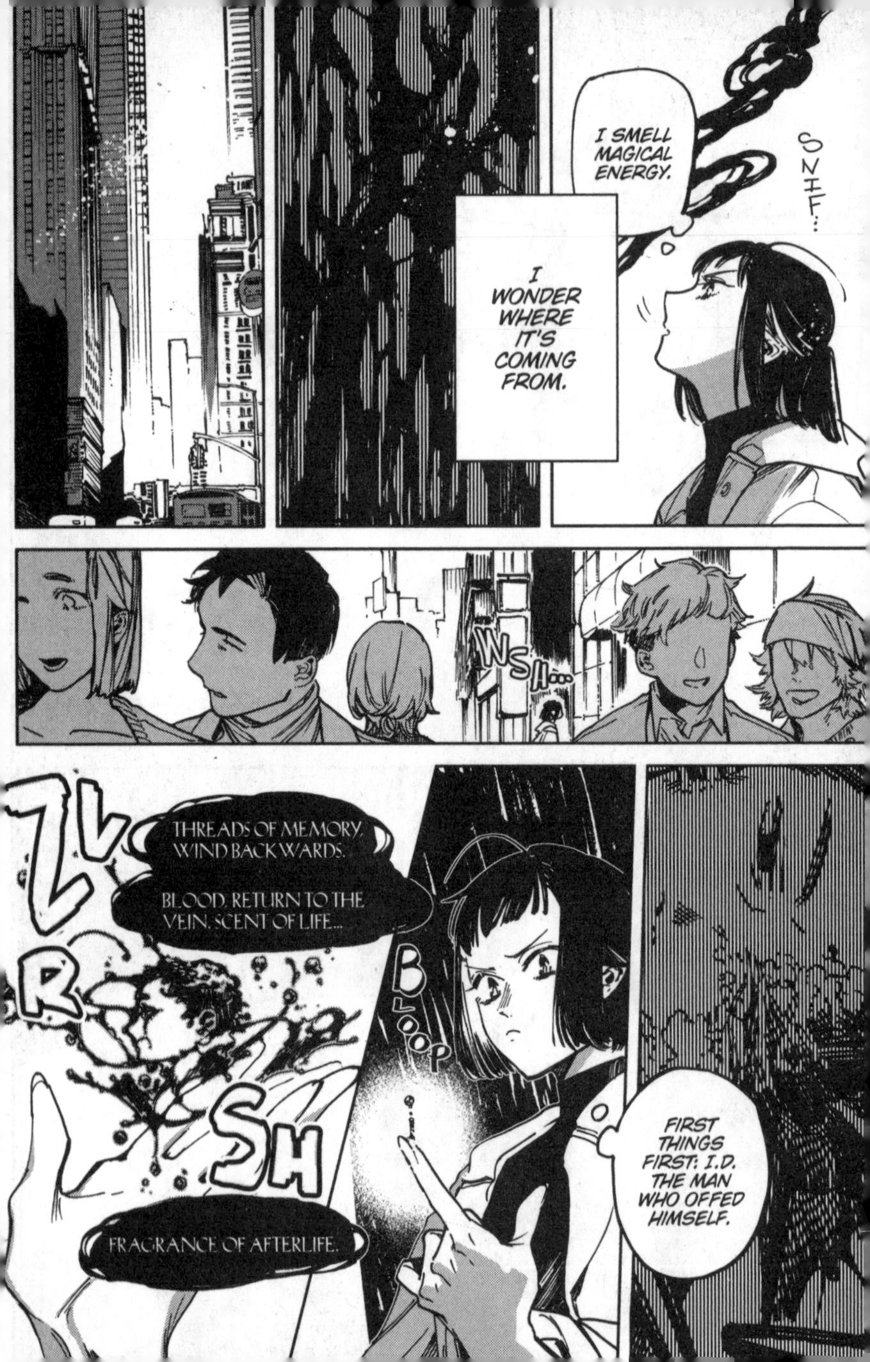
I SMELL MAGICAL ENERGY.
SNIF...
I WONDER WHERE IT'S COMING FROM.
WSH...
FIRST THINGS FIRST: I.D. THE MAN WHO OFFED HIMSELF.
BLOOP
ZV
THREADS OF MEMORY, WIND BACKWARDS.
BLOOD, RETURN TO THE VEIN. SCENT OF LIFE...
R
SH
FRAGRANCE OF AFTERLIFE.

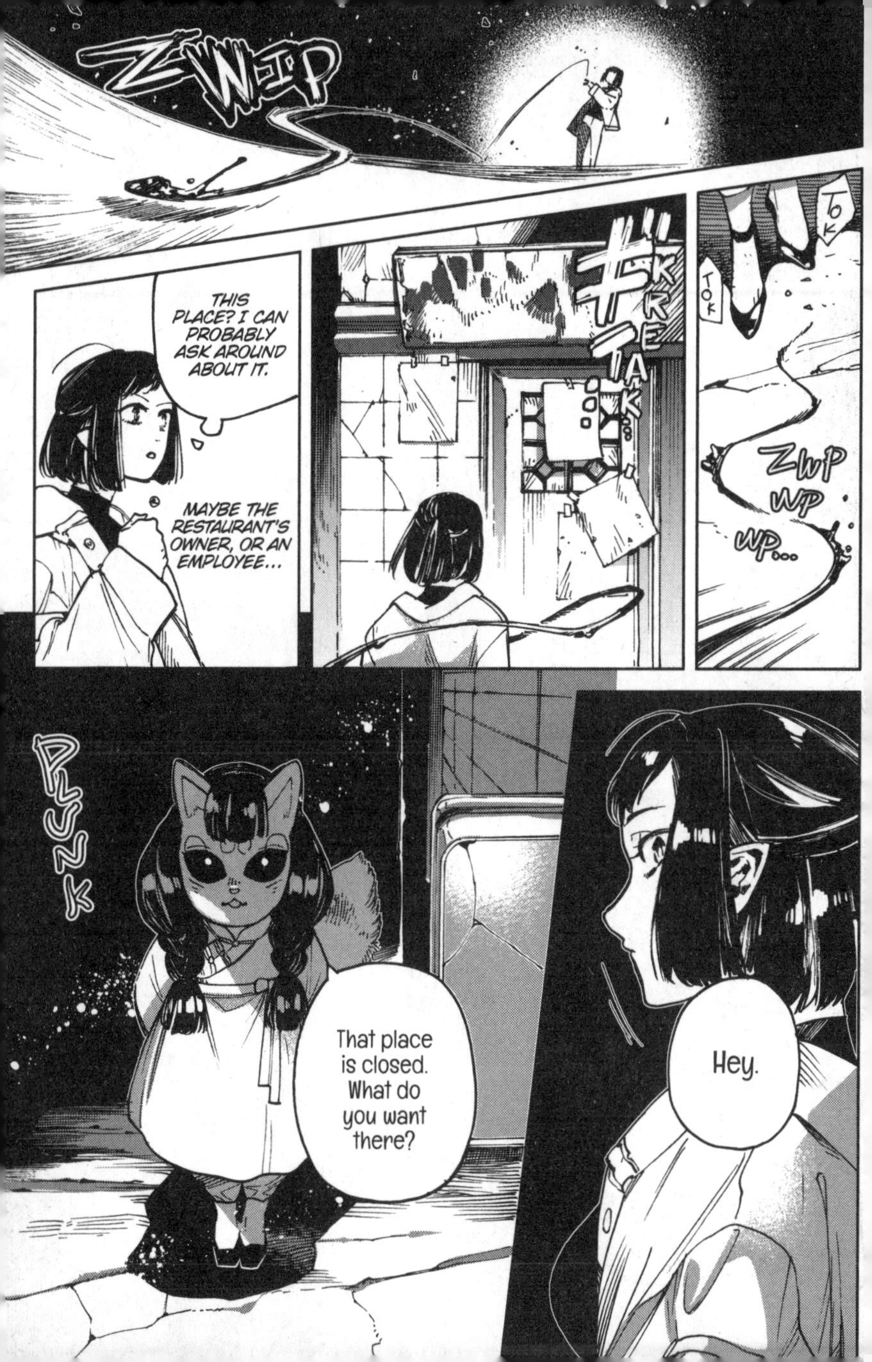
ZWIP
TOK
TOK
ZWP WP WP...
KREAK...
THIS PLACE? I CAN PROBABLY ASK AROUND ABOUT IT.
MAYBE THE RESTAURANT'S OWNER, OR AN EMPLOYEE...
Hey.
PLUNK
That place is closed. What do you want there?

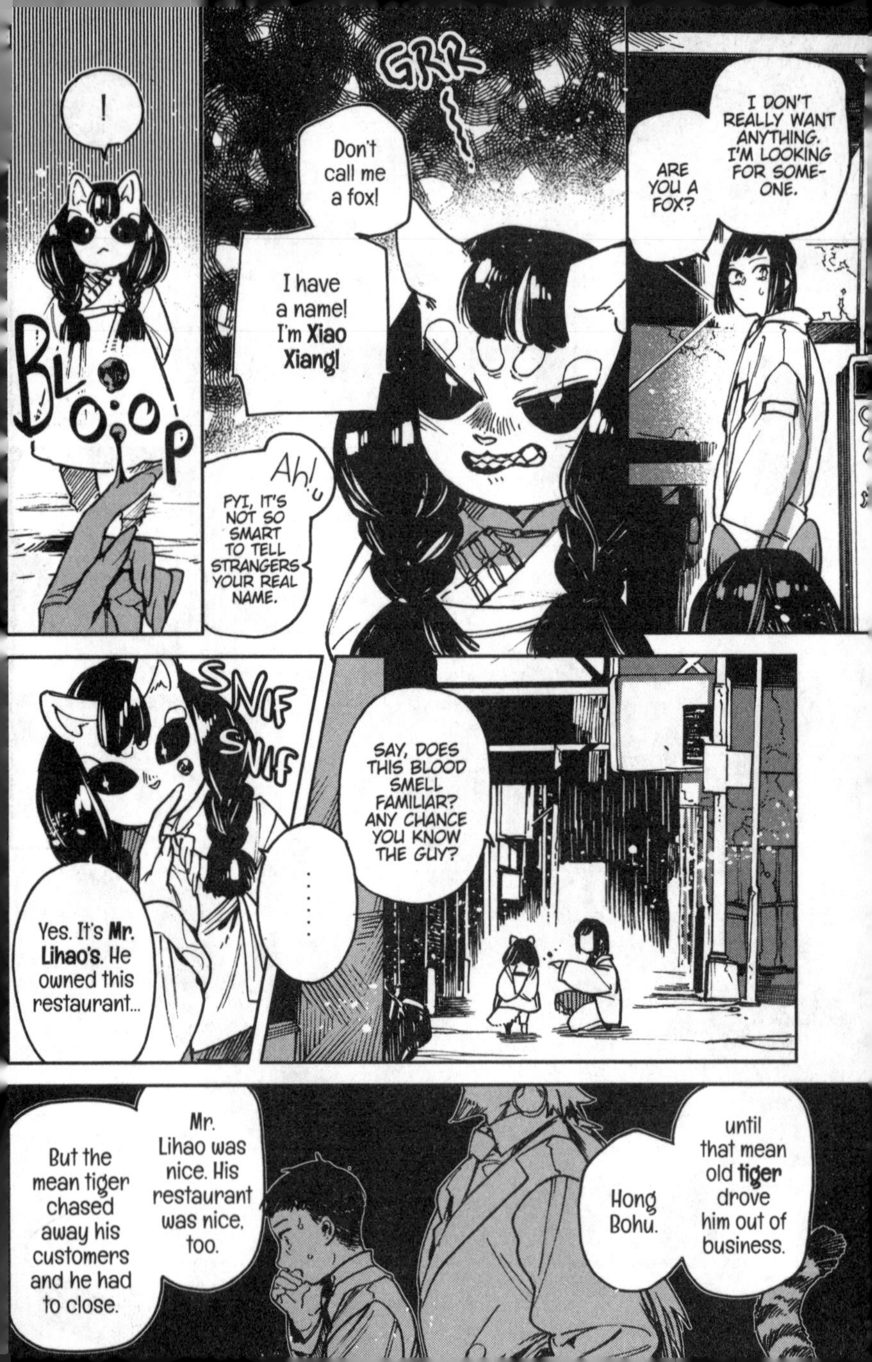
I DON'T REALLY WANT ANYTHING. I'M LOOKING FOR SOME-ONE.
ARE YOU A FOX?
GRR
Don't call me a fox!
I have a name! I'm **Xiao Xiang**!
Ah!
FYI, IT'S NOT SO SMART TO TELL STRANGERS YOUR REAL NAME.
!
BLOOP
SAY, DOES THIS BLOOD SMELL FAMILIAR? ANY CHANCE YOU KNOW THE GUY?
SNIF
SNIF
......
Yes. It's **Mr. Lihao's**. He owned this restaurant...
until that mean old **tiger** drove him out of business.
Hong Bohu.
Mr. Lihao was nice. His restaurant was nice, too.
But the mean tiger chased away his customers and he had to close.

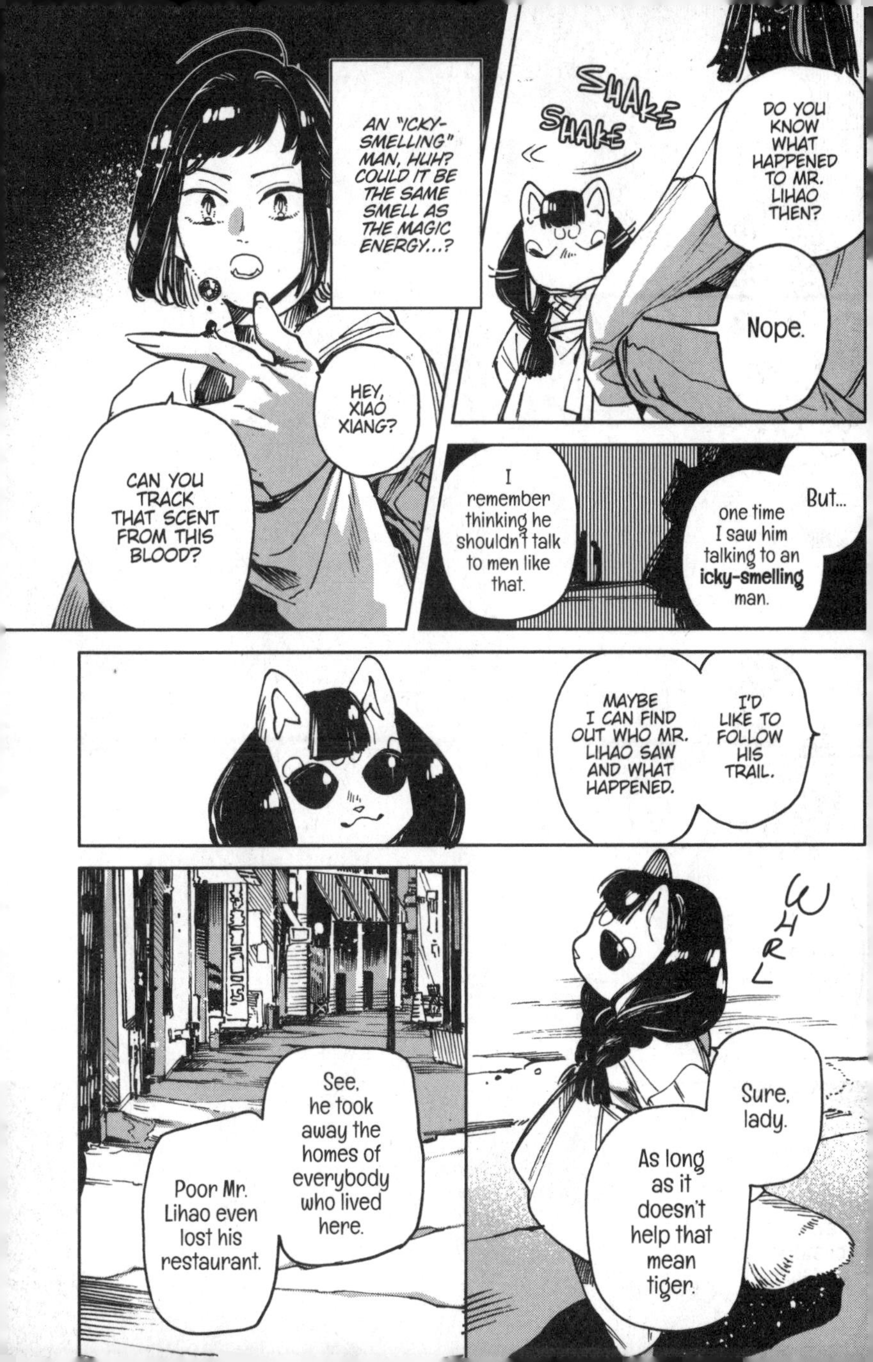
SHAKE SHAKE
DO YOU KNOW WHAT HAPPENED TO MR. LIHAO THEN?
Nope.
But...
one time I saw him talking to an **icky-smelling** man.
I remember thinking he shouldn't talk to men like that.
AN "ICKY-SMELLING" MAN, HUH? COULD IT BE THE SAME SMELL AS THE MAGIC ENERGY...?
HEY, XIAO XIANG?
CAN YOU TRACK THAT SCENT FROM THIS BLOOD?
I'D LIKE TO FOLLOW HIS TRAIL.
MAYBE I CAN FIND OUT WHO MR. LIHAO SAW AND WHAT HAPPENED.
WHRL
Sure, lady.
As long as it doesn't help that mean tiger.
See, he took away the homes of everybody who lived here.
Poor Mr. Lihao even lost his restaurant.

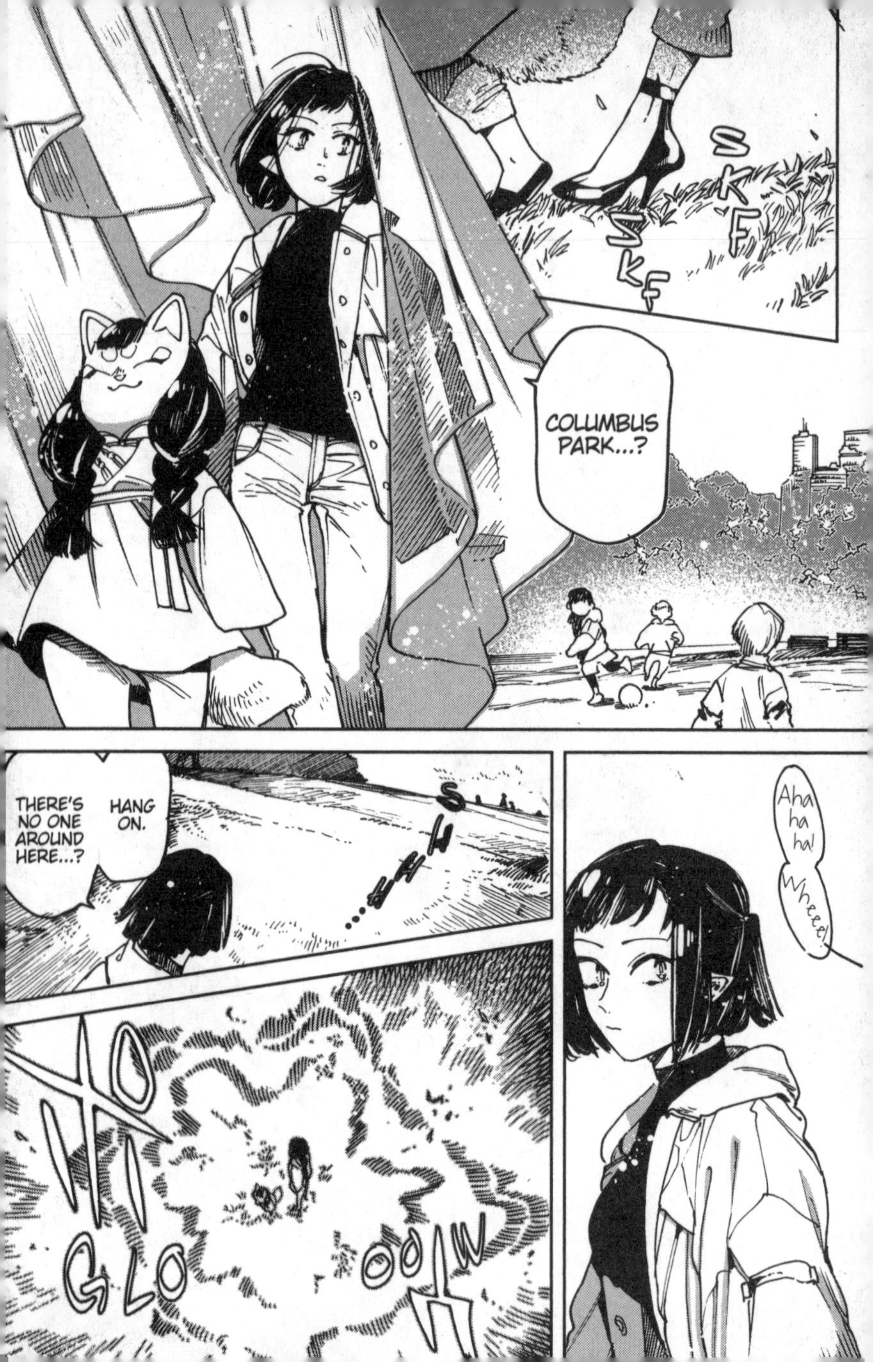

SKF
SKF
COLUMBUS PARK...?
Aha ha ha!
Wheee!
HANG ON.
THERE'S NO ONE AROUND HERE...?
SHHH...
GLOOOW

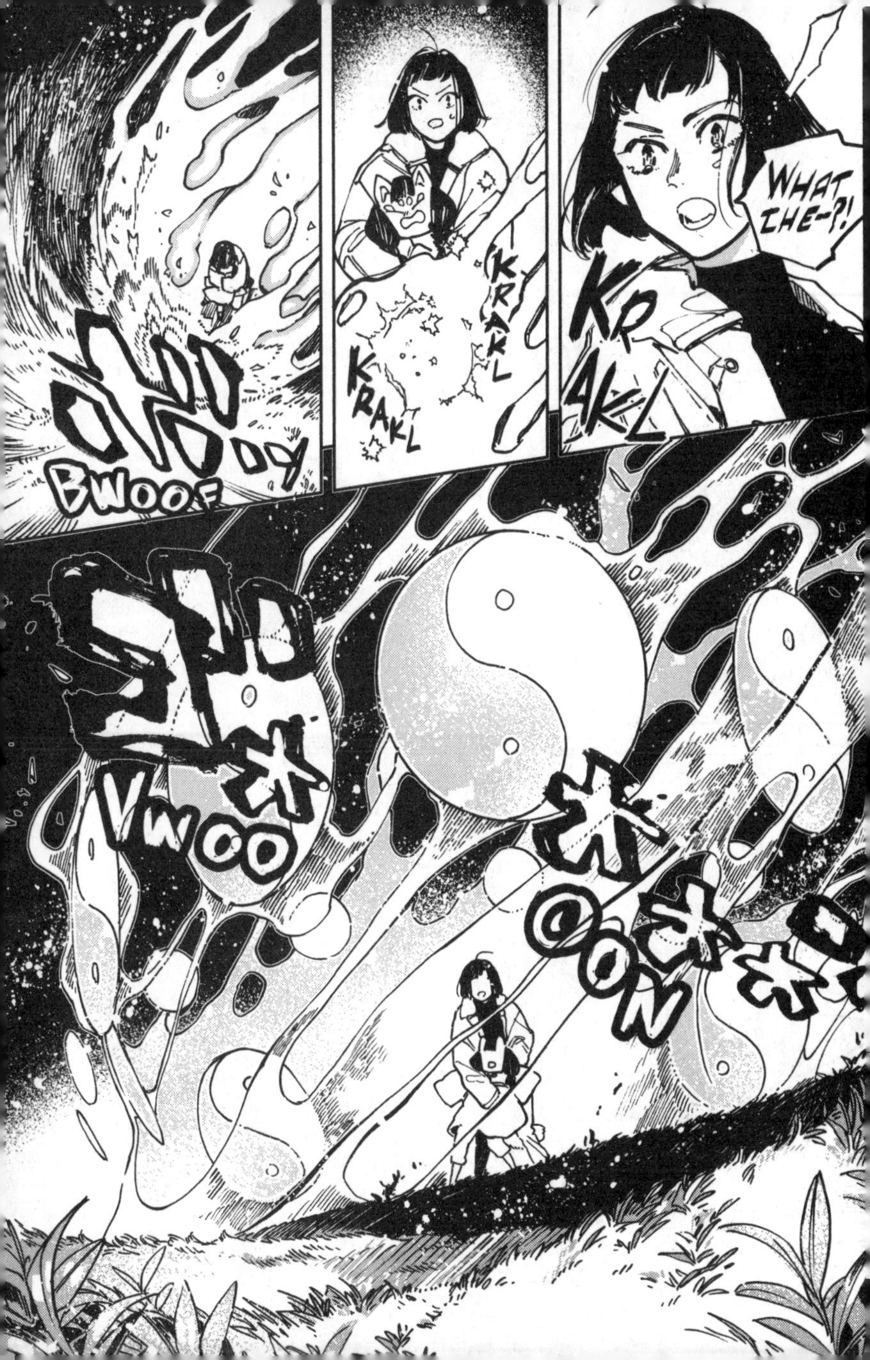
WHAT THE-?!
KRAKL
KRAKL
KRAKL
BWOOF
VWOO
OON

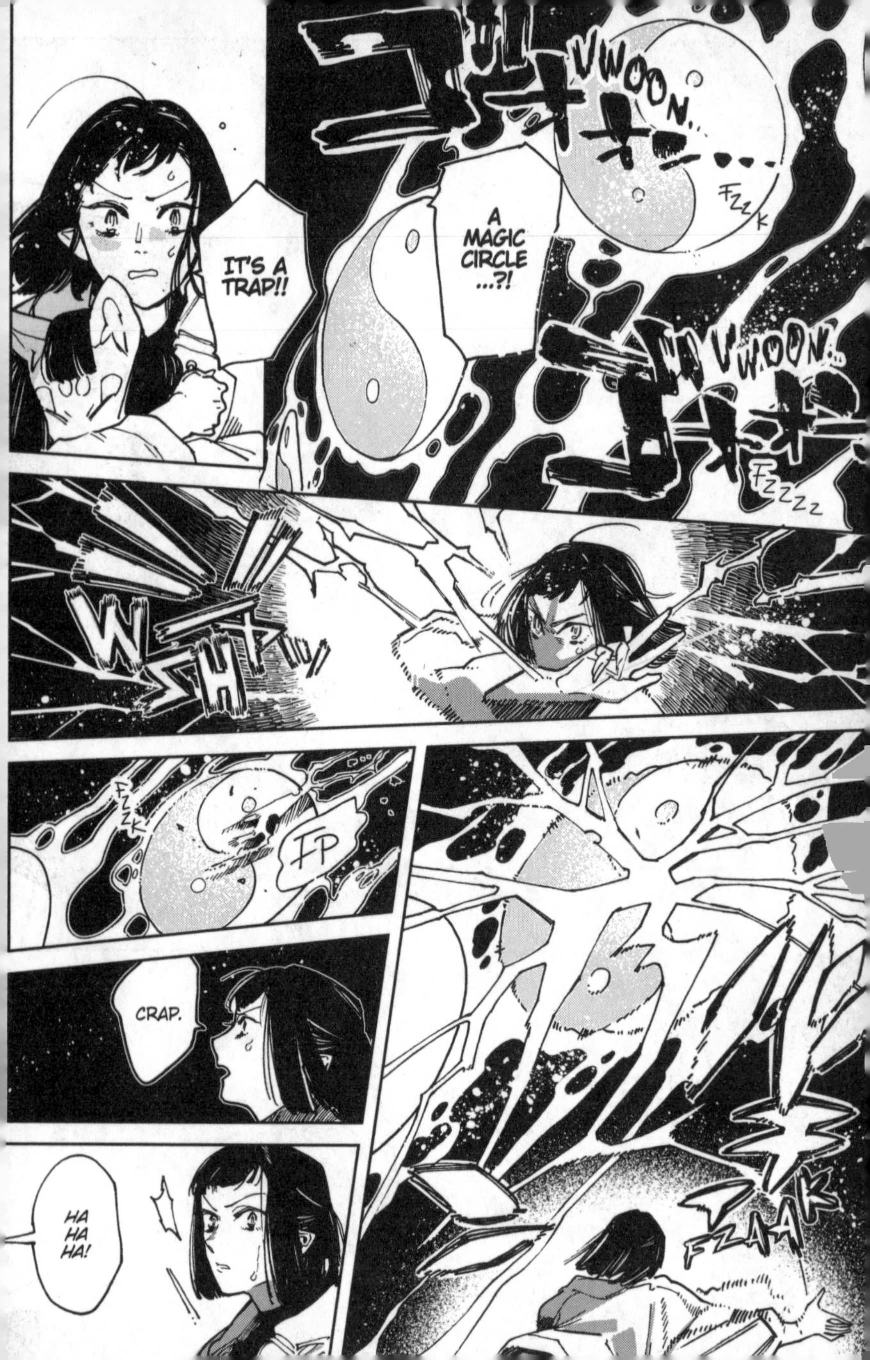
VWOON...
FZZK
A MAGIC CIRCLE ...?!
VWOON...
FZZZZ
IT'S A TRAP!!
WHSH
FZAAK
FZZK
FP
CRAP.
HA HA HA!

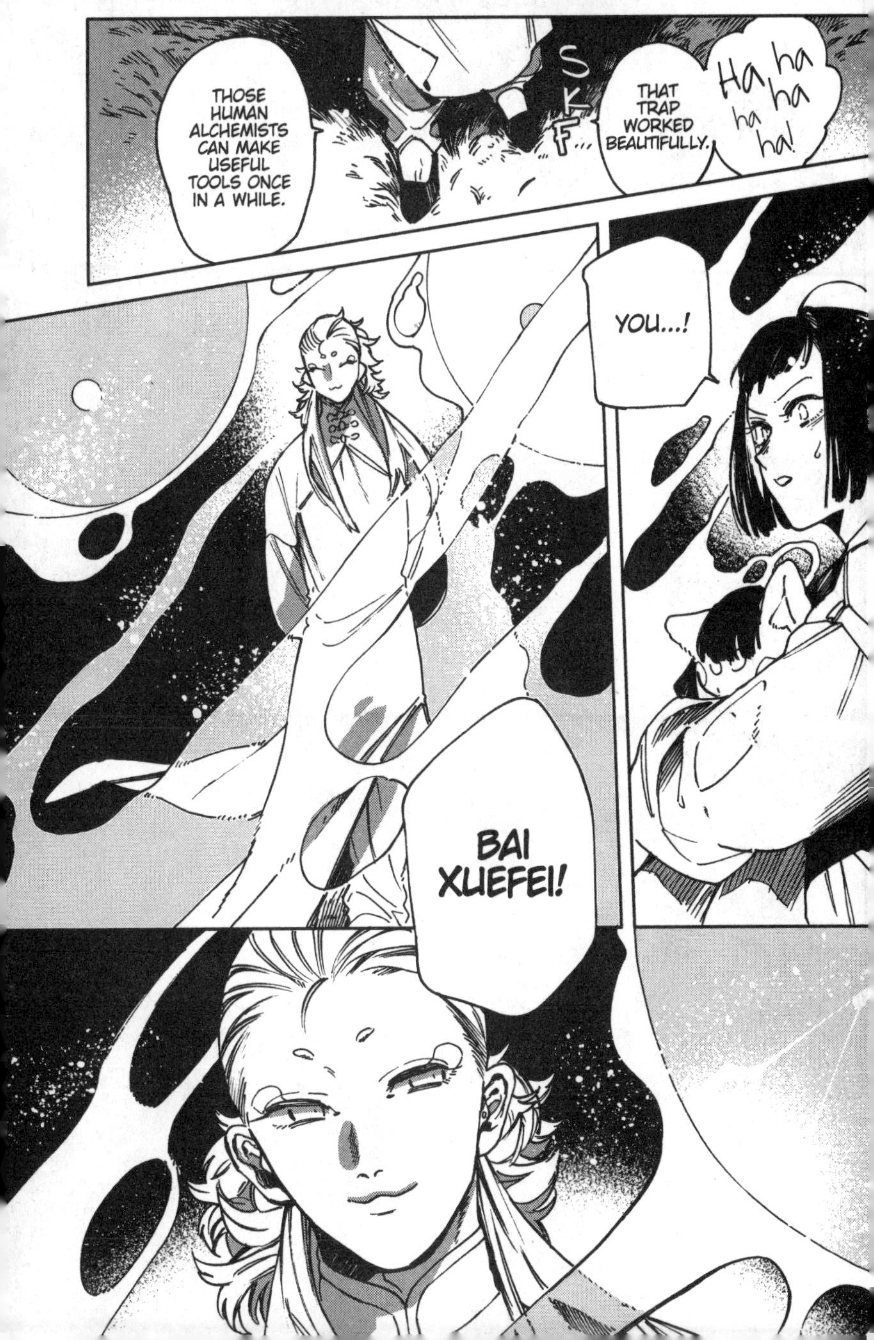
Ha ha ha ha ha!
THAT TRAP WORKED BEAUTIFULLY.
SKF...
THOSE HUMAN ALCHEMISTS CAN MAKE USEFUL TOOLS ONCE IN A WHILE.
YOU...!
BAI XUEFEI!

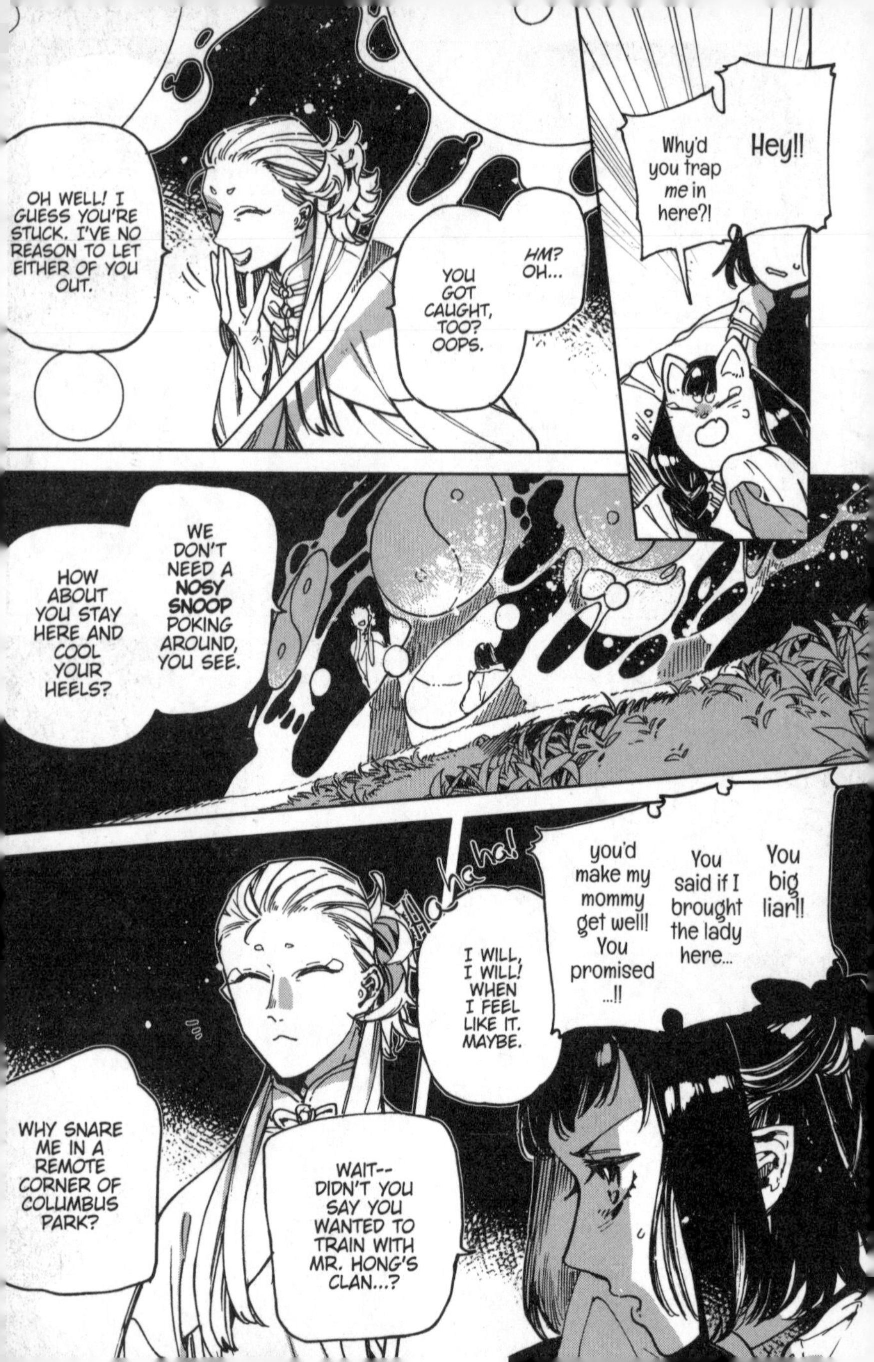
Hey!!
Why'd you trap *me* in here?!
HM? OH...
YOU GOT CAUGHT, TOO? OOPS.
OH WELL! I GUESS YOU'RE STUCK. I'VE NO REASON TO LET EITHER OF YOU OUT.
WE DON'T NEED A **NOSY SNOOP** POKING AROUND, YOU SEE.
HOW ABOUT YOU STAY HERE AND COOL YOUR HEELS?
You big liar!!
You said if I brought the lady here...
you'd make my mommy get well! You promised...!!
Ahahaha!
I WILL, I WILL! WHEN I FEEL LIKE IT. MAYBE.
WAIT-- DIDN'T YOU SAY YOU WANTED TO TRAIN WITH MR. HONG'S CLAN...?
WHY SNARE ME IN A REMOTE CORNER OF COLUMBUS PARK?

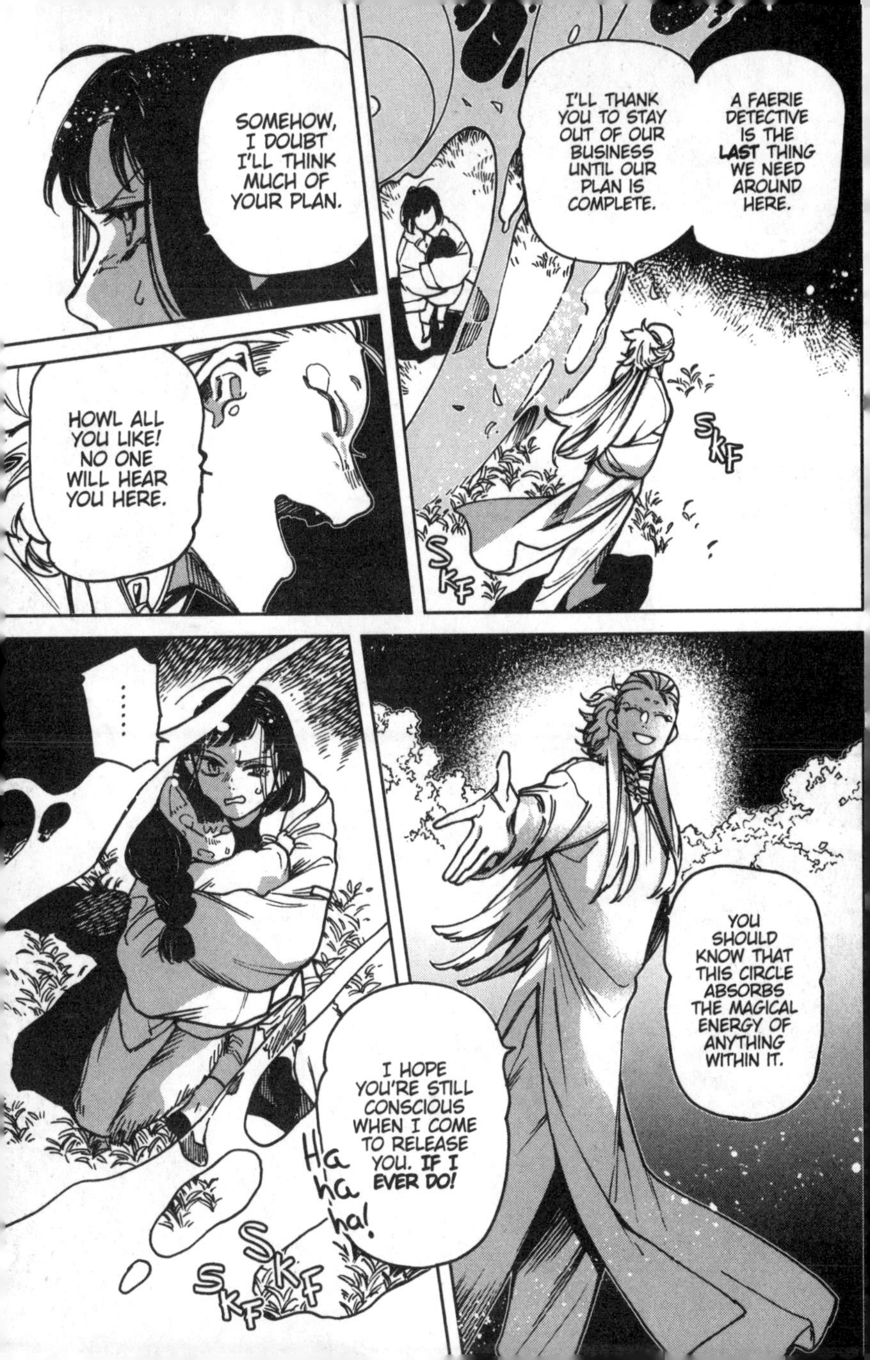
A FAERIE DETECTIVE IS THE **LAST** THING WE NEED AROUND HERE.
I'LL THANK YOU TO STAY OUT OF OUR BUSINESS UNTIL OUR PLAN IS COMPLETE.
SKF
SKF
SOMEHOW, I DOUBT I'LL THINK MUCH OF YOUR PLAN.
HOWL ALL YOU LIKE! NO ONE WILL HEAR YOU HERE.
YOU SHOULD KNOW THAT THIS CIRCLE ABSORBS THE MAGICAL ENERGY OF ANYTHING WITHIN IT.
I HOPE YOU'RE STILL CONSCIOUS WHEN I COME TO RELEASE YOU. **IF I EVER DO!**
Ha ha ha!
SKF
SKF
......

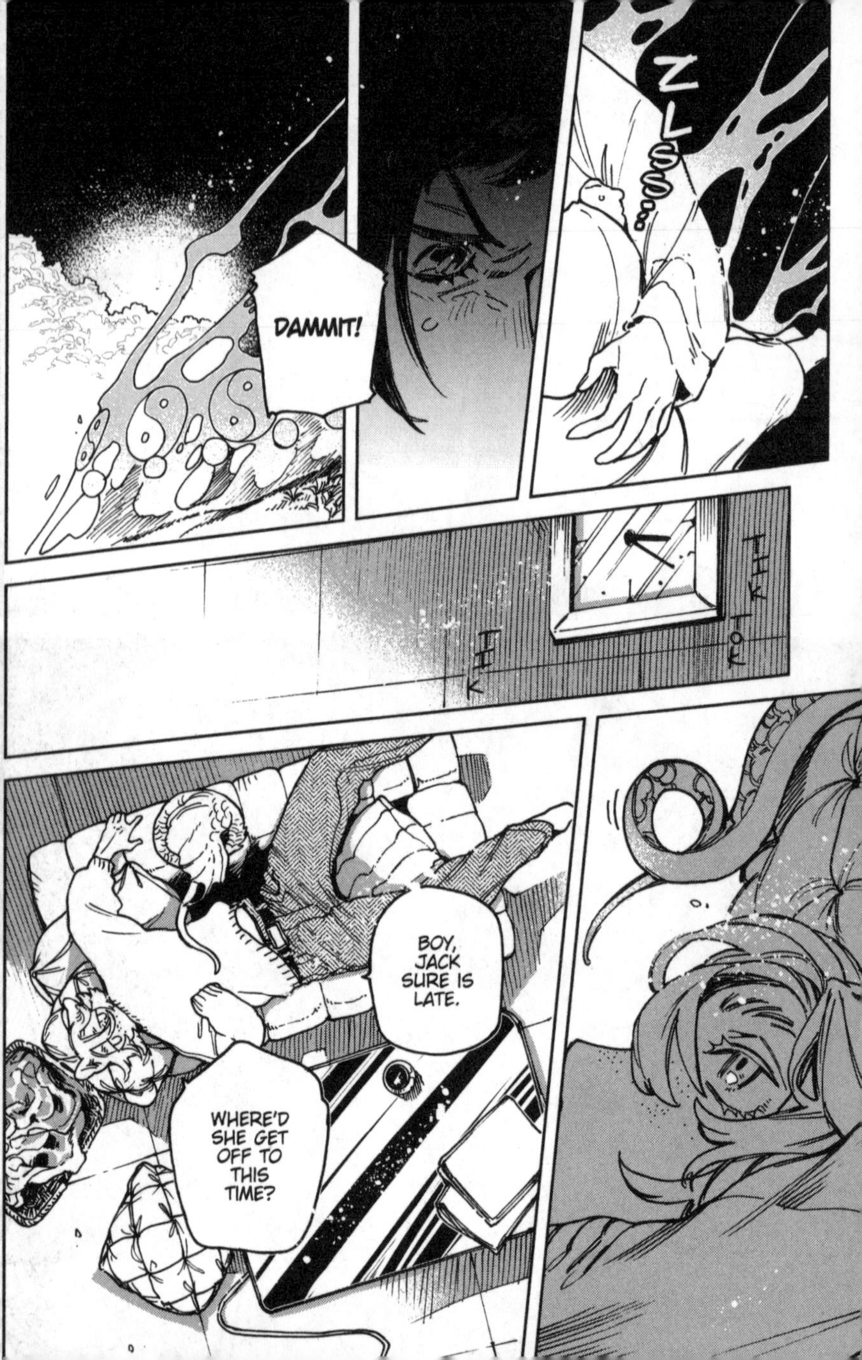
DAMMIT!
THK TOK
THK
BOY, JACK SURE IS LATE.
WHERE'D SHE GET OFF TO THIS TIME?

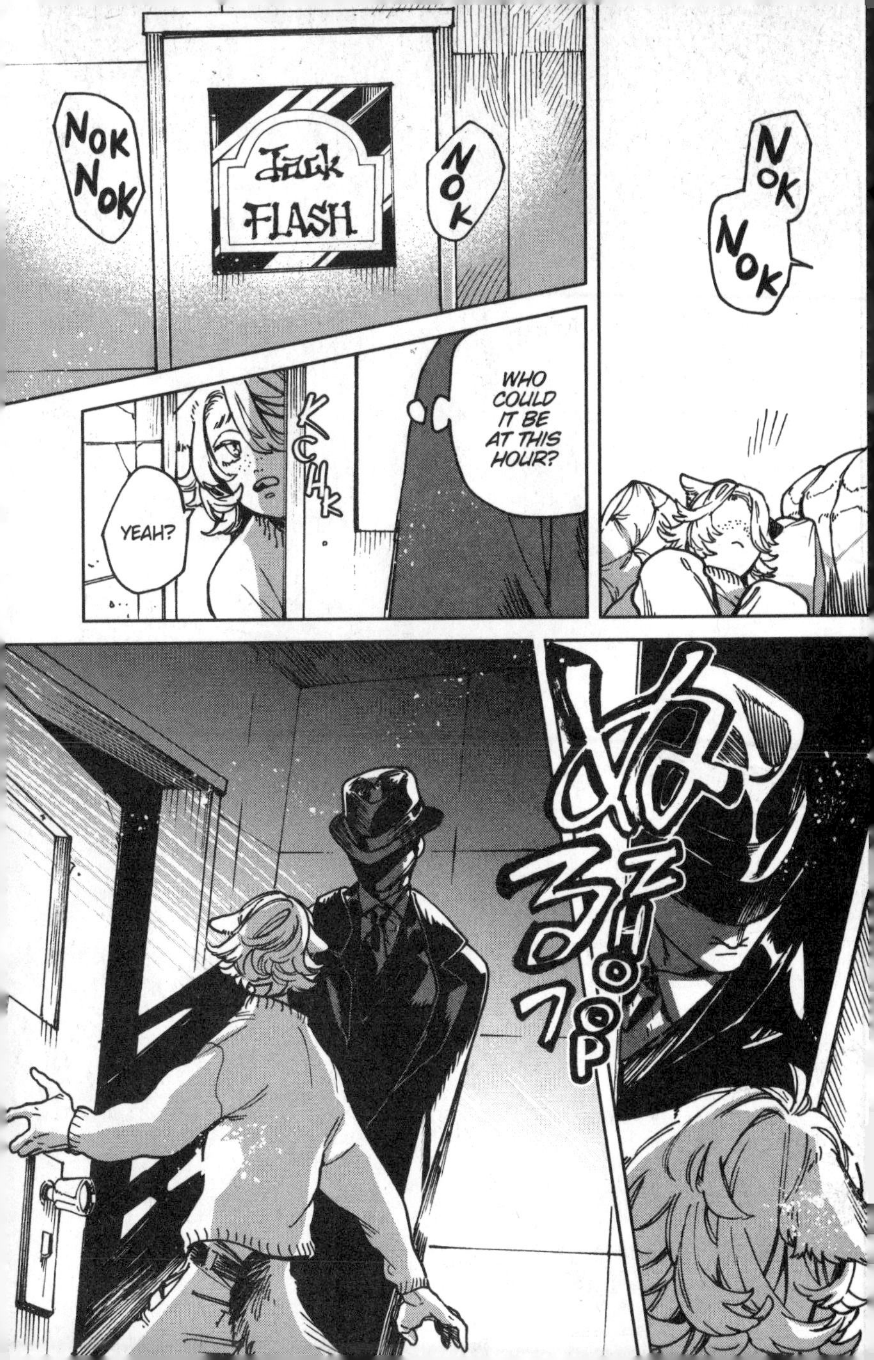
NOK NOK NOK NOK
NOK
Jack FLASH
NOK NOK
WHO COULD IT BE AT THIS HOUR?
KCHK
YEAH?
ZHOOP

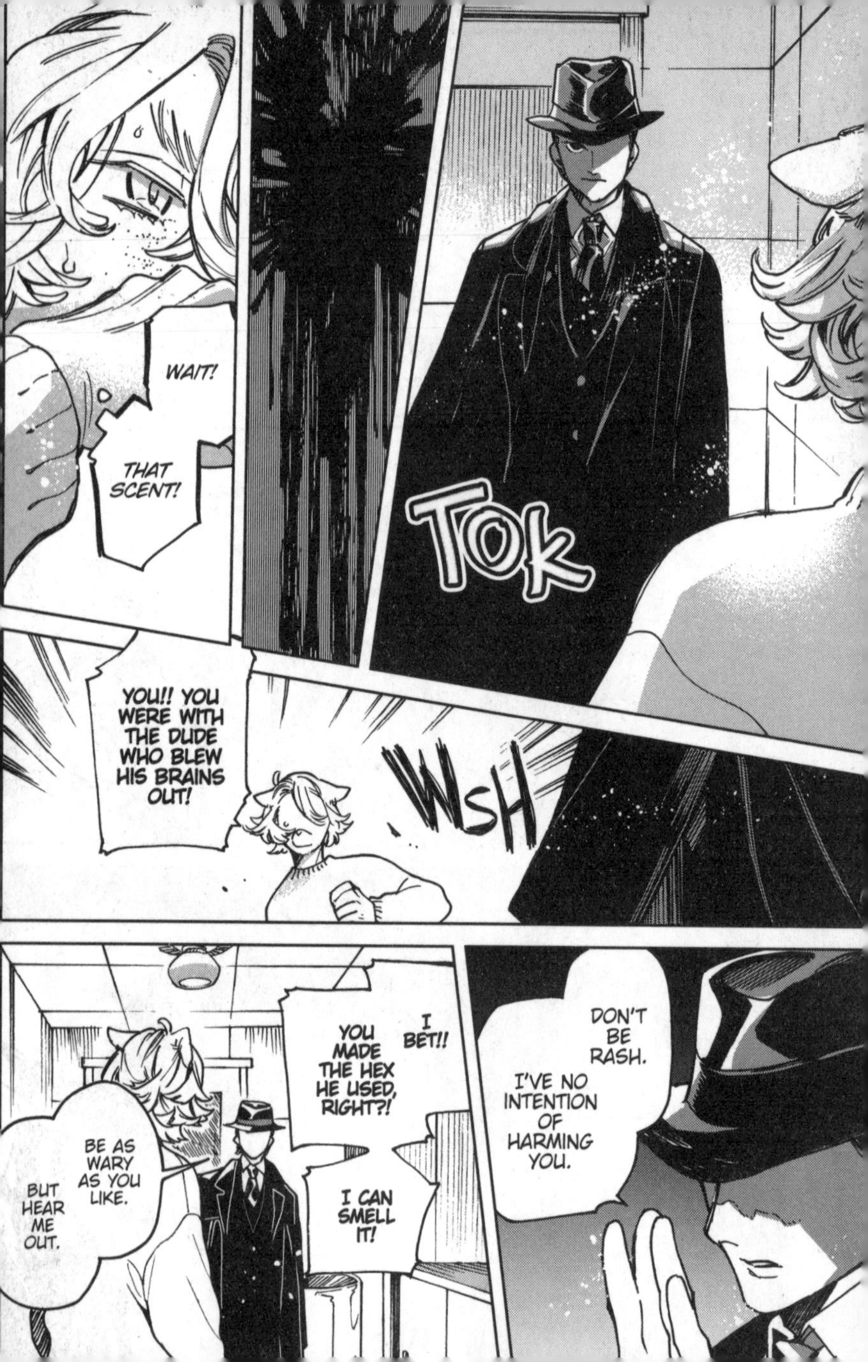
TOK
WAIT!
THAT SCENT!
WSH
YOU!! YOU WERE WITH THE DUDE WHO BLEW HIS BRAINS OUT!
DON'T BE RASH.
I'VE NO INTENTION OF HARMING YOU.
I BET!!
YOU MADE THE HEX HE USED, RIGHT?!
I CAN SMELL IT!
BE AS WARY AS YOU LIKE.
BUT HEAR ME OUT.

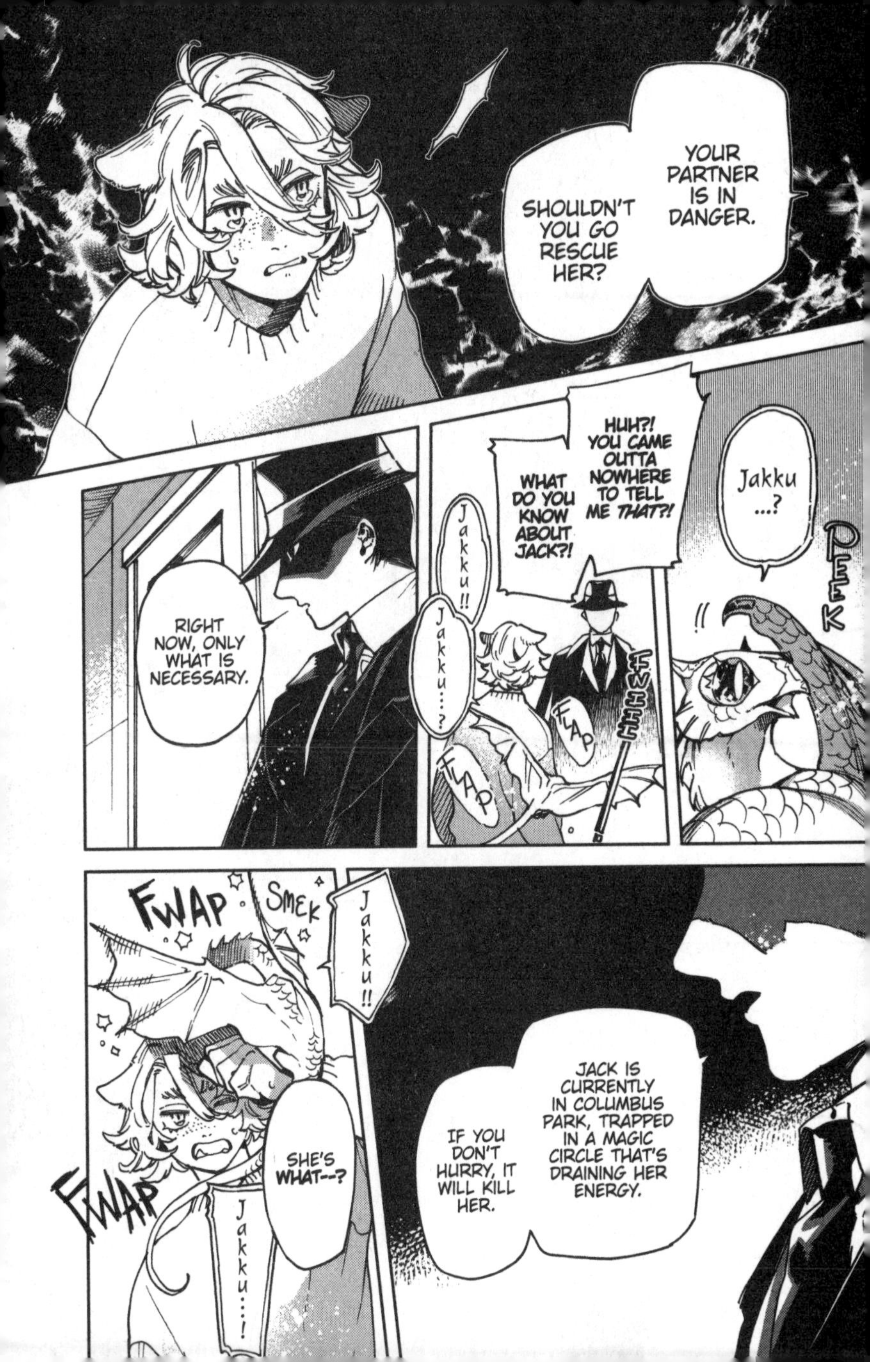
YOUR PARTNER IS IN DANGER.
SHOULDN'T YOU GO RESCUE HER?
Jakku ...?
PEEK
!!
HUH?! YOU CAME OUTTA NOWHERE TO TELL ME *THAT?!*
WHAT DO YOU KNOW ABOUT JACK?!
Jakku!!
Jakku...?
FWIII
FLAP
FLAP
RIGHT NOW, ONLY WHAT IS NECESSARY.
JACK IS CURRENTLY IN COLUMBUS PARK, TRAPPED IN A MAGIC CIRCLE THAT'S DRAINING HER ENERGY.
IF YOU DON'T HURRY, IT WILL KILL HER.
Jakku!!
SMEK
FWAP
SHE'S **WHAT--?**
Jakku...!
FWAP

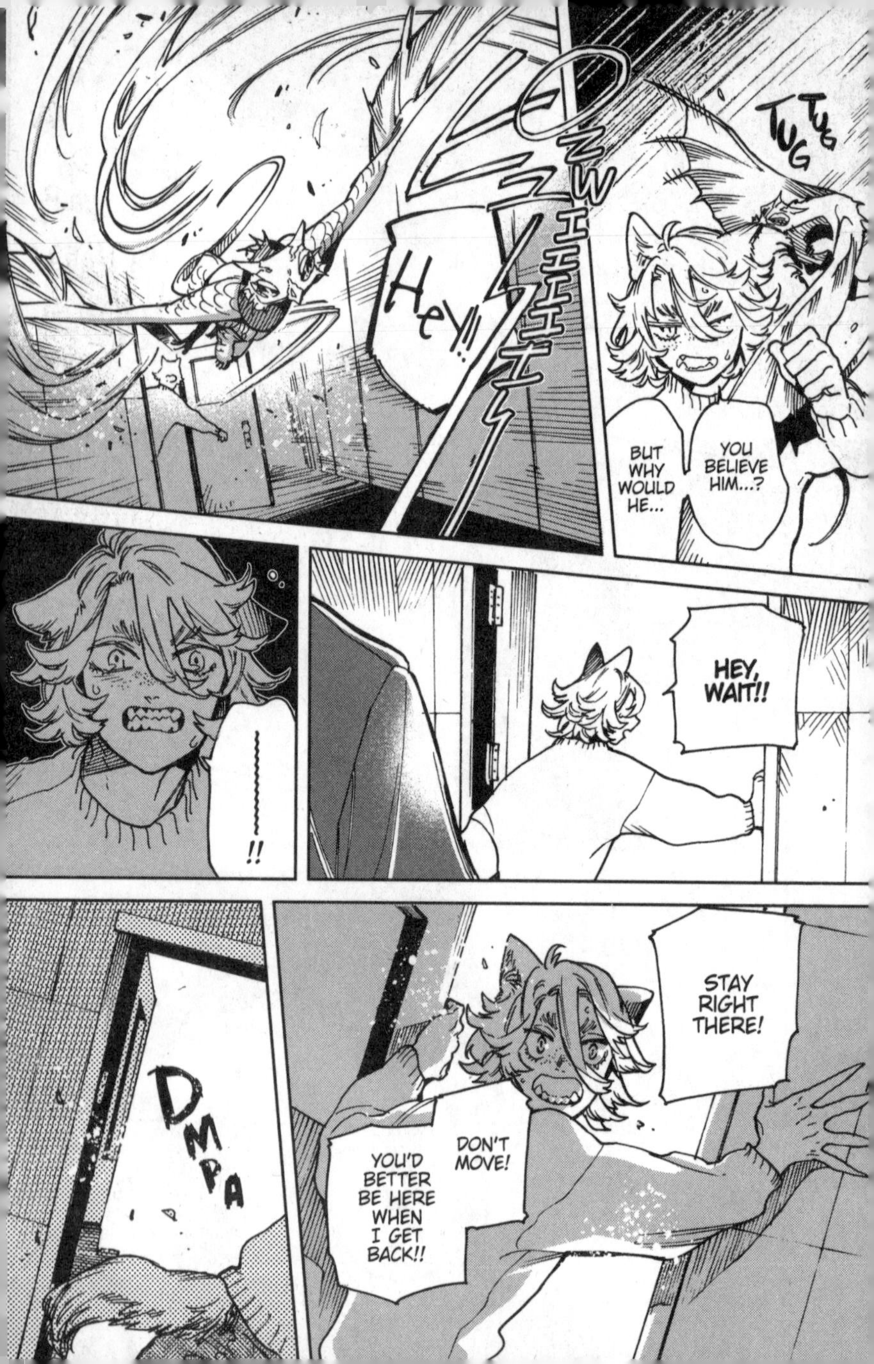
TUG TUG
YOU BELIEVE HIM...?
BUT WHY WOULD HE...
Hey!!
HEY, WAIT!!
......!!
STAY RIGHT THERE!
DON'T MOVE!
YOU'D BETTER BE HERE WHEN I GET BACK!!

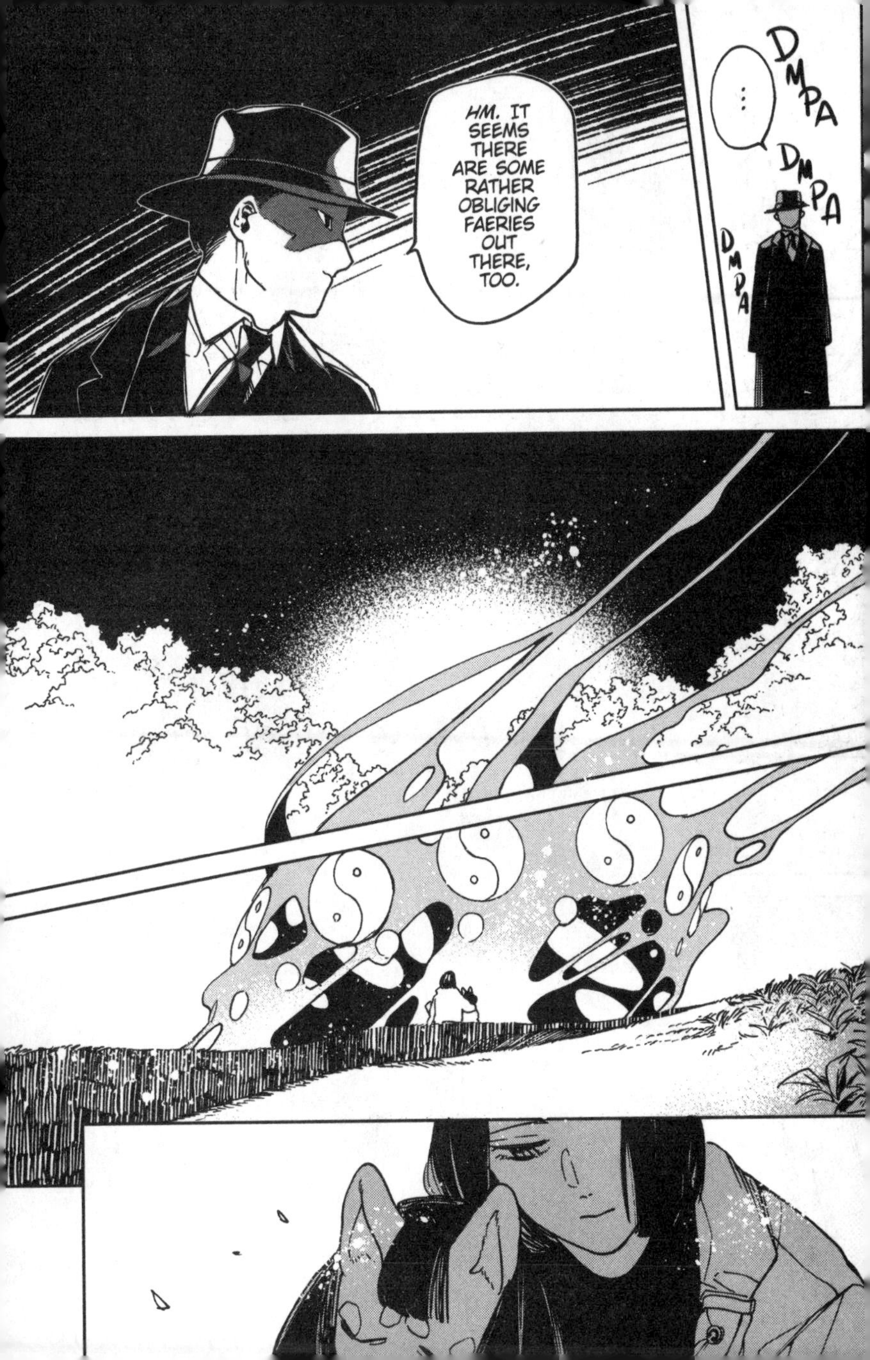
...
DMPA
DMPA
DMPA
HM. IT SEEMS THERE ARE SOME RATHER OBLIGING FAERIES OUT THERE, TOO.

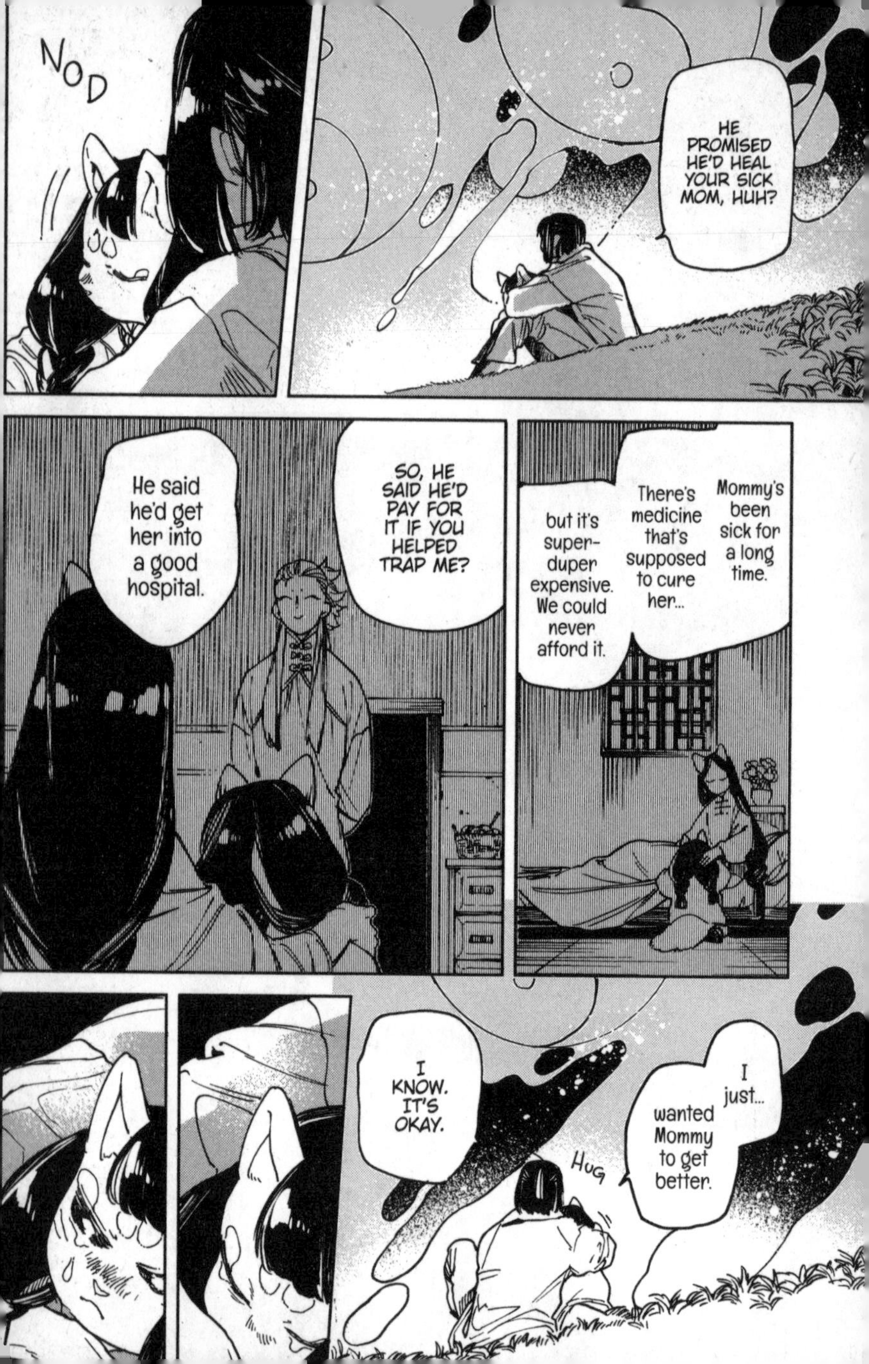

HE PROMISED HE'D HEAL YOUR SICK MOM, HUH?
NOD
Mommy's been sick for a long time.
There's medicine that's supposed to cure her...
but it's super-duper expensive. We could never afford it.
SO, HE SAID HE'D PAY FOR IT IF YOU HELPED TRAP ME?
He said he'd get her into a good hospital.
I just...
wanted Mommy to get better.
HUG
I KNOW. IT'S OKAY.

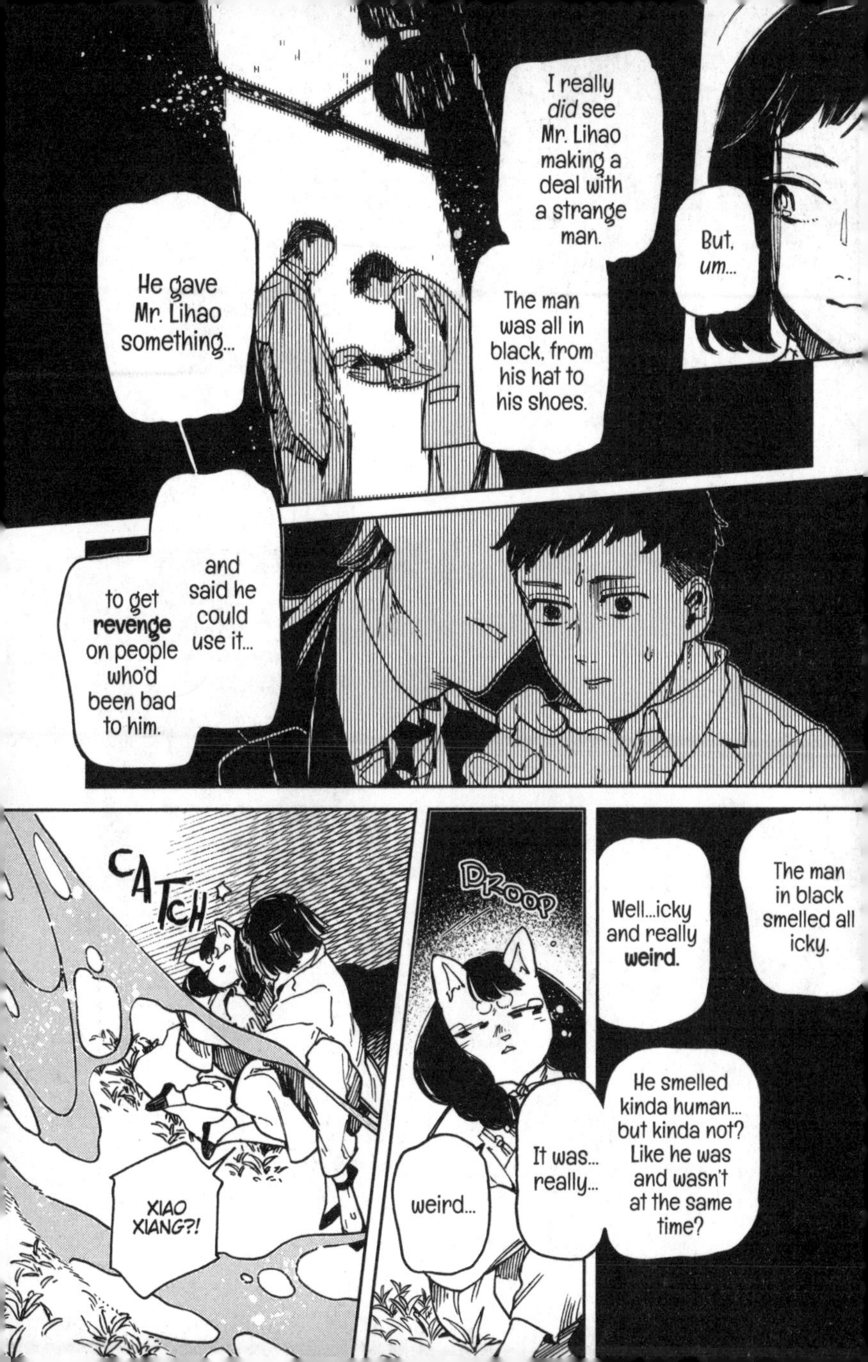
But, um...
I really *did* see Mr. Lihao making a deal with a strange man.
The man was all in black, from his hat to his shoes.
He gave Mr. Lihao something...
and said he could use it...
to get **revenge** on people who'd been bad to him.
The man in black smelled all icky.
Well...icky and really **weird**.
DROOP
He smelled kinda human... but kinda not? Like he was and wasn't at the same time?
It was... really...
weird...
CATCH
XIAO XIANG?!

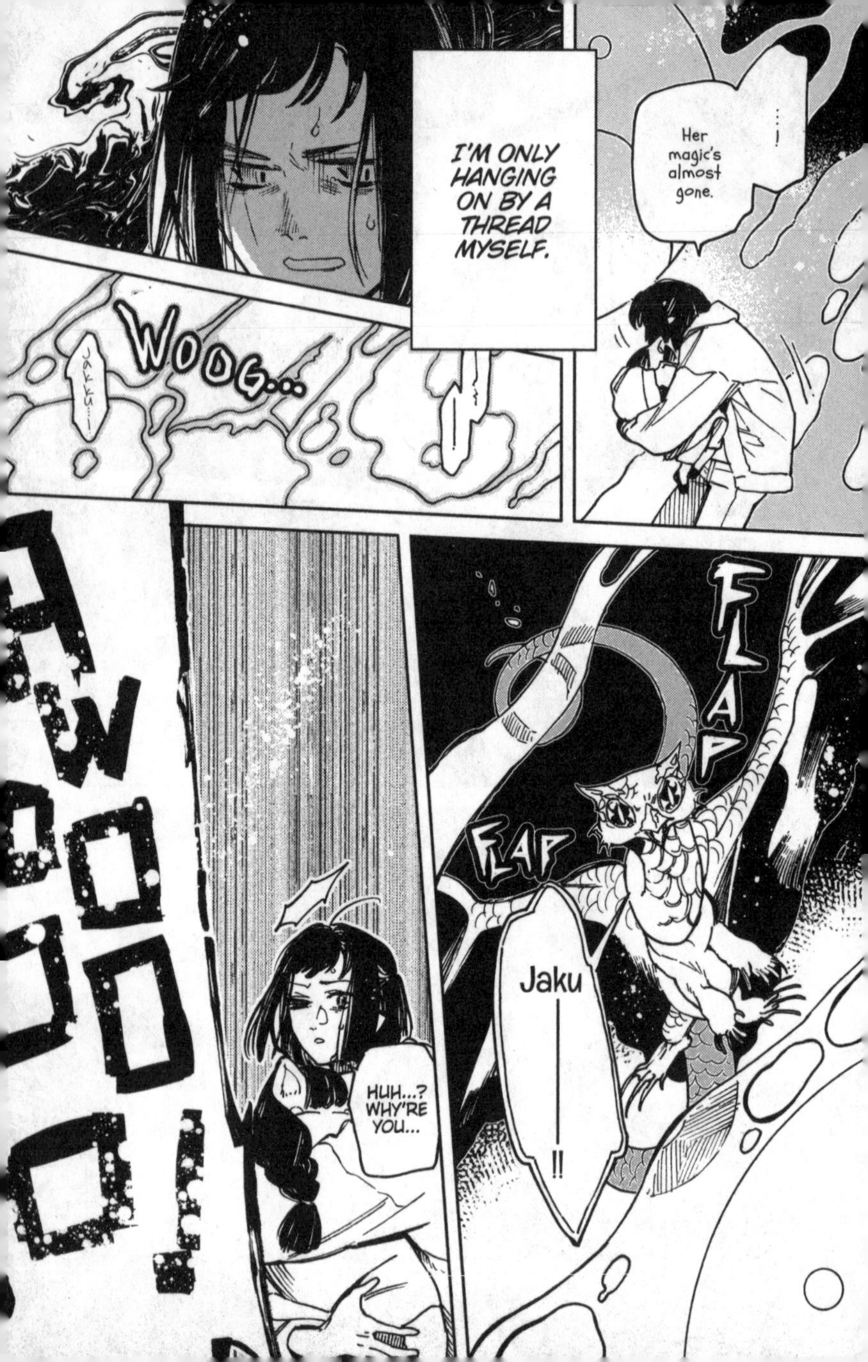
...!
Her magic's almost gone.
I'M ONLY HANGING ON BY A THREAD MYSELF.
...!
WOOG...
Jakku...!
FLAP
FLAP
Jaku—!!
HUH...? WHY'RE YOU...
AWOOOOO!

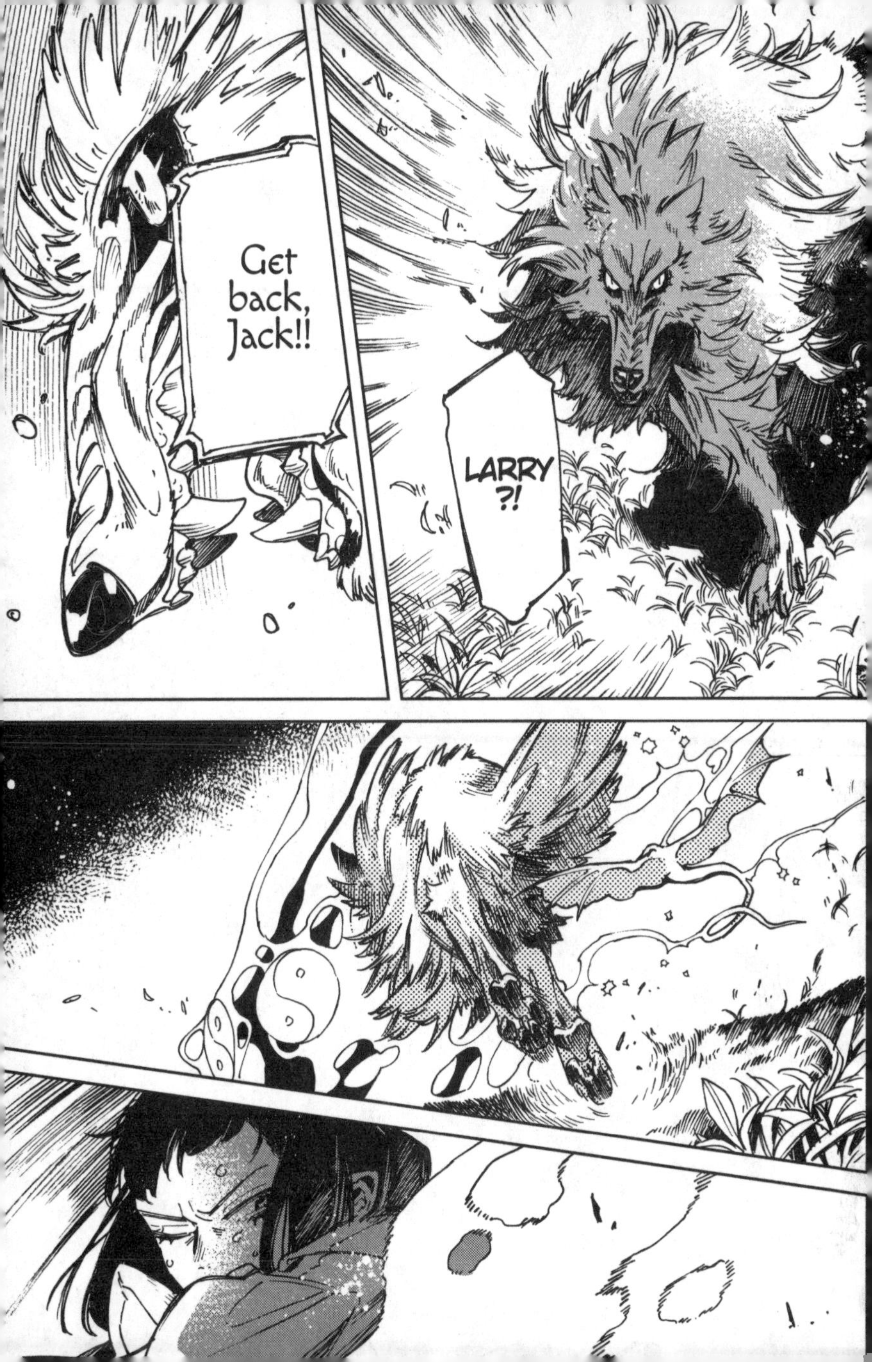
LARRY?!
Get back, Jack!!

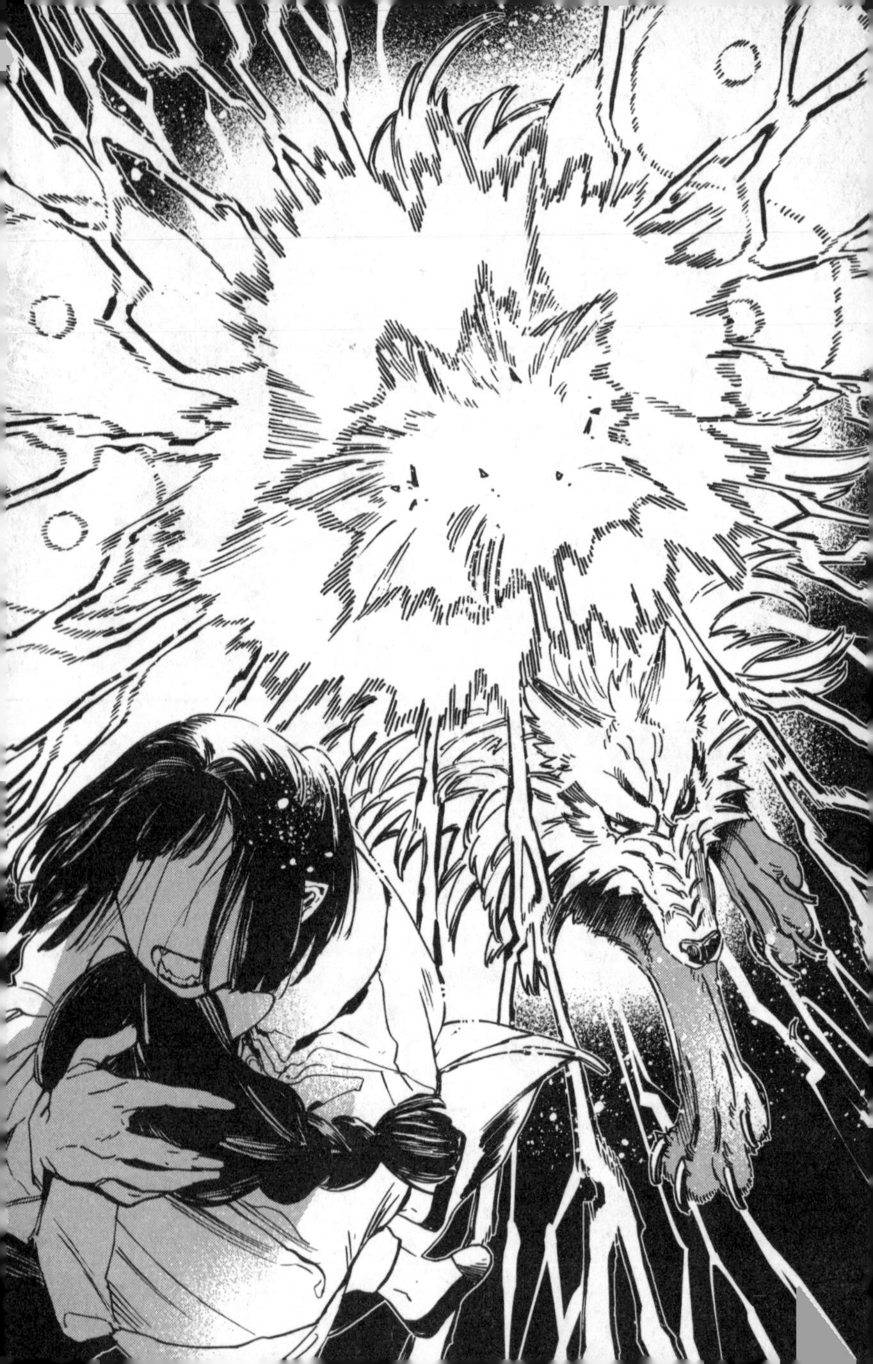

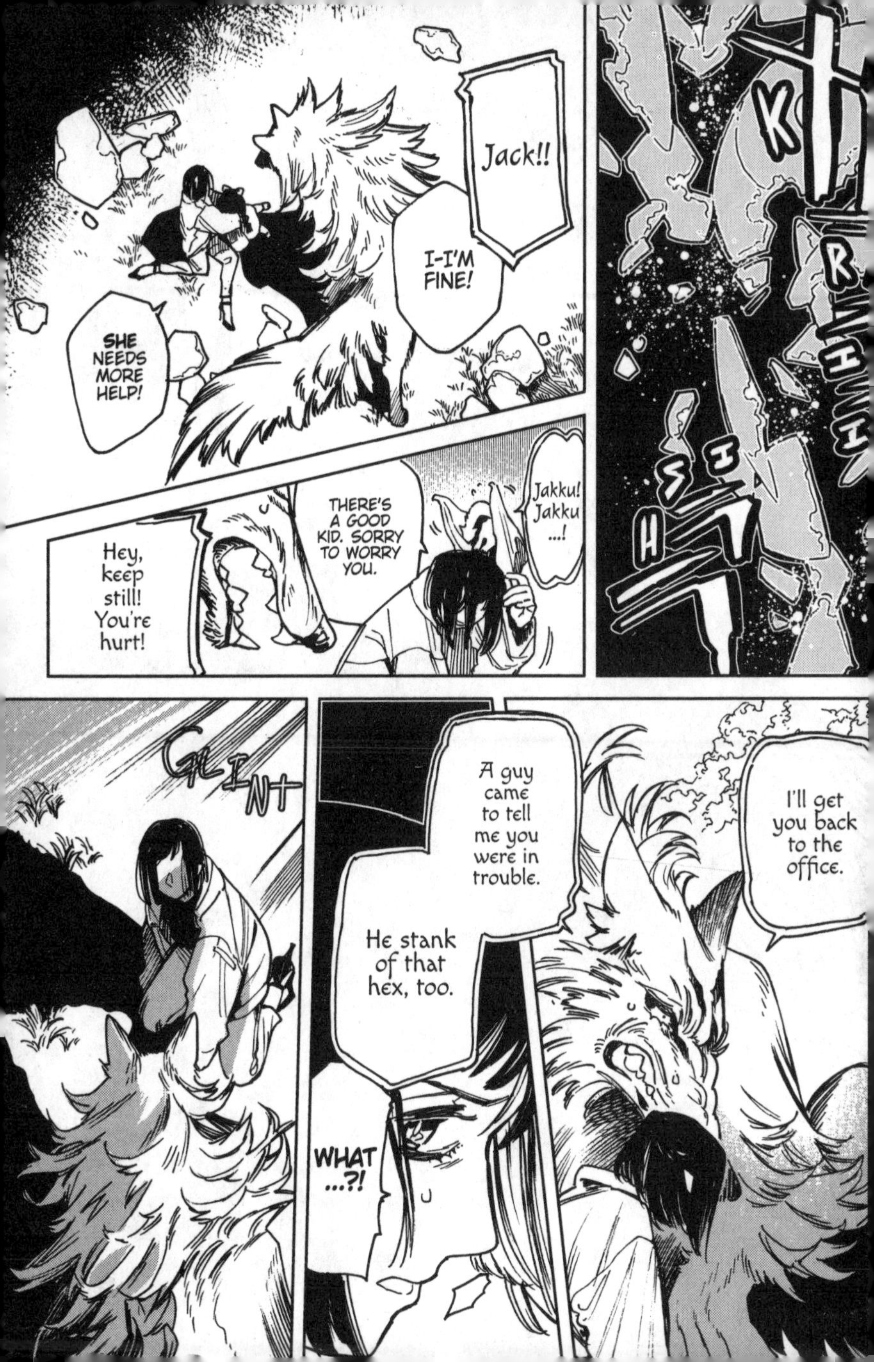
KRHH
Jack!!
I-I'M FINE!
SHE NEEDS MORE HELP!
Jakku! Jakku ...!
THERE'S A GOOD KID. SORRY TO WORRY YOU.
Hey, keep still! You're hurt!
I'll get you back to the office.
A guy came to tell me you were in trouble.
He stank of that hex, too.
WHAT ...?!
GLINT

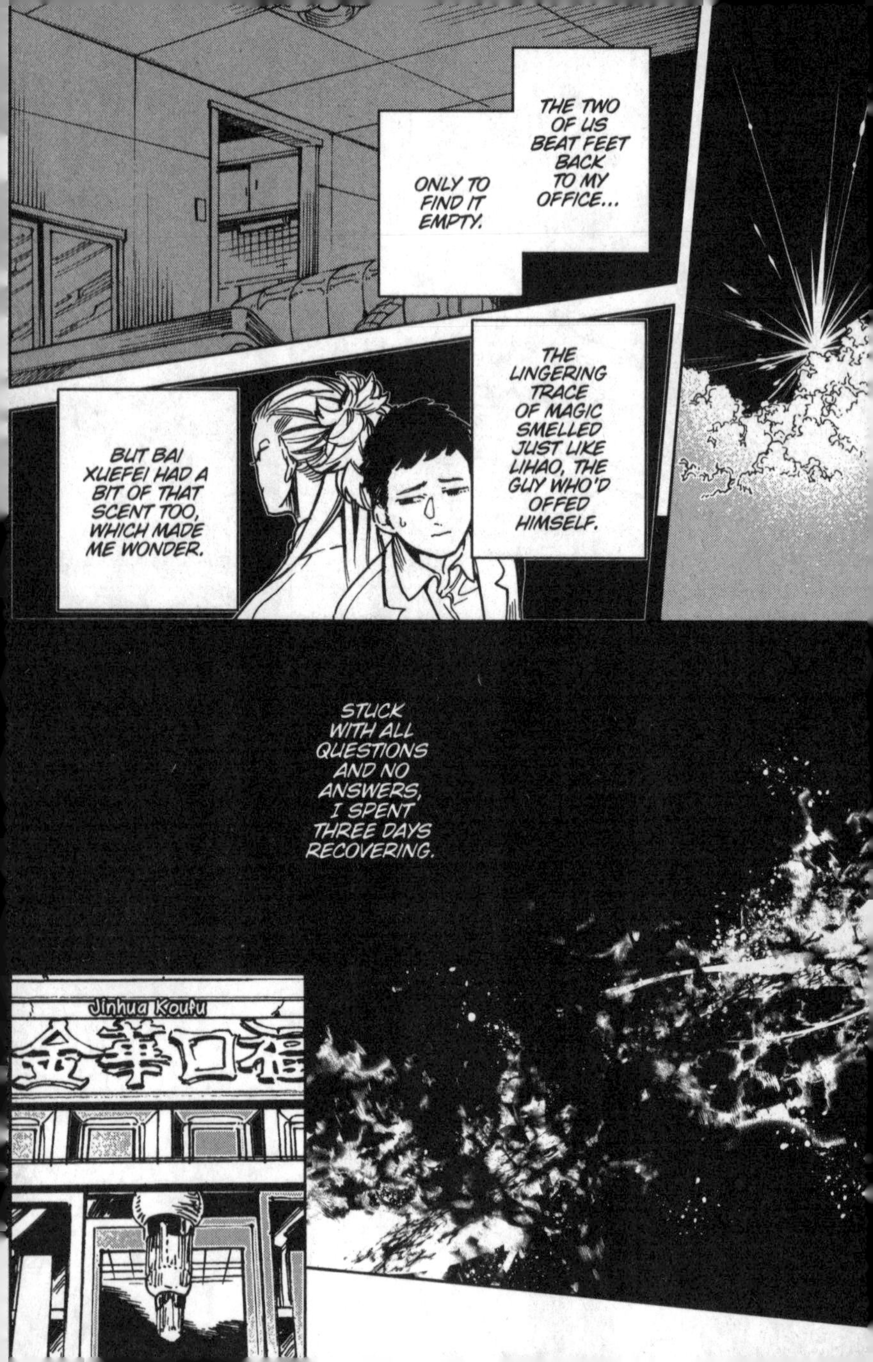
THE TWO OF US BEAT FEET BACK TO MY OFFICE...
ONLY TO FIND IT EMPTY.
THE LINGERING TRACE OF MAGIC SMELLED JUST LIKE LIHAO, THE GUY WHO'D OFFED HIMSELF.
BUT BAI XUEFEI HAD A BIT OF THAT SCENT TOO, WHICH MADE ME WONDER.
STUCK WITH ALL QUESTIONS AND NO ANSWERS, I SPENT THREE DAYS RECOVERING.
Jinhua Koufu

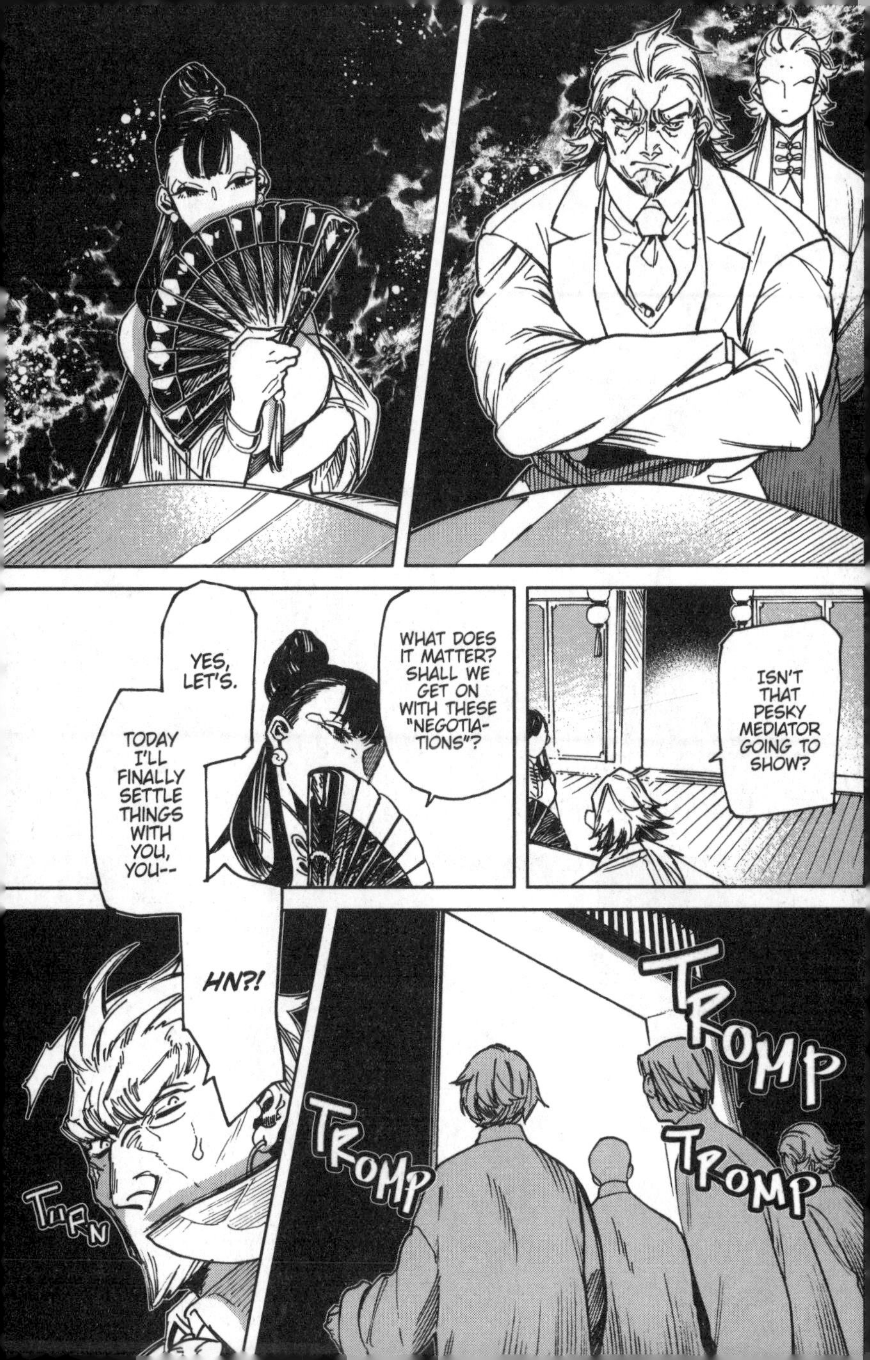
ISN'T THAT PESKY MEDIATOR GOING TO SHOW?
WHAT DOES IT MATTER? SHALL WE GET ON WITH THESE "NEGOTIATIONS"?
YES, LET'S.
TODAY I'LL FINALLY SETTLE THINGS WITH YOU, YOU--
TROMP
TROMP
TROMP
HN?!
TURN

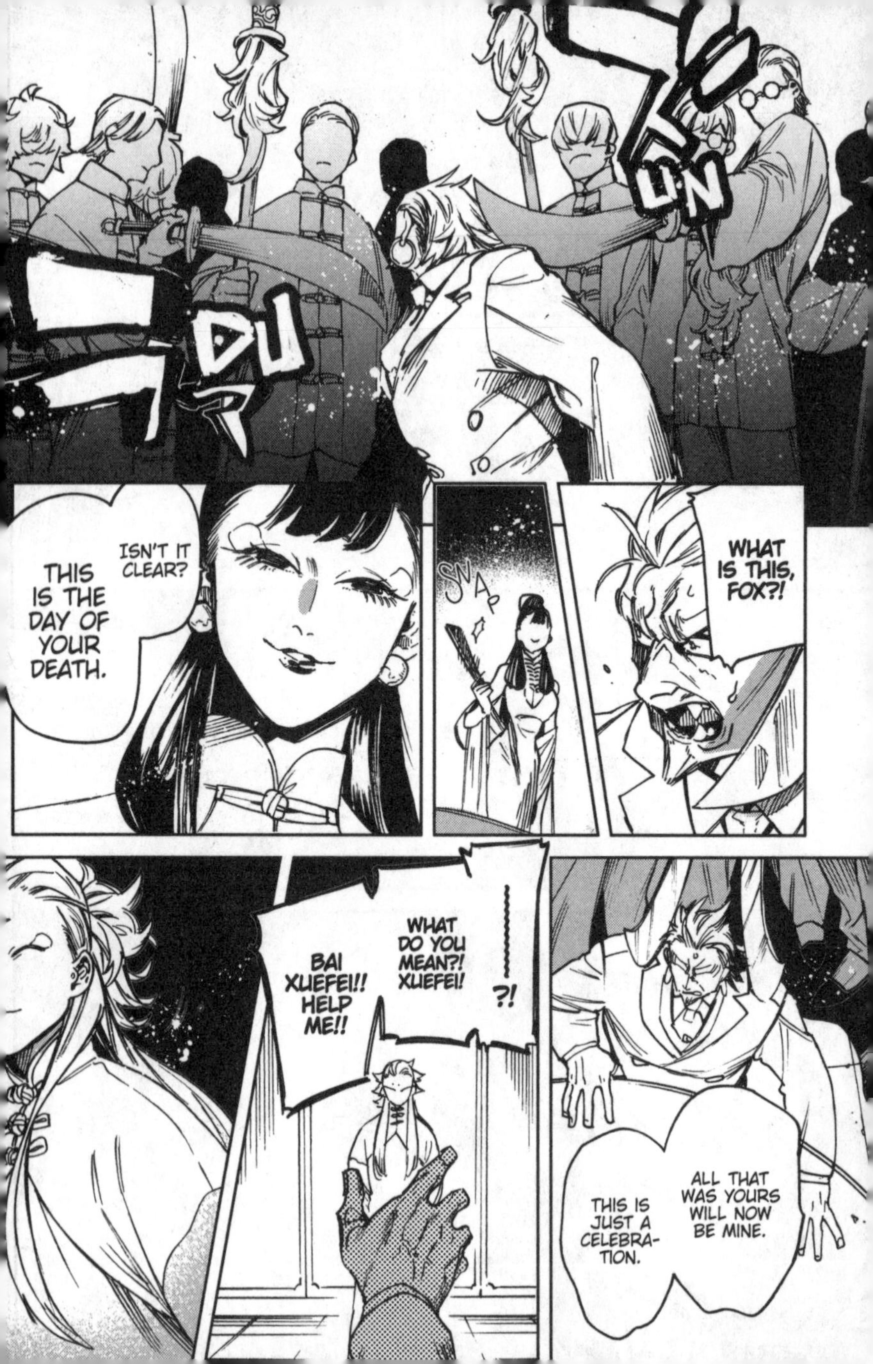
DU
WHAT IS THIS, FOX?!
SNAP
ISN'T IT CLEAR?
THIS IS THE DAY OF YOUR DEATH.
ALL THAT WAS YOURS WILL NOW BE MINE.
THIS IS JUST A CELEBRATION.
——?!
WHAT DO YOU MEAN?! XUEFEI!
BAI XUEFEI!! HELP ME!!

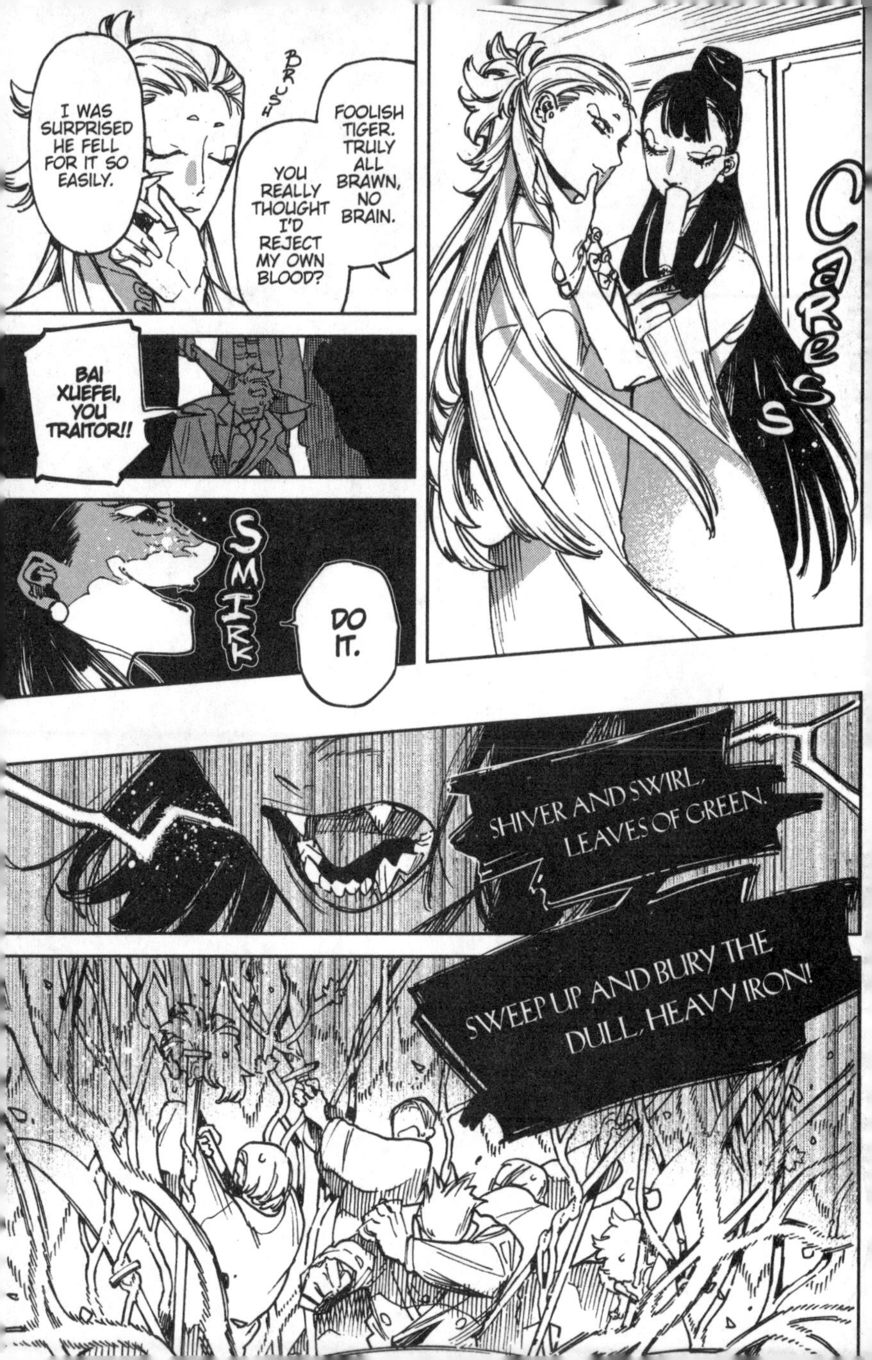
Caresss
FOOLISH TIGER. TRULY ALL BRAWN, NO BRAIN.
YOU REALLY THOUGHT I'D REJECT MY OWN BLOOD?
BRUSH
I WAS SURPRISED HE FELL FOR IT SO EASILY.
BAI XUEFEI, YOU TRAITOR!!
SMIRK
DO IT.
SHIVER AND SWIRL, LEAVES OF GREEN.
SWEEP UP AND BURY THE DULL, HEAVY IRON!

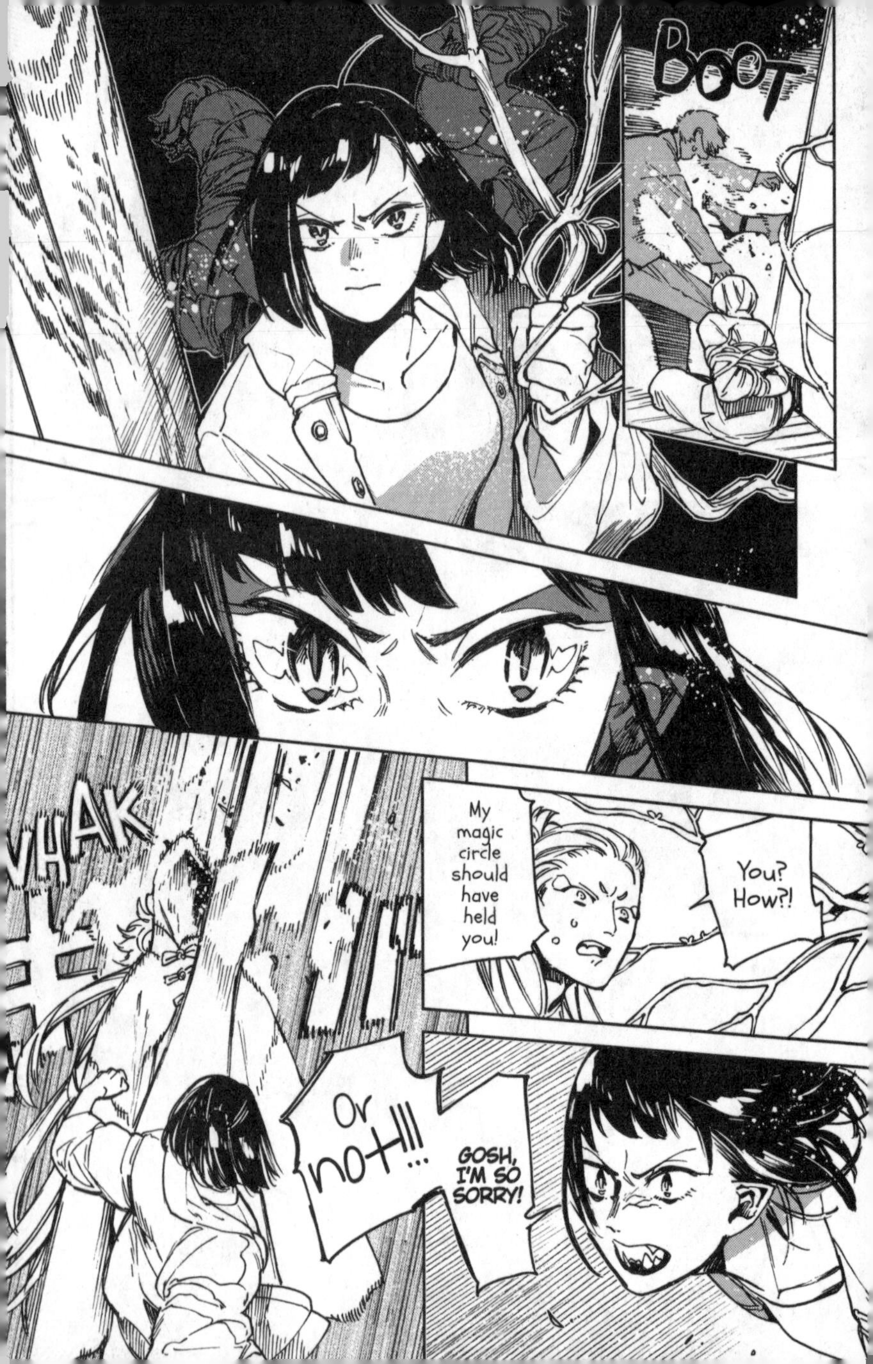
BOOT
You? How?!
My magic circle should have held you!
Or not!!!...
GOSH, I'M SO SORRY!

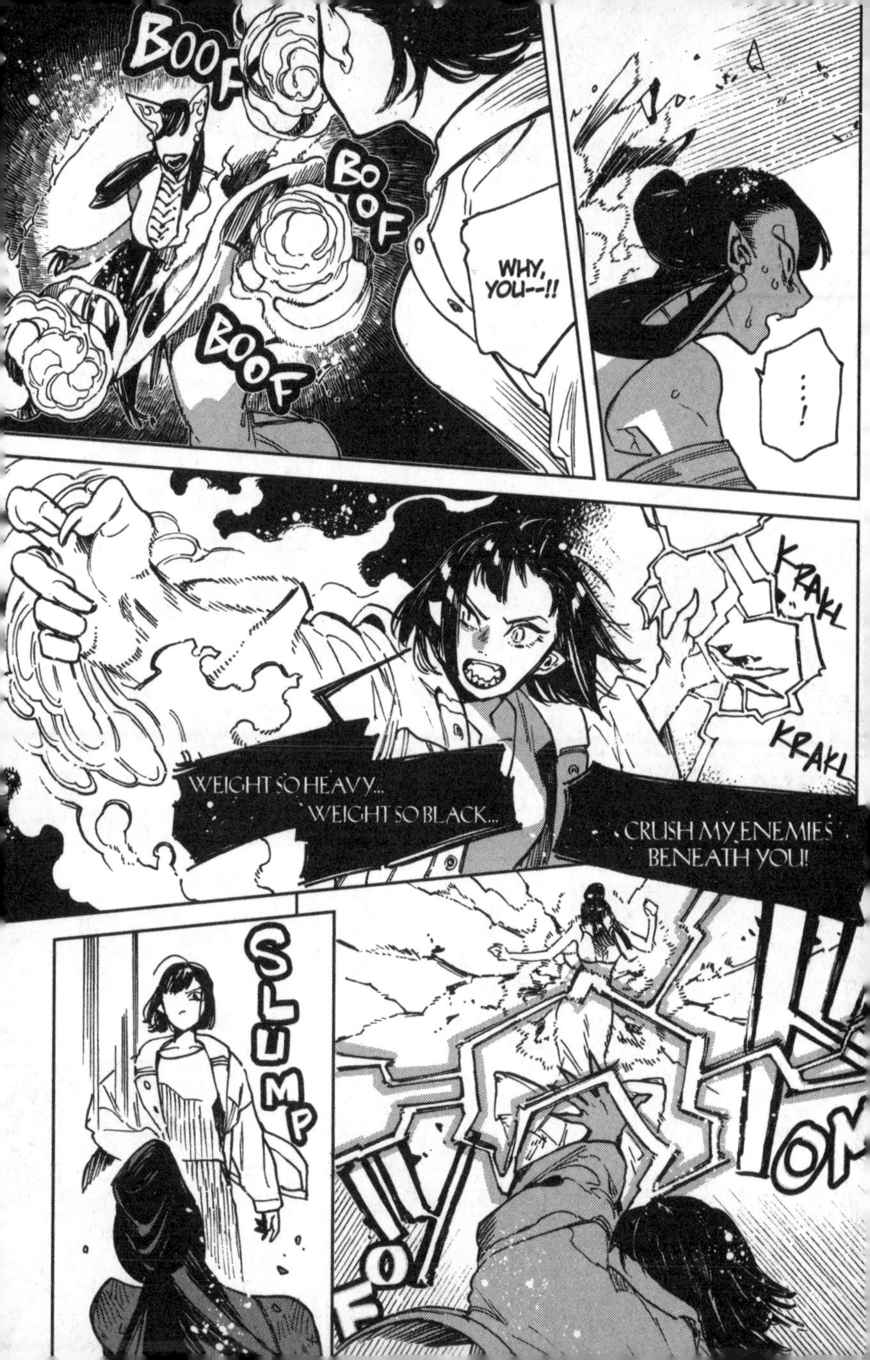
...!
WHY, YOU--!!
BOOF
BOOF
BOOF
KRAKL
KRAKL
CRUSH MY ENEMIES BENEATH YOU!
WEIGHT SO HEAVY...
WEIGHT SO BLACK...
SLUMP

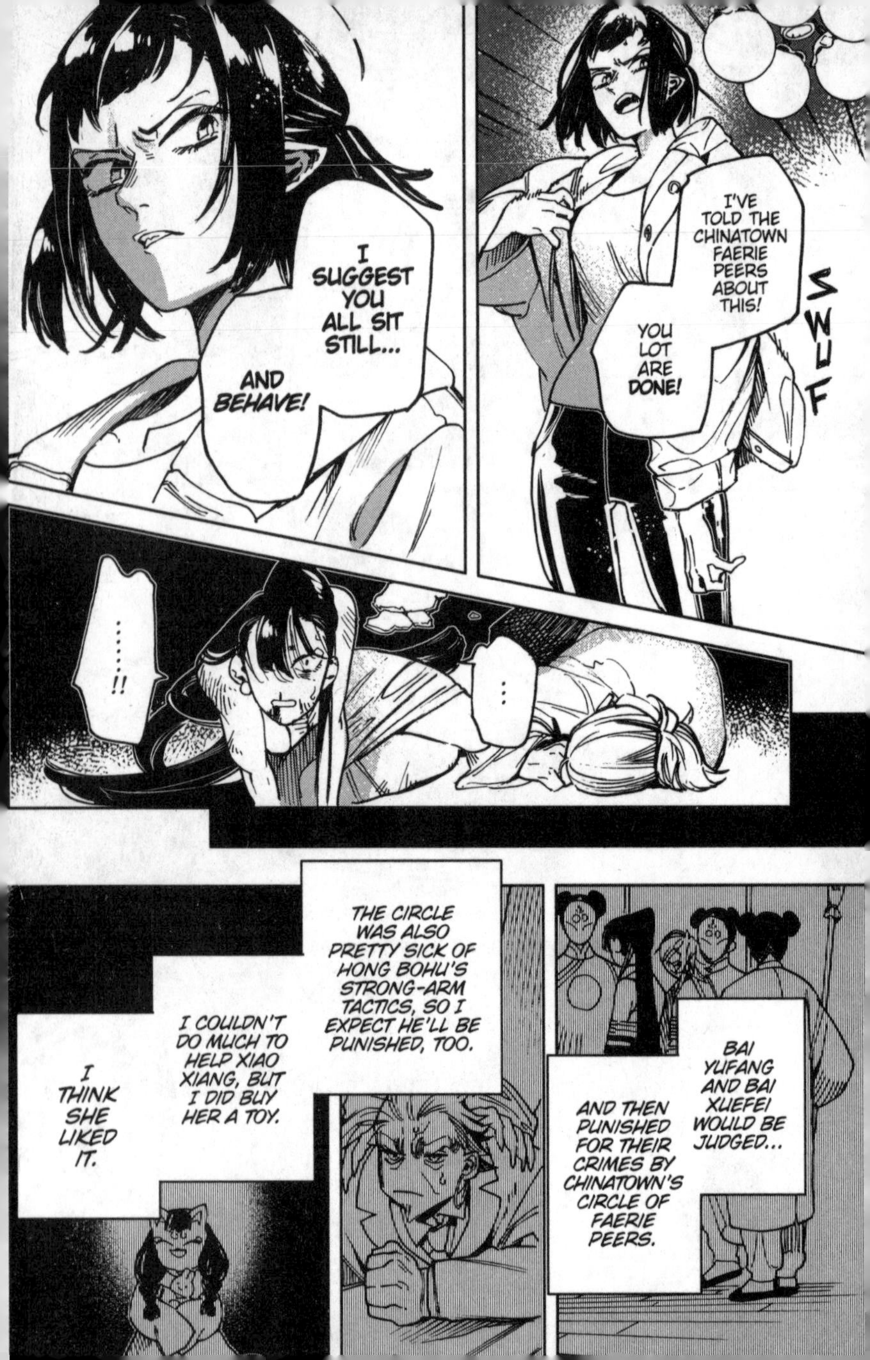
I'VE TOLD THE CHINATOWN FAERIE PEERS ABOUT THIS!
YOU LOT ARE DONE!
SWUF
I SUGGEST YOU ALL SIT STILL...
AND BEHAVE!
...
......!!
BAI YUFANG AND BAI XUEFEI WOULD BE JUDGED...
AND THEN PUNISHED FOR THEIR CRIMES BY CHINATOWN'S CIRCLE OF FAERIE PEERS.
THE CIRCLE WAS ALSO PRETTY SICK OF HONG BOHU'S STRONG-ARM TACTICS, SO I EXPECT HE'LL BE PUNISHED, TOO.
I COULDN'T DO MUCH TO HELP XIAO XIANG, BUT I DID BUY HER A TOY.
I THINK SHE LIKED IT.

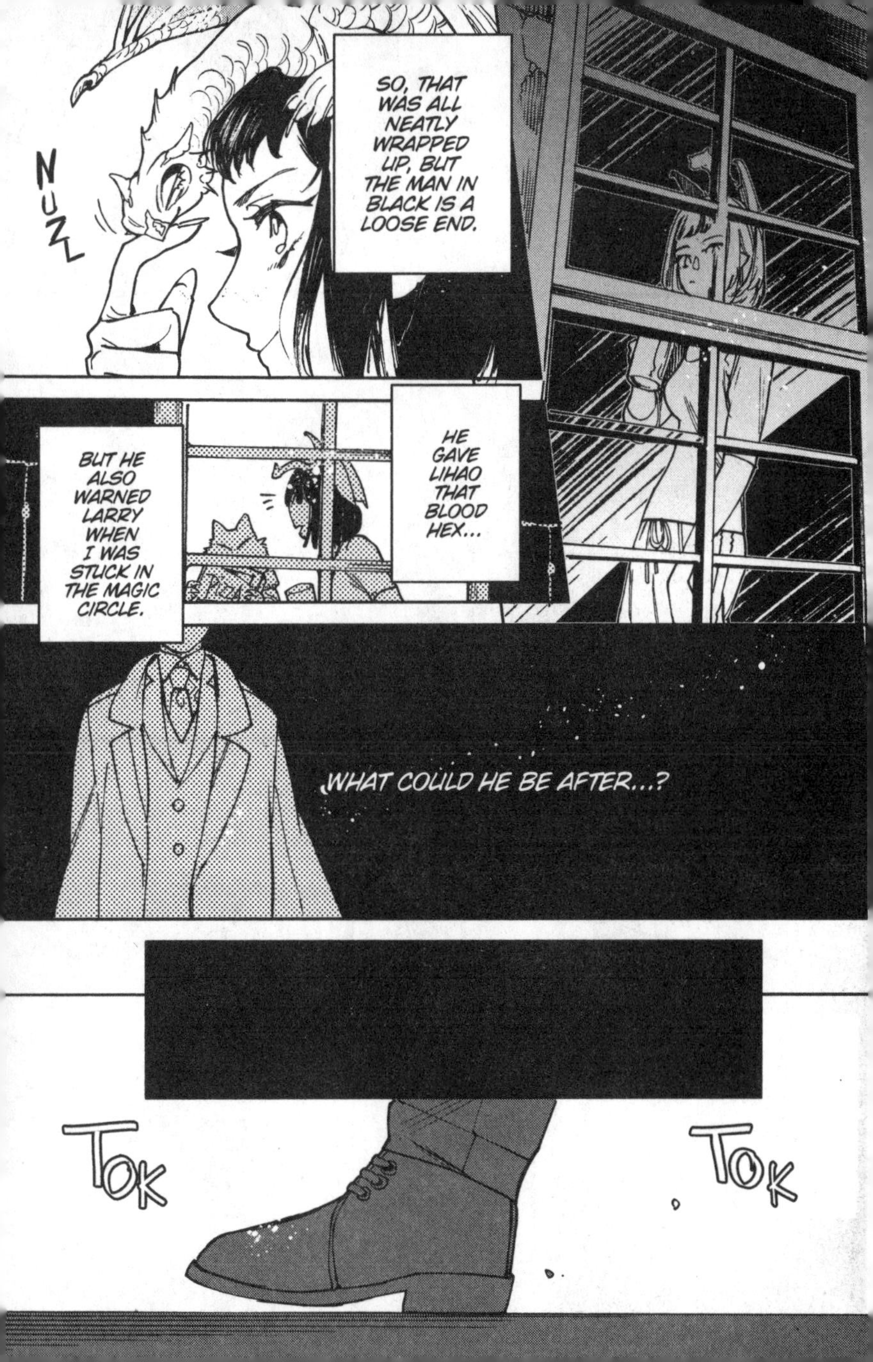
SO, THAT WAS ALL NEATLY WRAPPED UP, BUT THE MAN IN BLACK IS A LOOSE END.
NUZL
HE GAVE LIHAO THAT BLOOD HEX...
BUT HE ALSO WARNED LARRY WHEN I WAS STUCK IN THE MAGIC CIRCLE.
WHAT COULD HE BE AFTER...?
TOK
TOK

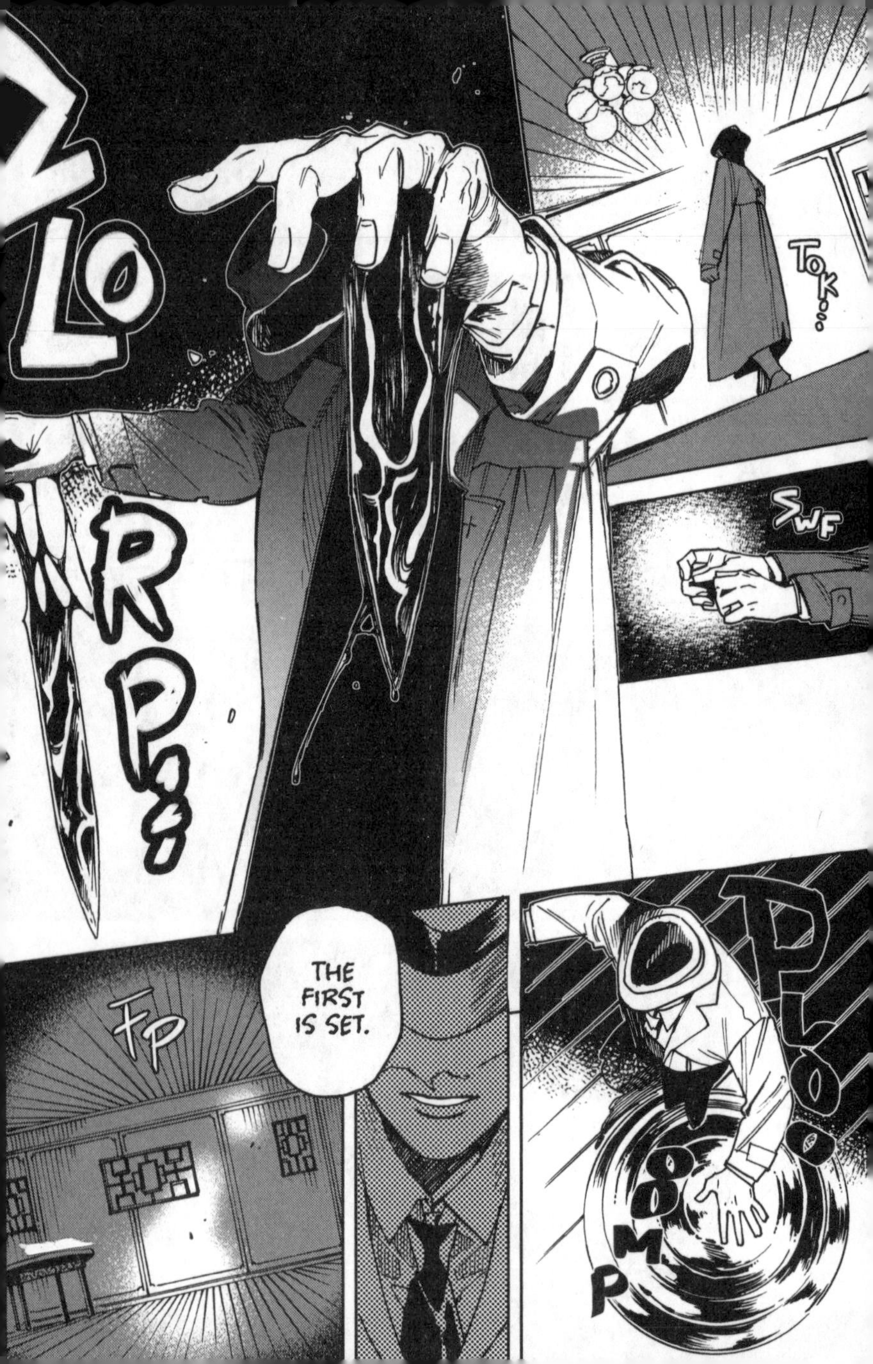
TOK...
SWF
ZLO
THE FIRST IS SET.
FP

The Ancient
Magus' Bride

JACK FLASH AND THE FAERIE CASE FILES

The Ancient
Magus' Bride

JACK FLASH AND THE FAERIE CASE FILES

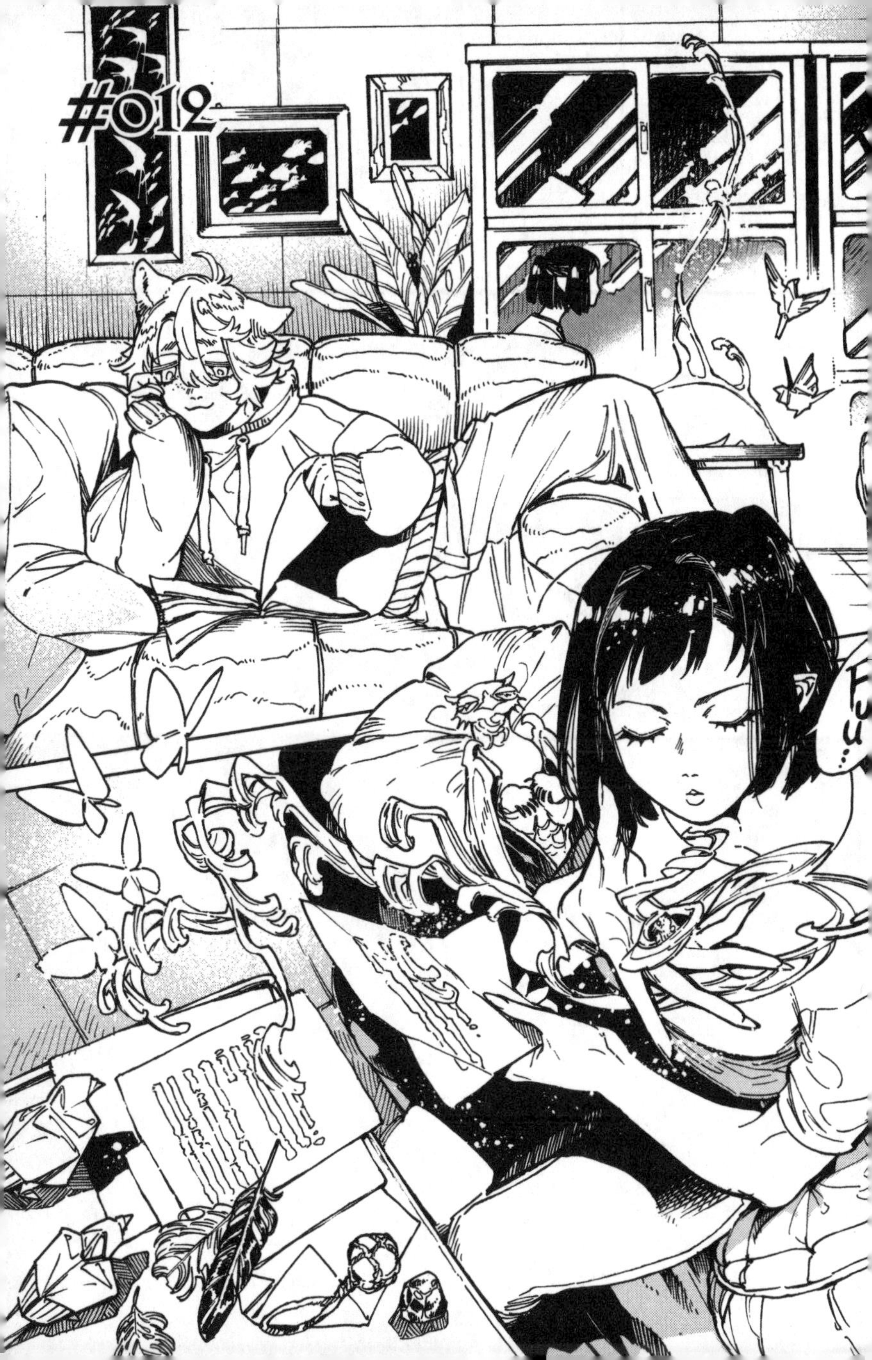
#012
Fuu...

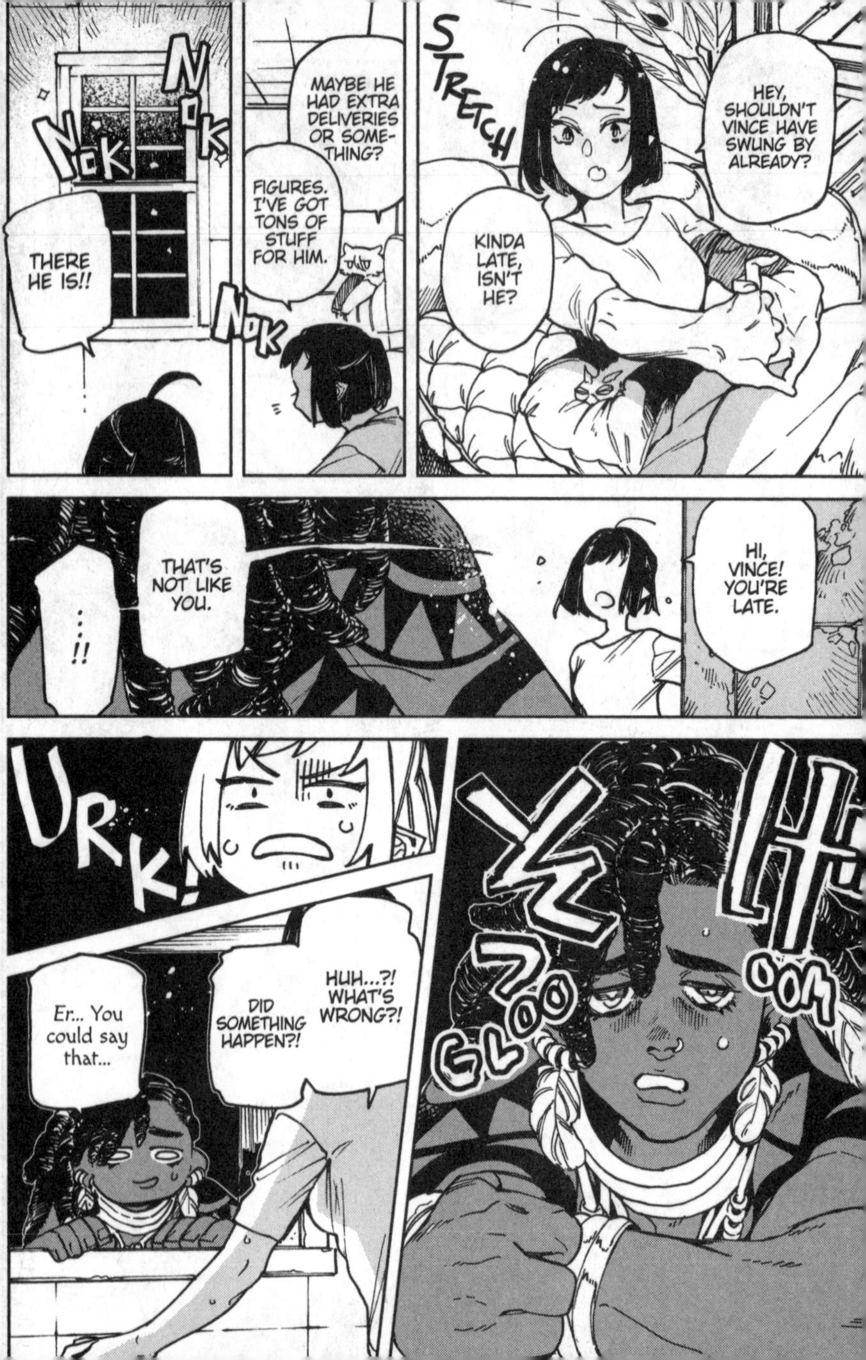
STRETCH
HEY, SHOULDN'T VINCE HAVE SWUNG BY ALREADY?
KINDA LATE, ISN'T HE?
MAYBE HE HAD EXTRA DELIVERIES OR SOME-THING?
FIGURES. I'VE GOT TONS OF STUFF FOR HIM.
NOK
NOK
NOK
THERE HE IS!!
...
HI, VINCE! YOU'RE LATE.
THAT'S NOT LIKE YOU.
...!!
URK!
HUH...?! WHAT'S WRONG?!
DID SOMETHING HAPPEN?!
Er... You could say that...

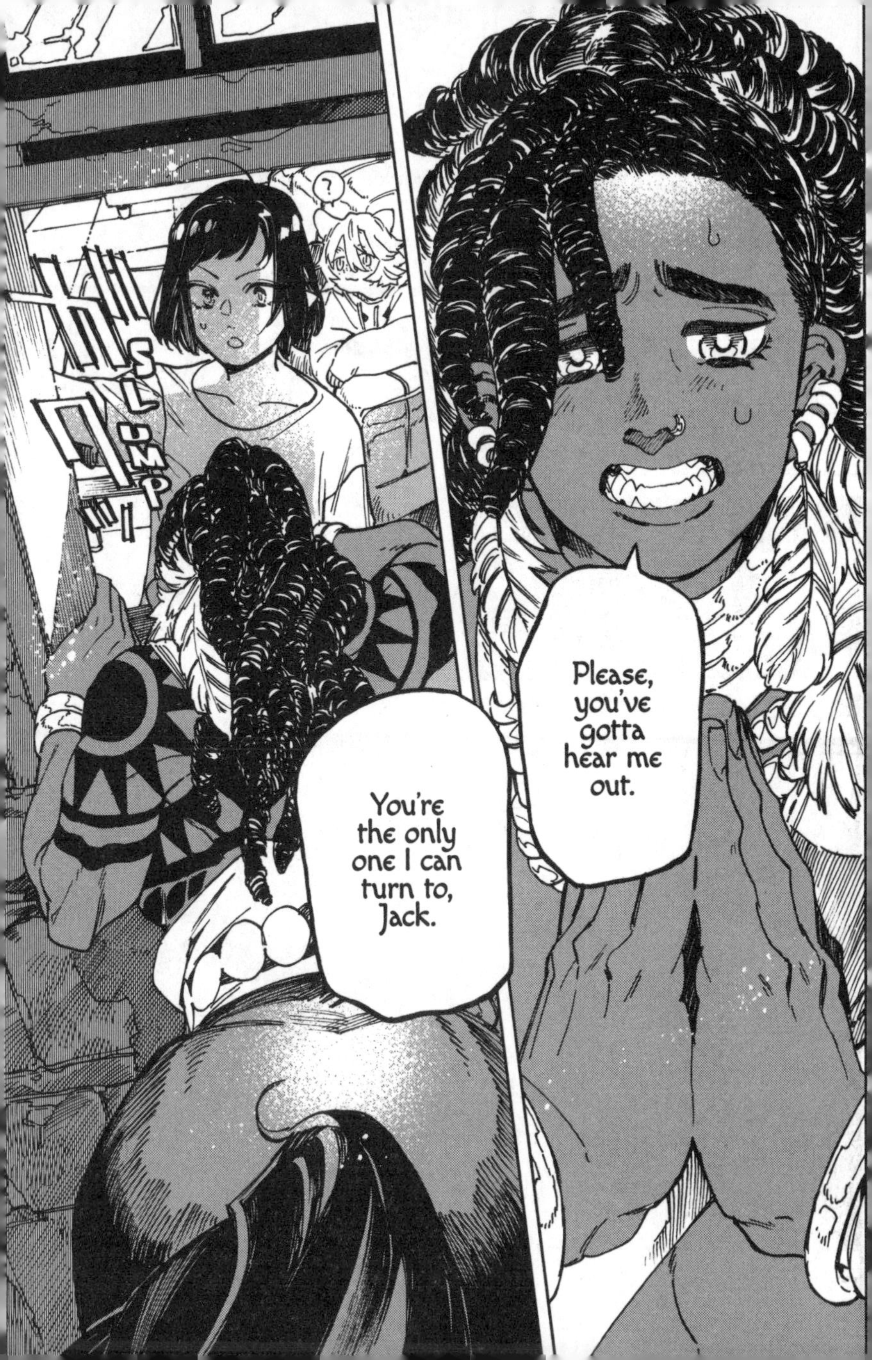
Please, you've gotta hear me out.
SLUMP
You're the only one I can turn to, Jack.

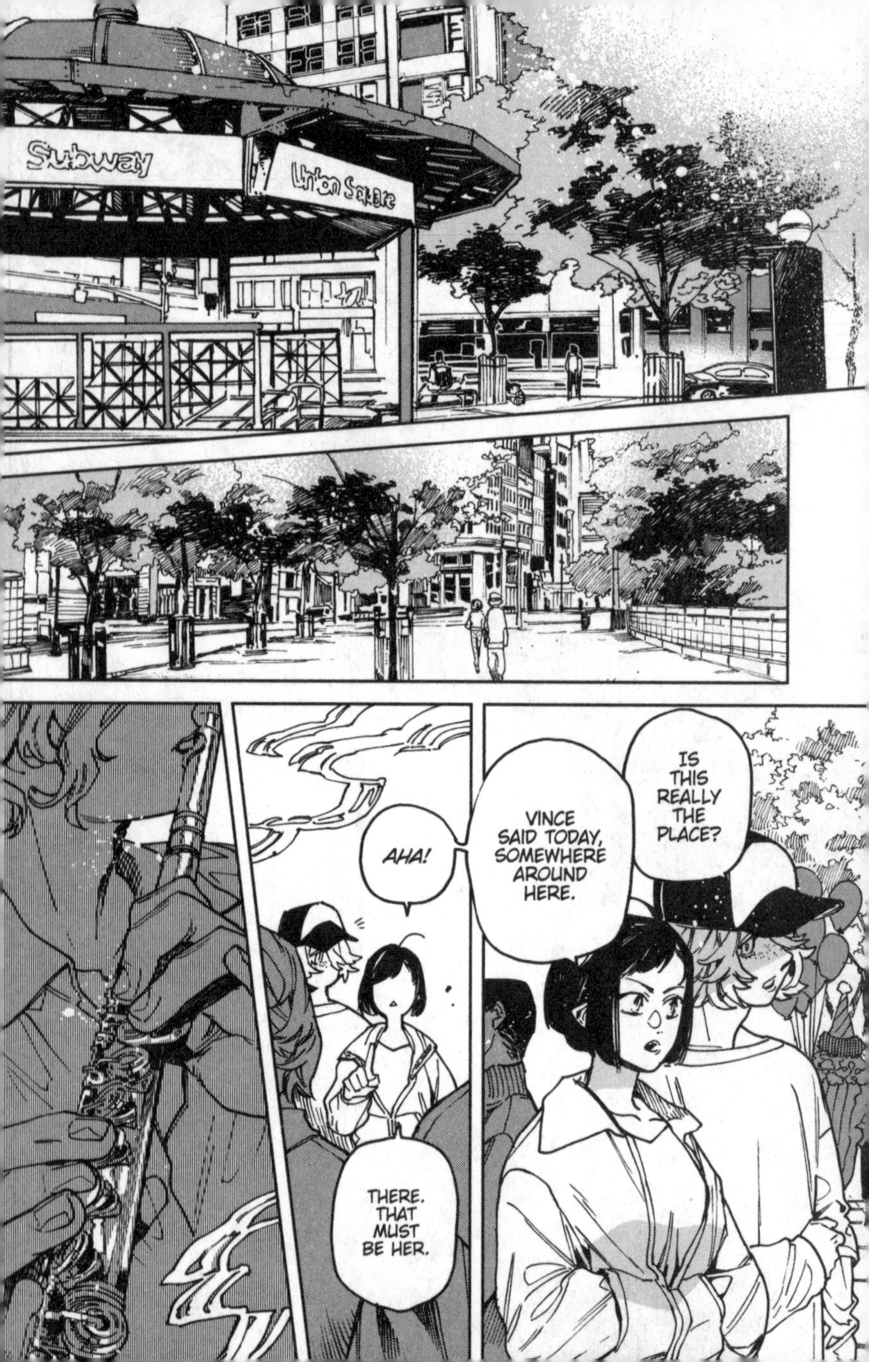
Subway
Union Square
IS THIS REALLY THE PLACE?
VINCE SAID TODAY, SOMEWHERE AROUND HERE.
AHA!
THERE. THAT MUST BE HER.

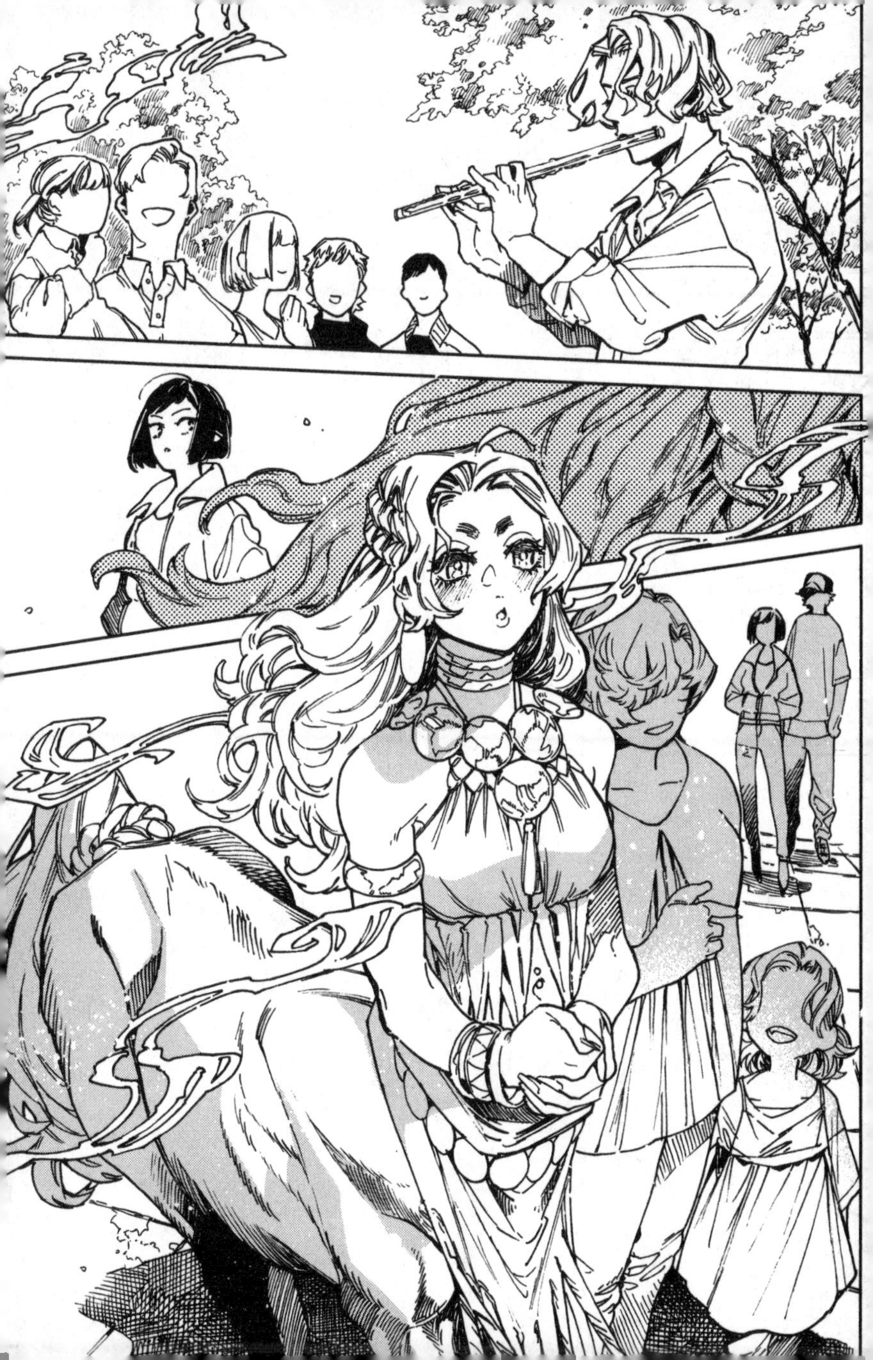

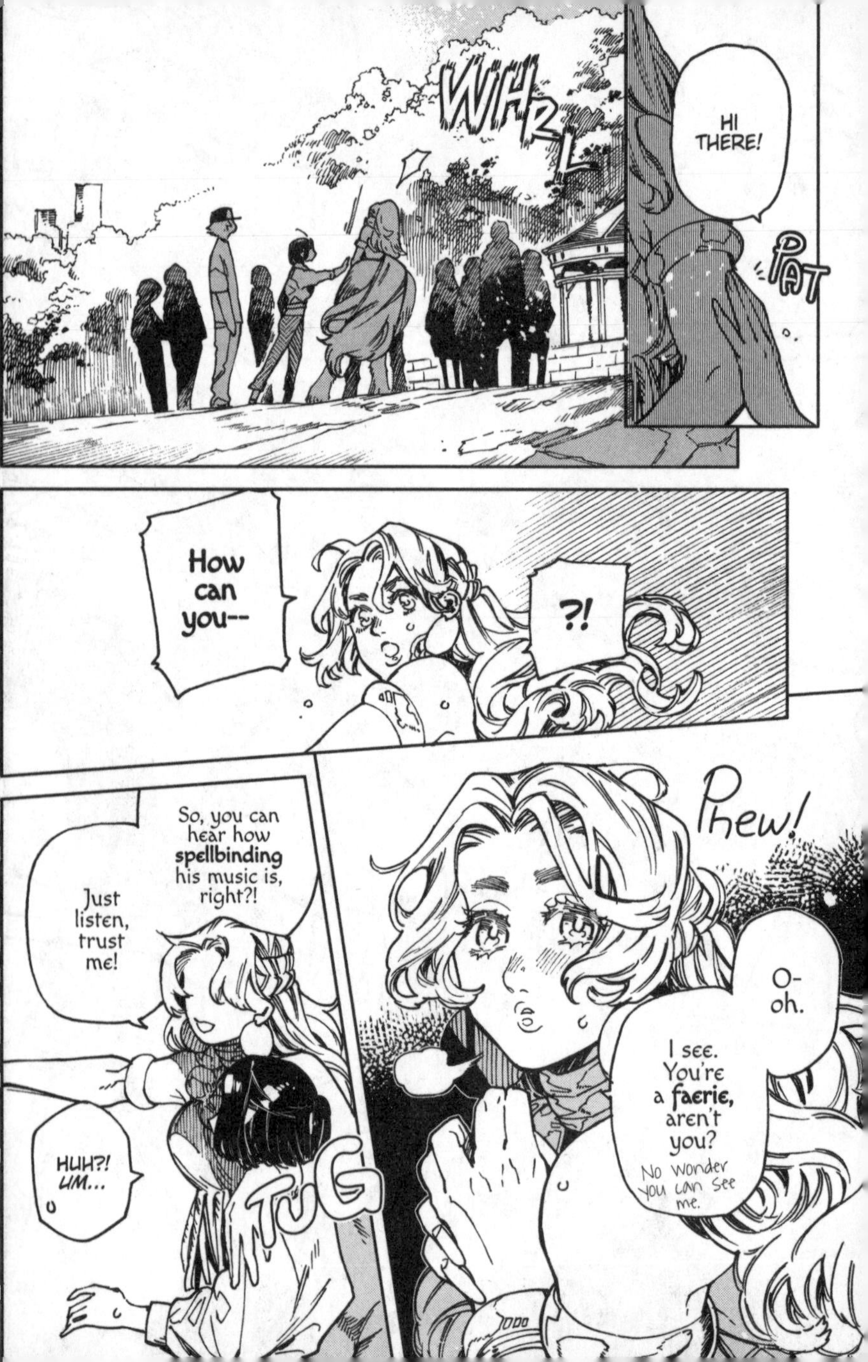
HI THERE!
PAT
WHRL
?!
How can you--
Phew!
O-oh.
I see. You're a faerie, aren't you?
No wonder you can see me.
So, you can hear how spellbinding his music is, right?!
Just listen, trust me!
HUH?! UM...
TUG

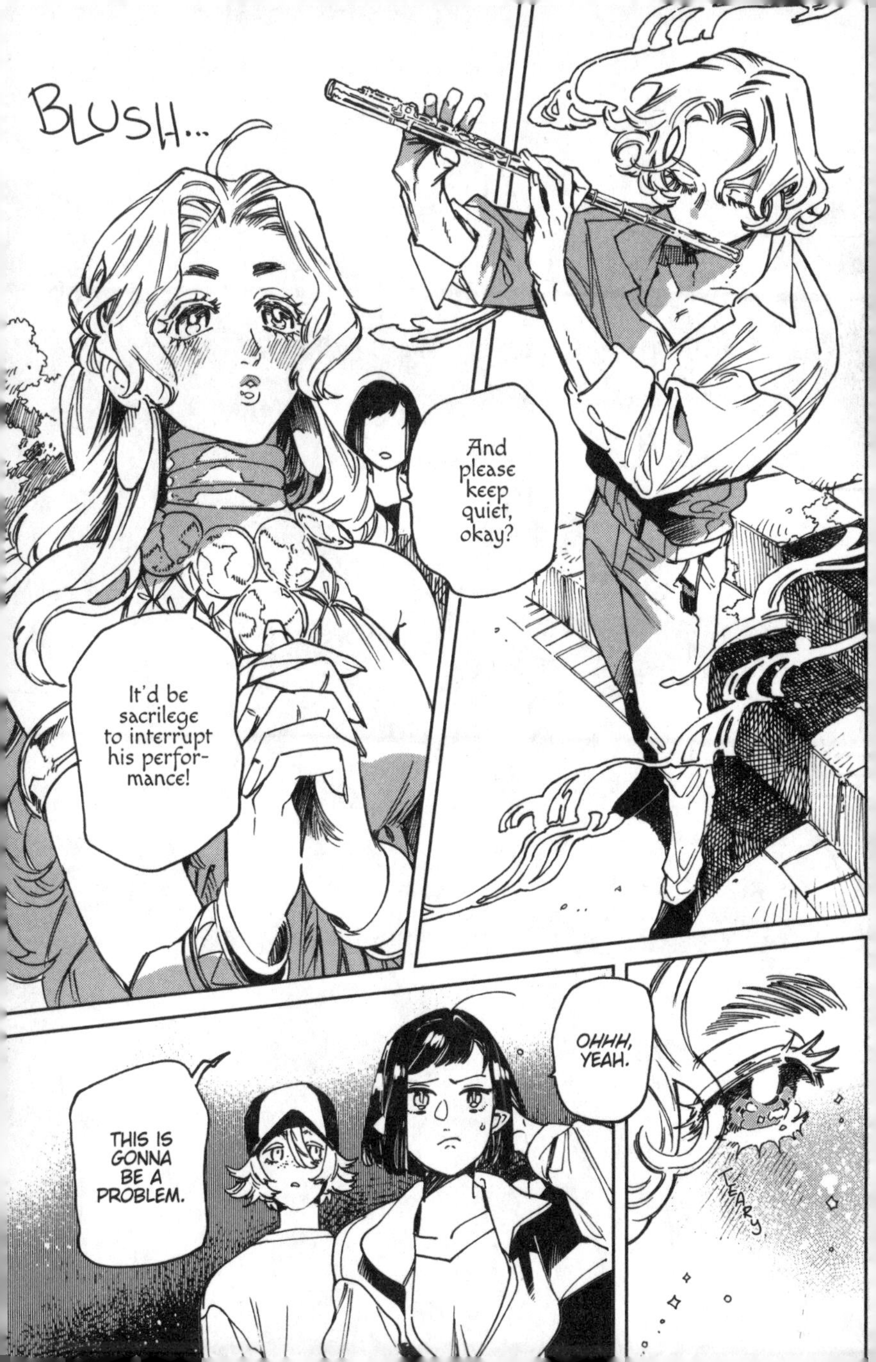
BLUSH...
It'd be sacrilege to interrupt his performance!
And please keep quiet, okay?
OHHH, YEAH.
TEARY
THIS IS GONNA BE A PROBLEM.

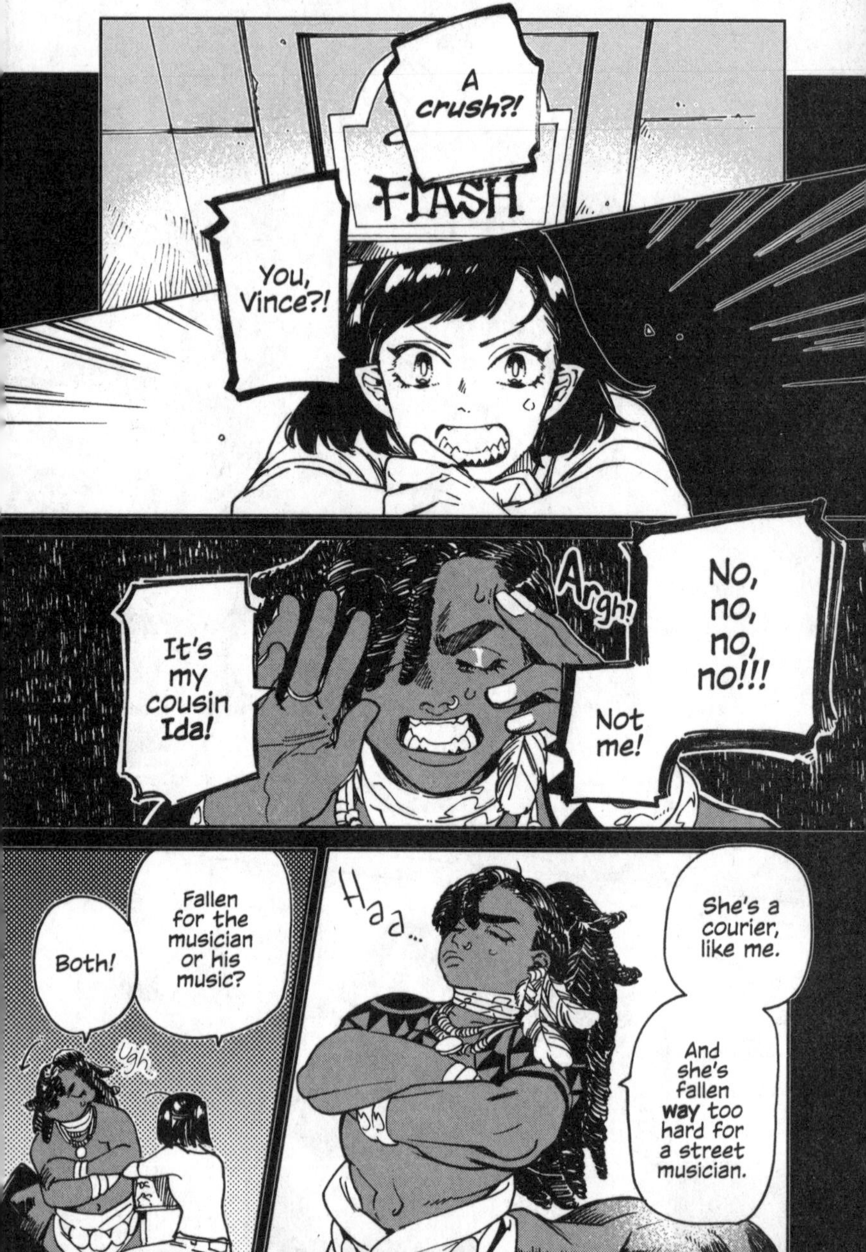
FLASH
A crush?!
You, Vince?!
Argh!
No, no, no, no!!!
Not me!
It's my cousin Ida!
Haa...
She's a courier, like me.
And she's fallen **way** too hard for a street musician.
Fallen for the musician or his music?
Both!
Ugh

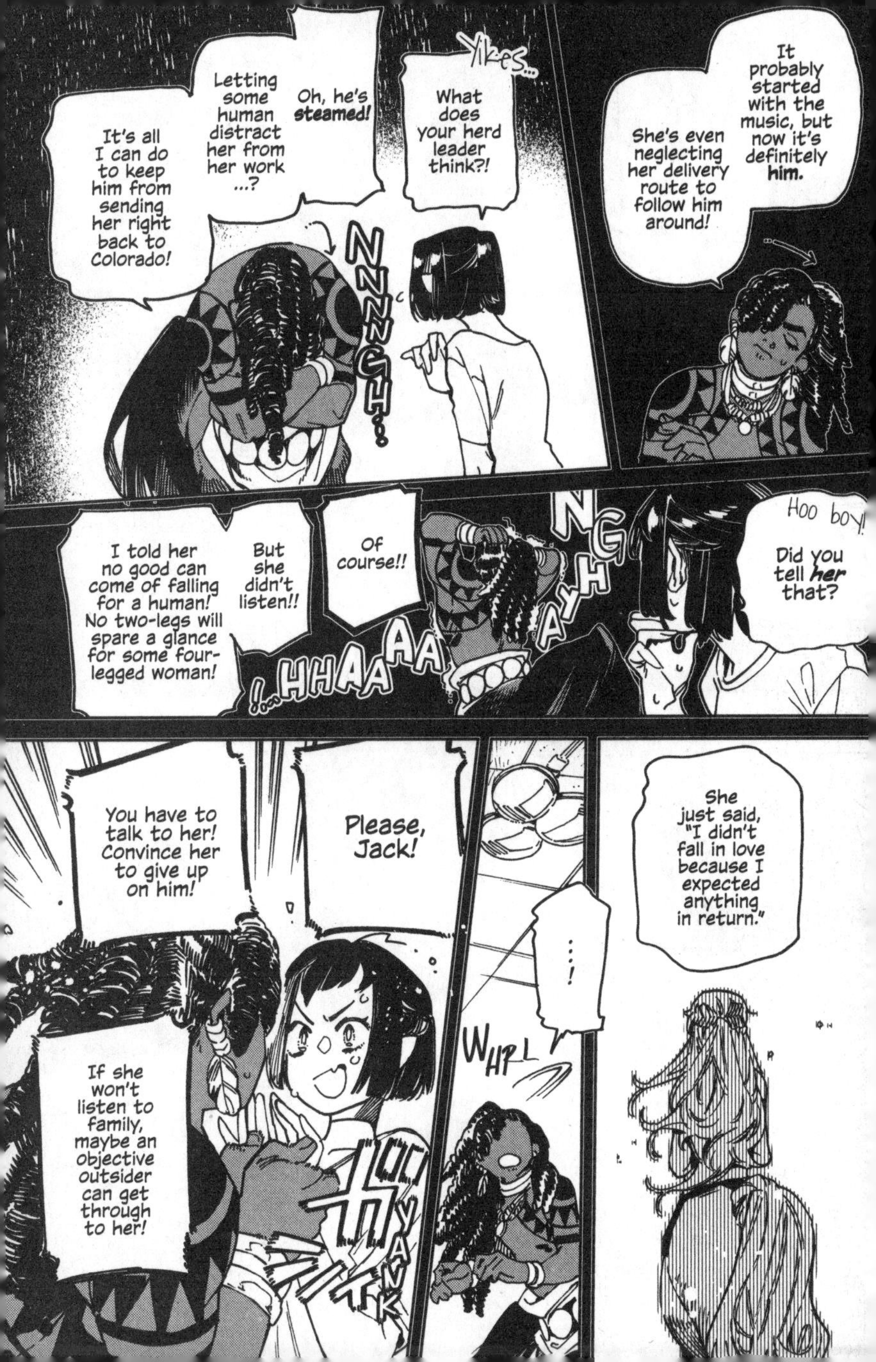

It probably started with the music, but now it's definitely **him.**
She's even neglecting her delivery route to follow him around!
Yikes...
What does your herd leader think?!
Oh, he's **steamed!**
Letting some human distract her from her work ...?
It's all I can do to keep him from sending her right back to Colorado!
NNNNNGH...
Hoo boy!
Did you tell ***her*** that?
NGHYAAAAAHH...!
Of course!!
But she didn't listen!!
I told her no good can come of falling for a human! No two-legs will spare a glance for some four-legged woman!
She just said, "I didn't fall in love because I expected anything in return."
...!
WHRL
Please, Jack!
You have to talk to her! Convince her to give up on him!
YANK
If she won't listen to family, maybe an objective outsider can get through to her!

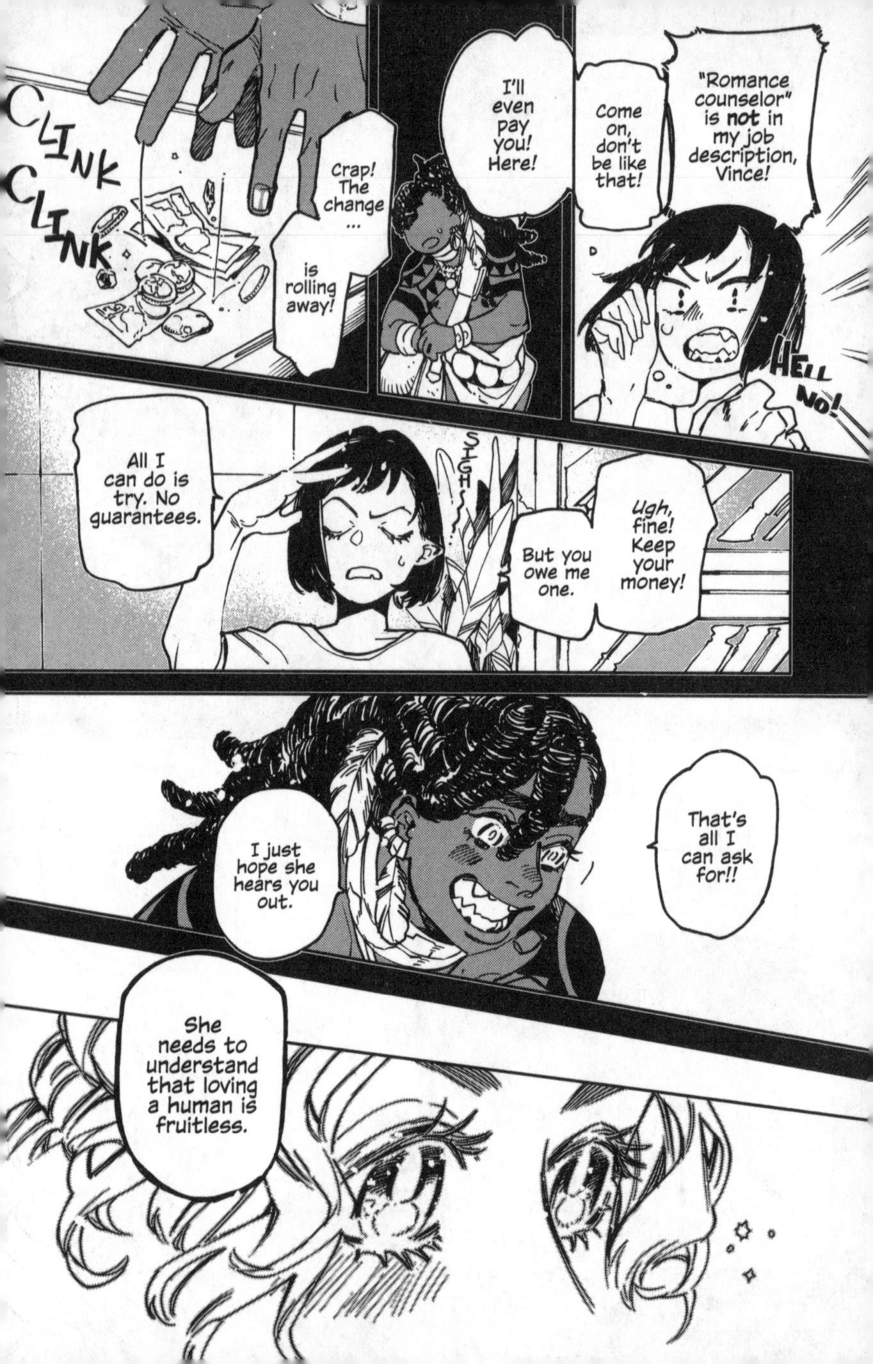
"Romance counselor" is **not** in my job description, Vince!
HELL NO!
Come on, don't be like that!
I'll even pay you! Here!
Crap! The change ...
is rolling away!
CLINK
CLINK
Ugh, fine! Keep your money!
But you owe me one.
SIGH
All I can do is try. No guarantees.
That's all I can ask for!!
I just hope she hears you out.
She needs to understand that loving a human is fruitless.

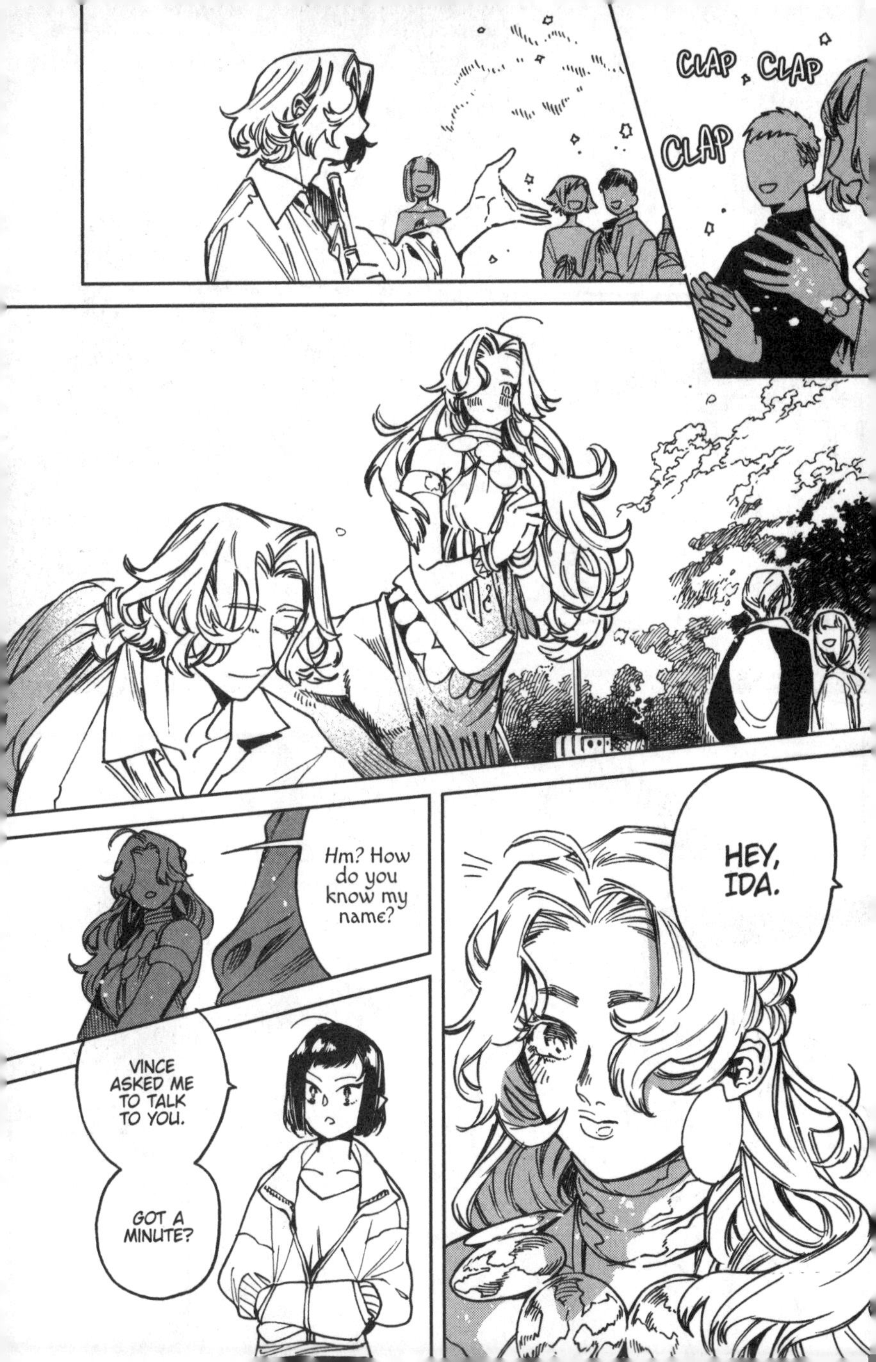
CLAP CLAP
CLAP
HEY, IDA.
Hm? How do you know my name?
VINCE ASKED ME TO TALK TO YOU.
GOT A MINUTE?

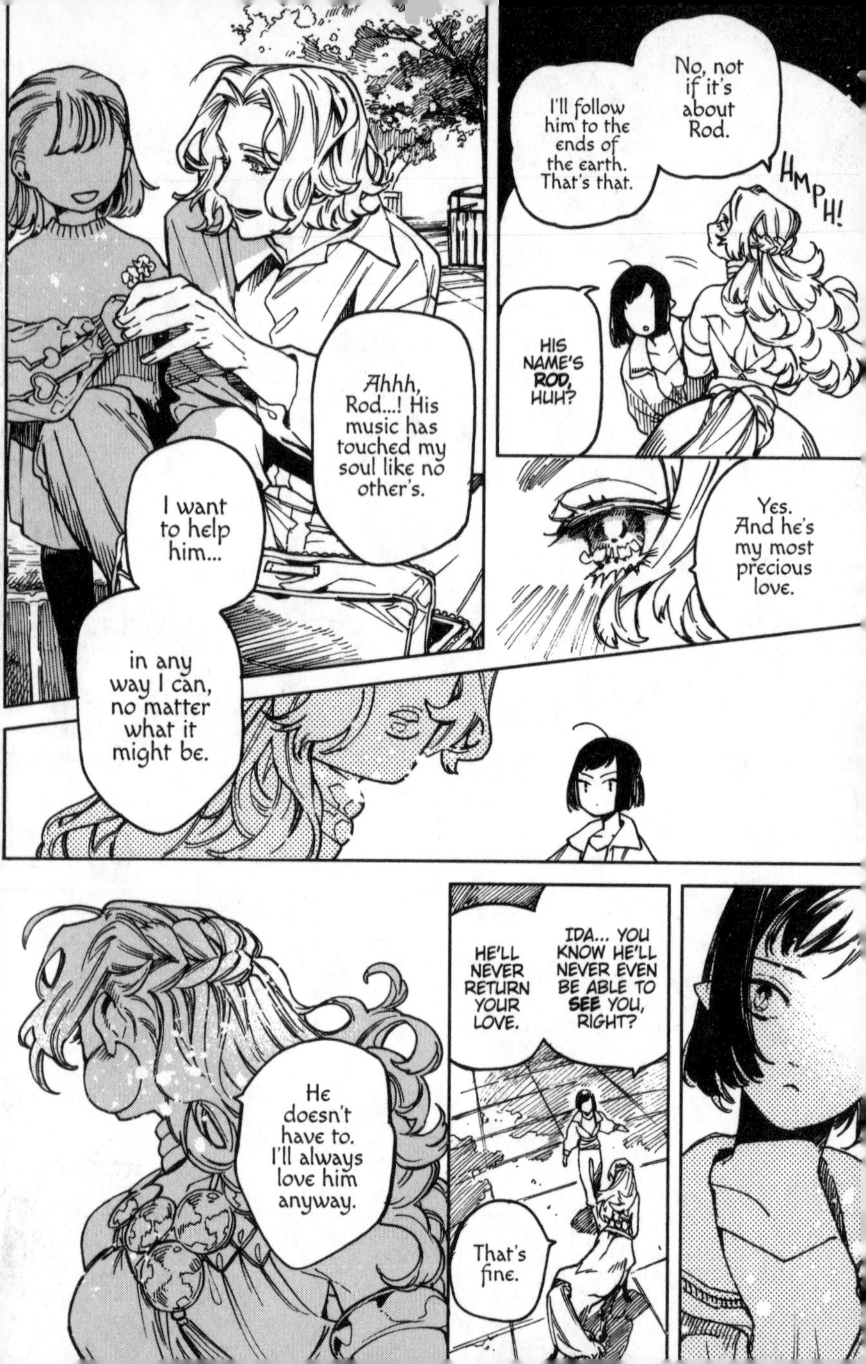

No, not if it's about Rod.
I'll follow him to the ends of the earth. That's that.
HMPH!
HIS NAME'S **ROD,** HUH?
Yes. And he's my most precious love.
Ahhh, Rod...! His music has touched my soul like no other's.
I want to help him...
in any way I can, no matter what it might be.
IDA... YOU KNOW HE'LL NEVER EVEN BE ABLE TO **SEE** YOU, RIGHT?
HE'LL NEVER RETURN YOUR LOVE.
That's fine.
He doesn't have to. I'll always love him anyway.

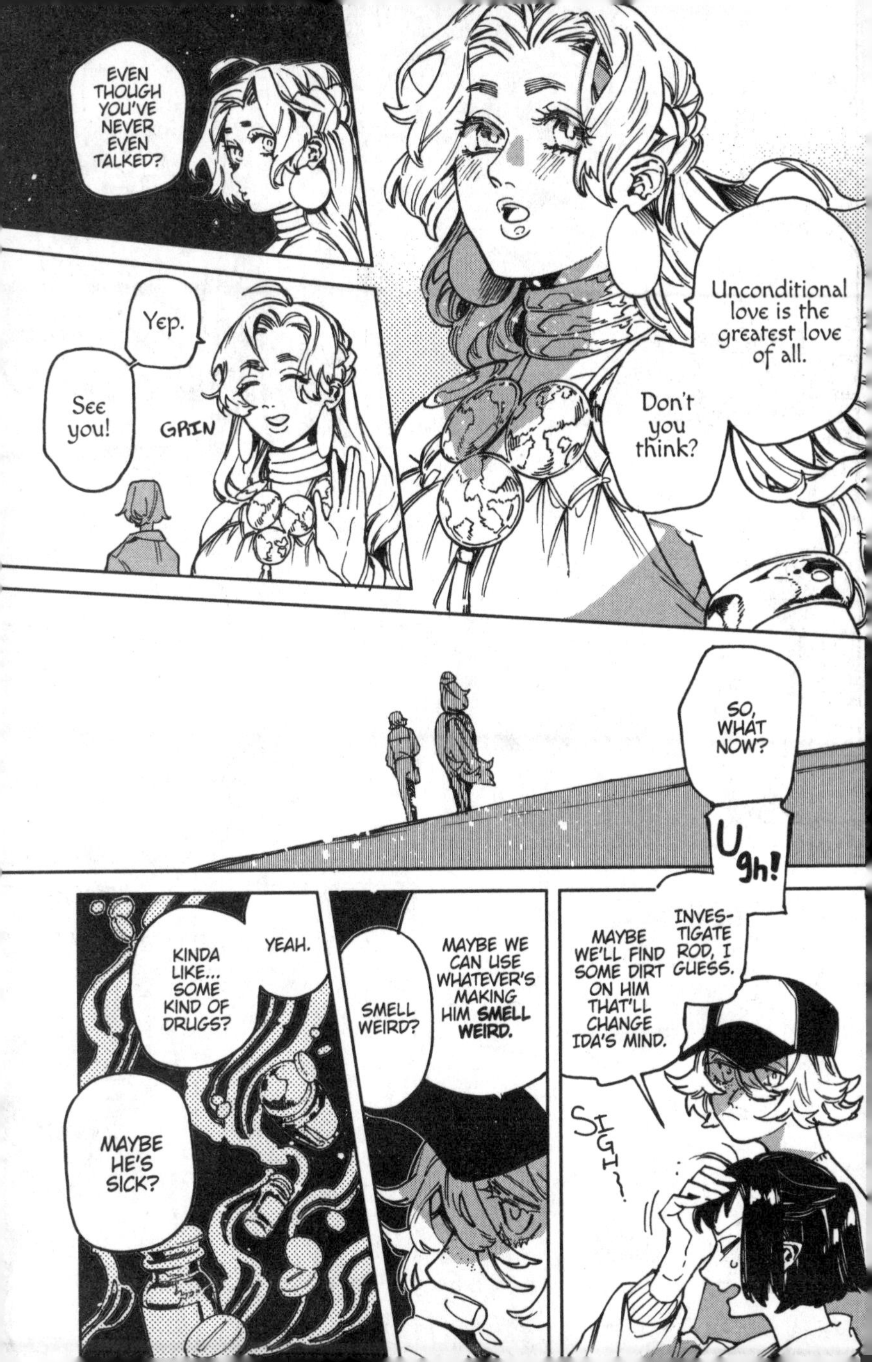
Unconditional love is the greatest love of all.
Don't you think?
EVEN THOUGH YOU'VE NEVER EVEN TALKED?
Yep.
See you!
GRIN
SO, WHAT NOW?
Ugh!
INVESTIGATE ROD, I GUESS.
MAYBE WE'LL FIND SOME DIRT ON HIM THAT'LL CHANGE IDA'S MIND.
SIGH~...
MAYBE WE CAN USE WHATEVER'S MAKING HIM **SMELL WEIRD.**
SMELL WEIRD?
YEAH.
KINDA LIKE... SOME KIND OF DRUGS?
MAYBE HE'S SICK?

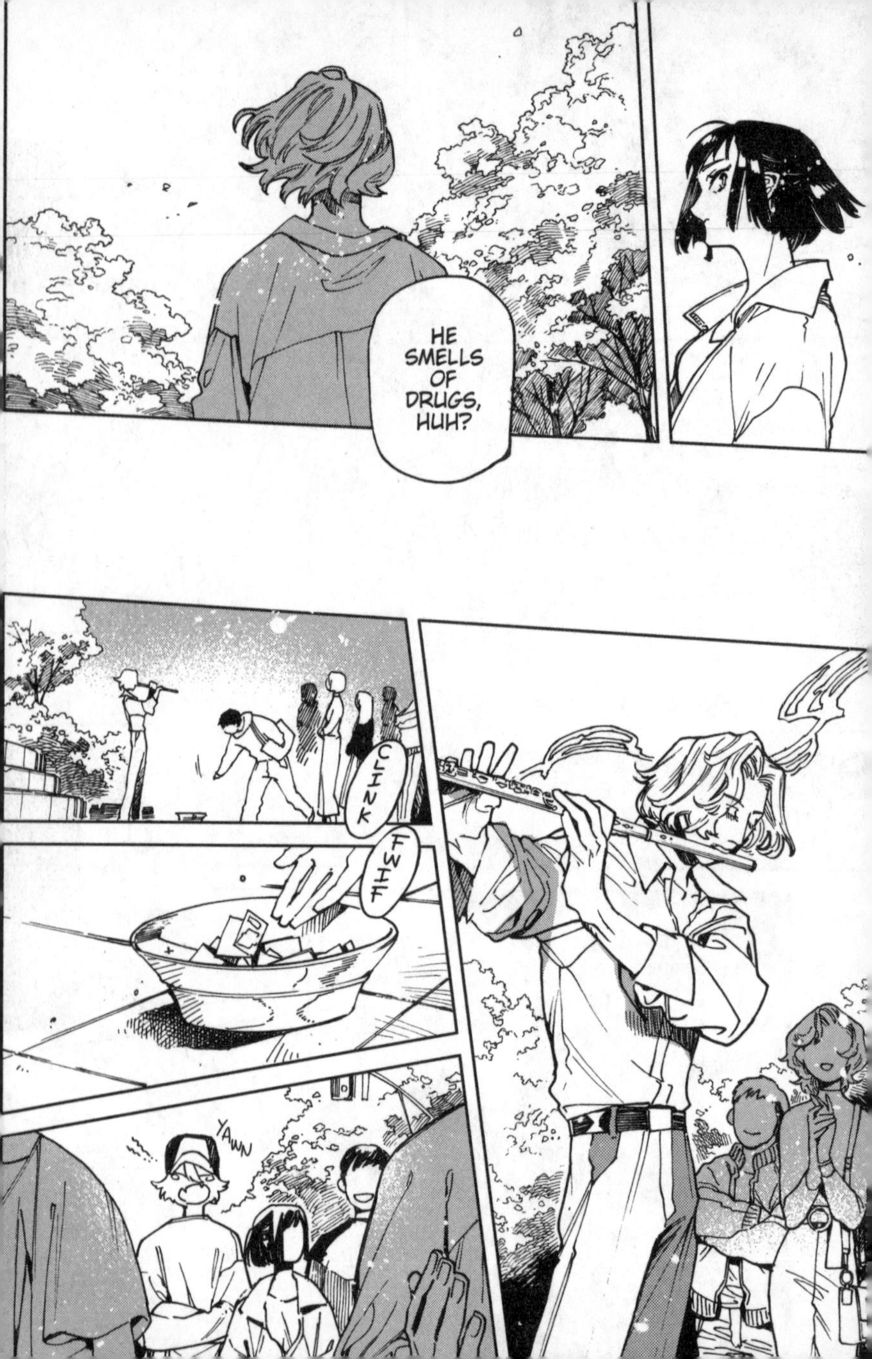
HE SMELLS OF DRUGS, HUH?
CLINK
FWIFF
YAWN

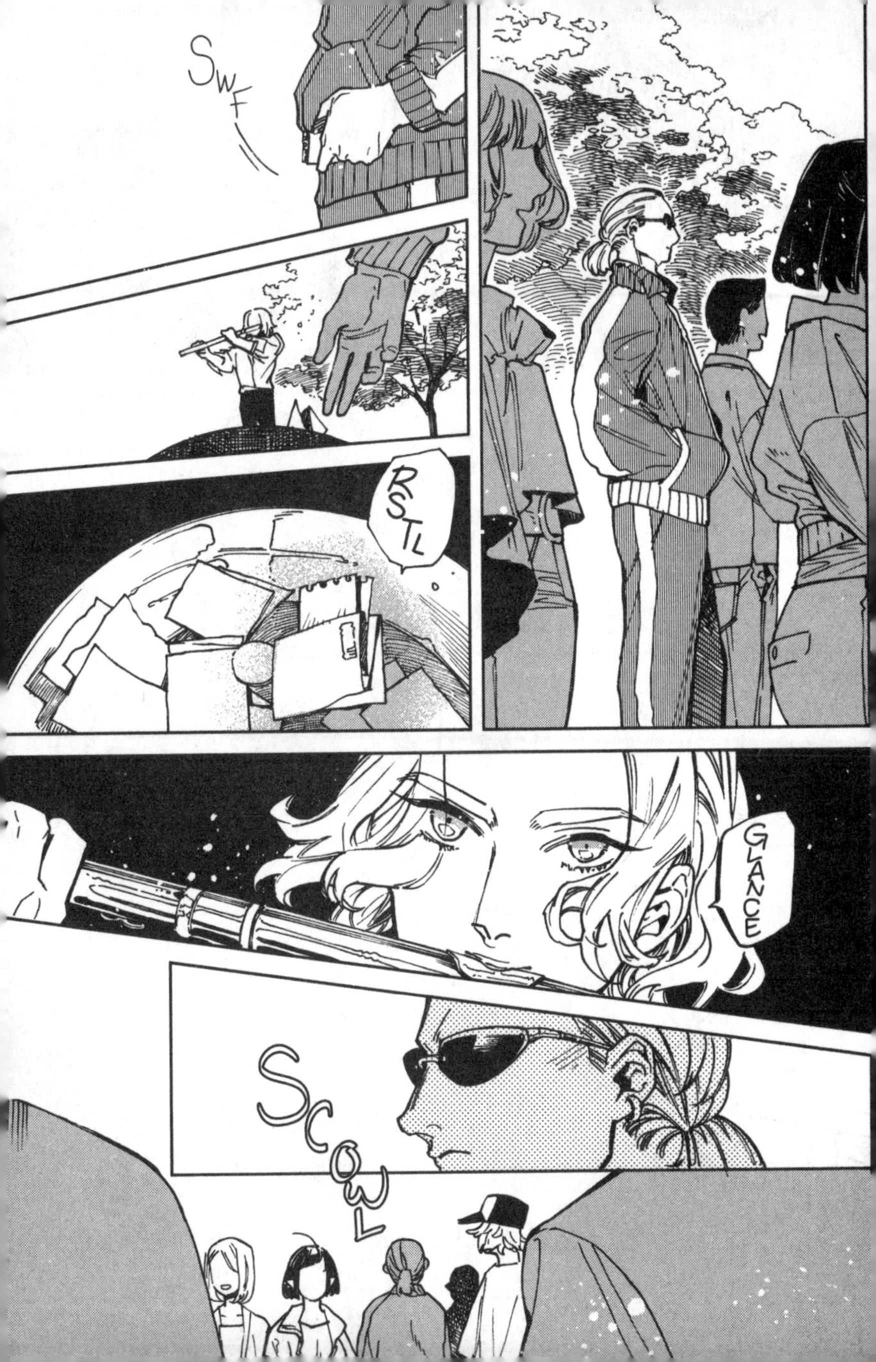
SWF
RSTL
GLANCE
SCOWL

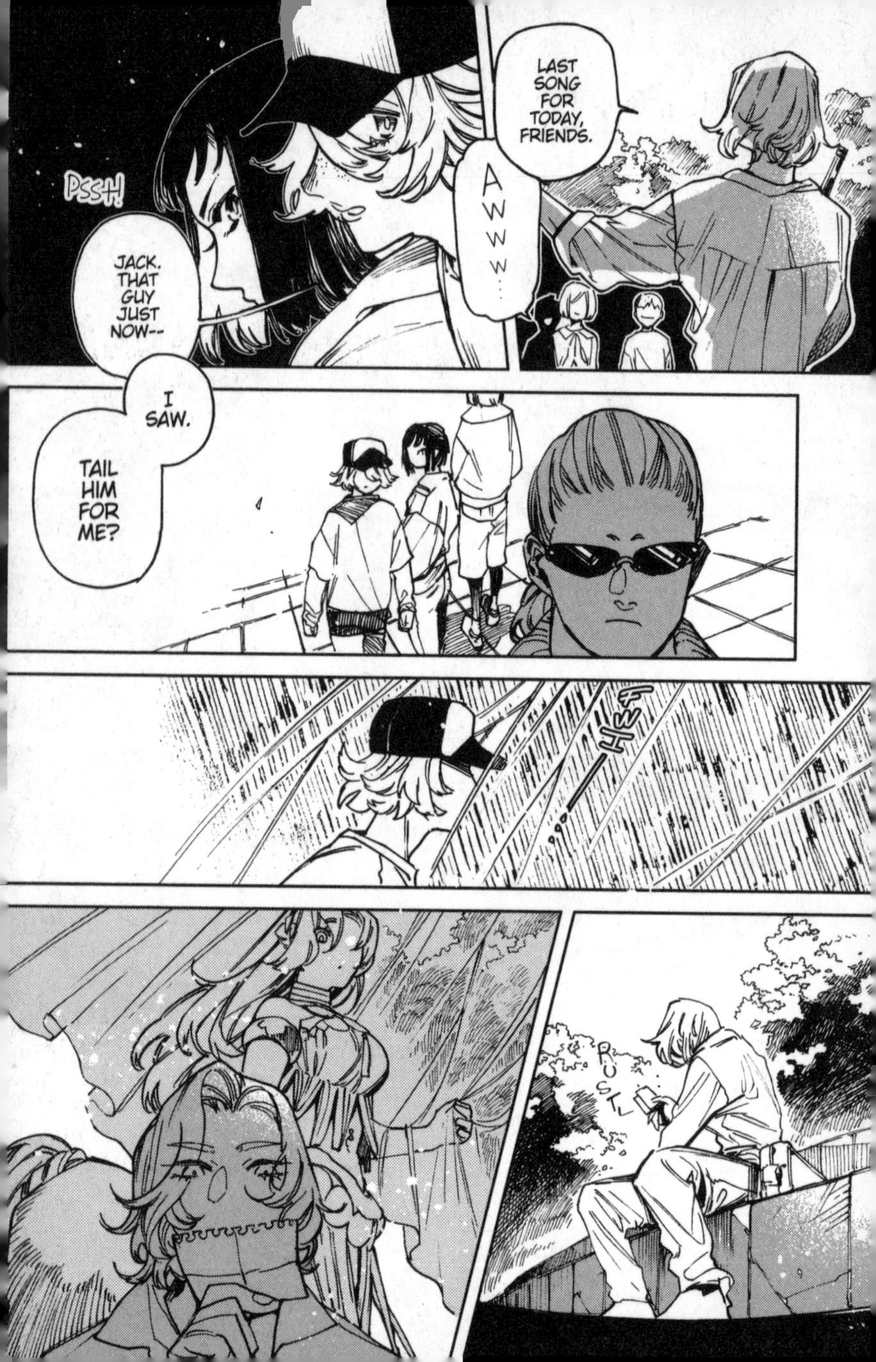
LAST SONG FOR TODAY, FRIENDS.
AWWW...
PSSH!
JACK. THAT GUY JUST NOW--
I SAW.
TAIL HIM FOR ME?
FWHI—
RUSTL

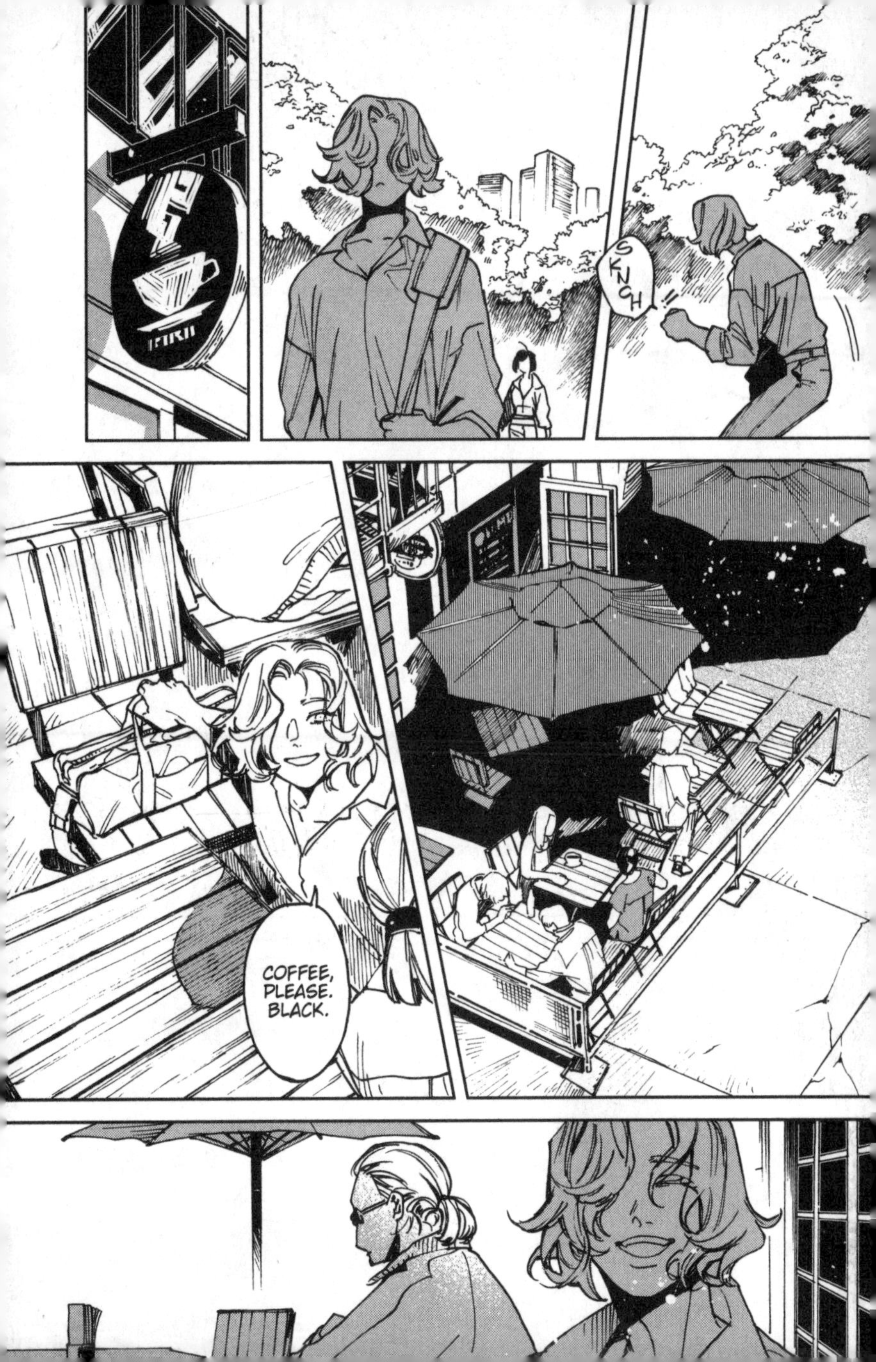
SKNCH
COFFEE, PLEASE. BLACK.

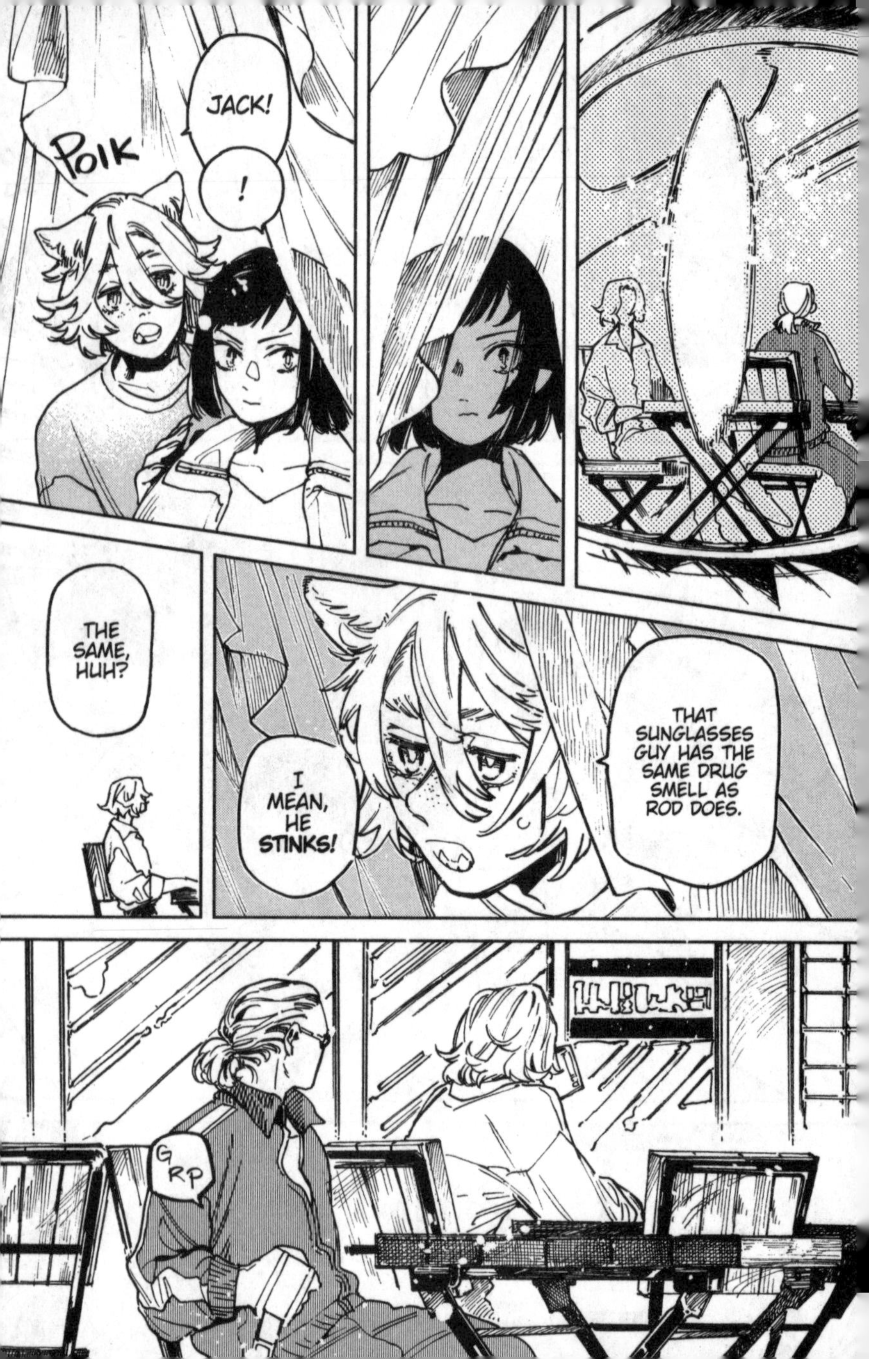
JACK!
POIK
!
THAT SUNGLASSES GUY HAS THE SAME DRUG SMELL AS ROD DOES.
I MEAN, HE STINKS!
THE SAME, HUH?
GRP

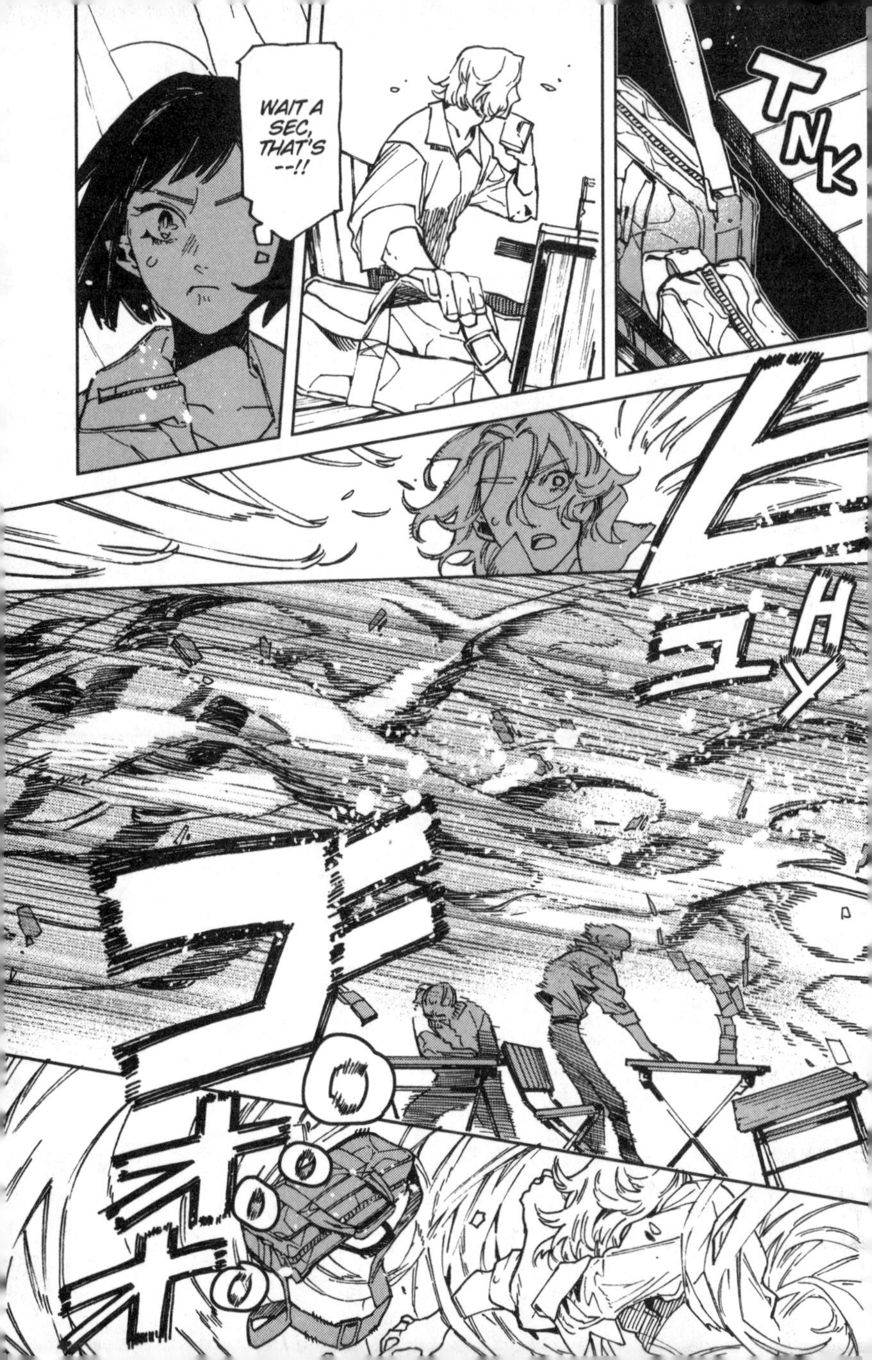
TNK
WAIT A SEC, THAT'S --!!
HY

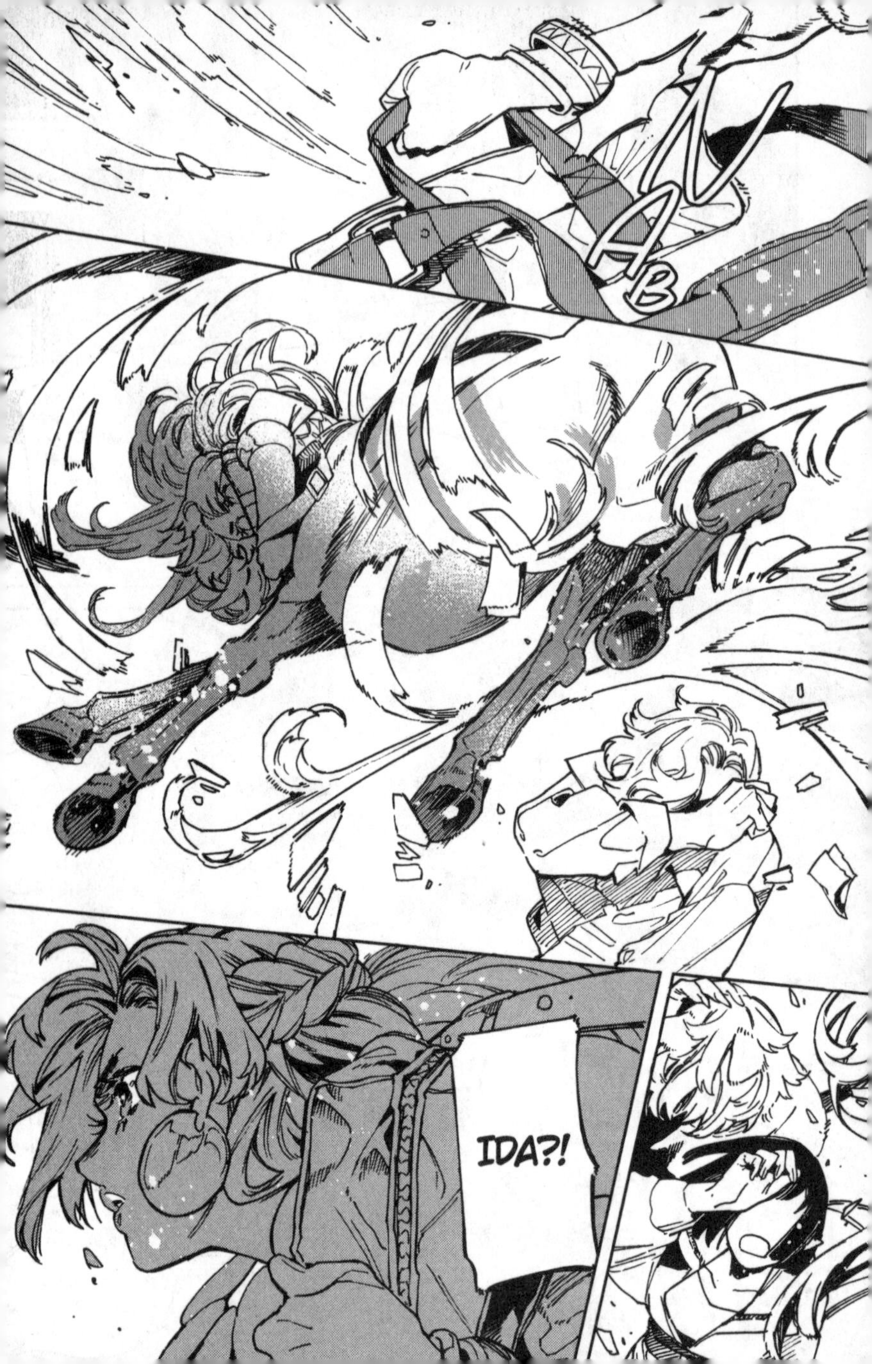
BANG
IDA?!

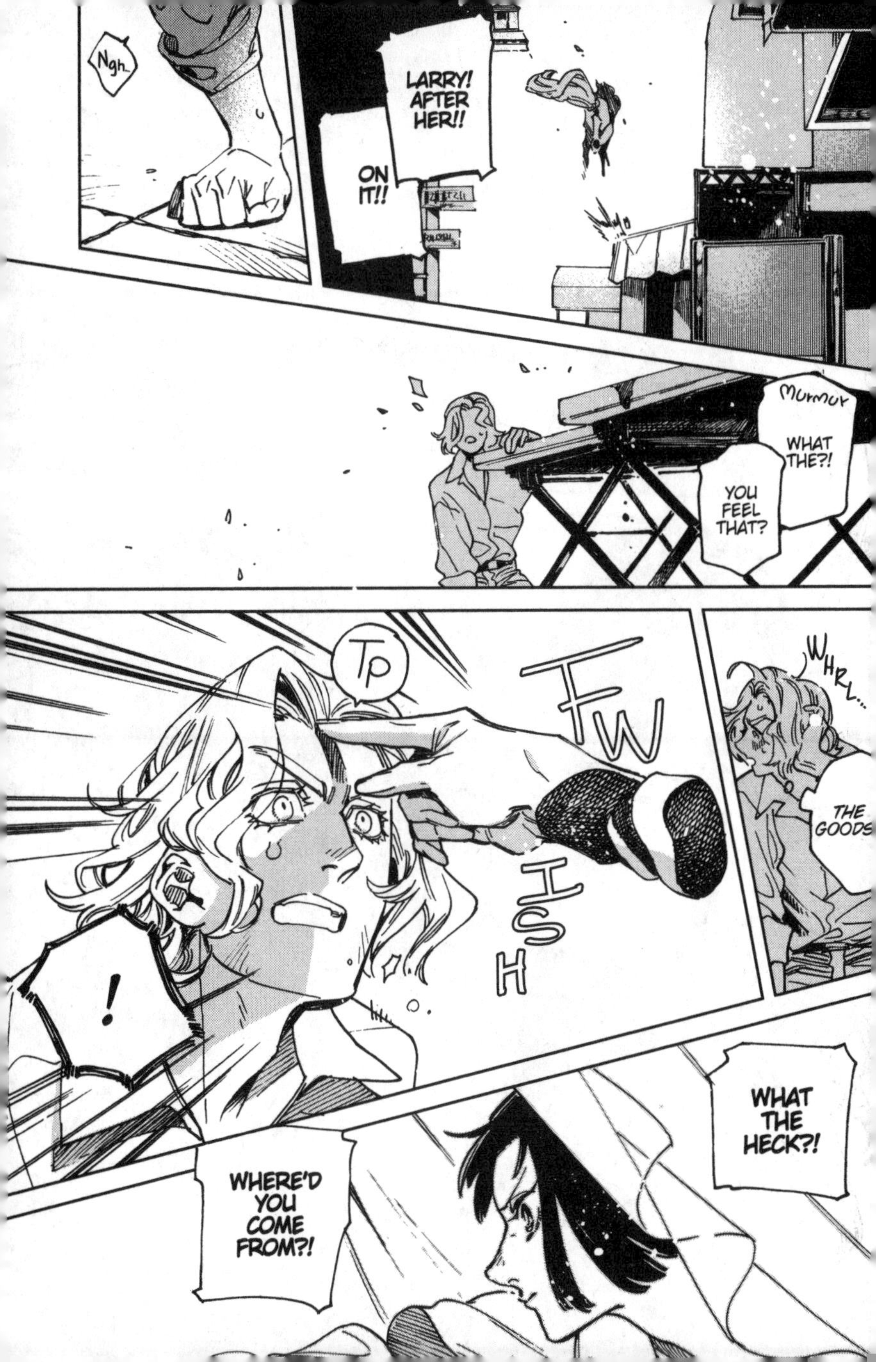
LARRY! AFTER HER!!
ON IT!!
Ngh...
Murmur
WHAT THE?!
YOU FEEL THAT?
WHRL...
THE GOODS
Tp
FWISH
!
WHAT THE HECK?!
WHERE'D YOU COME FROM?!

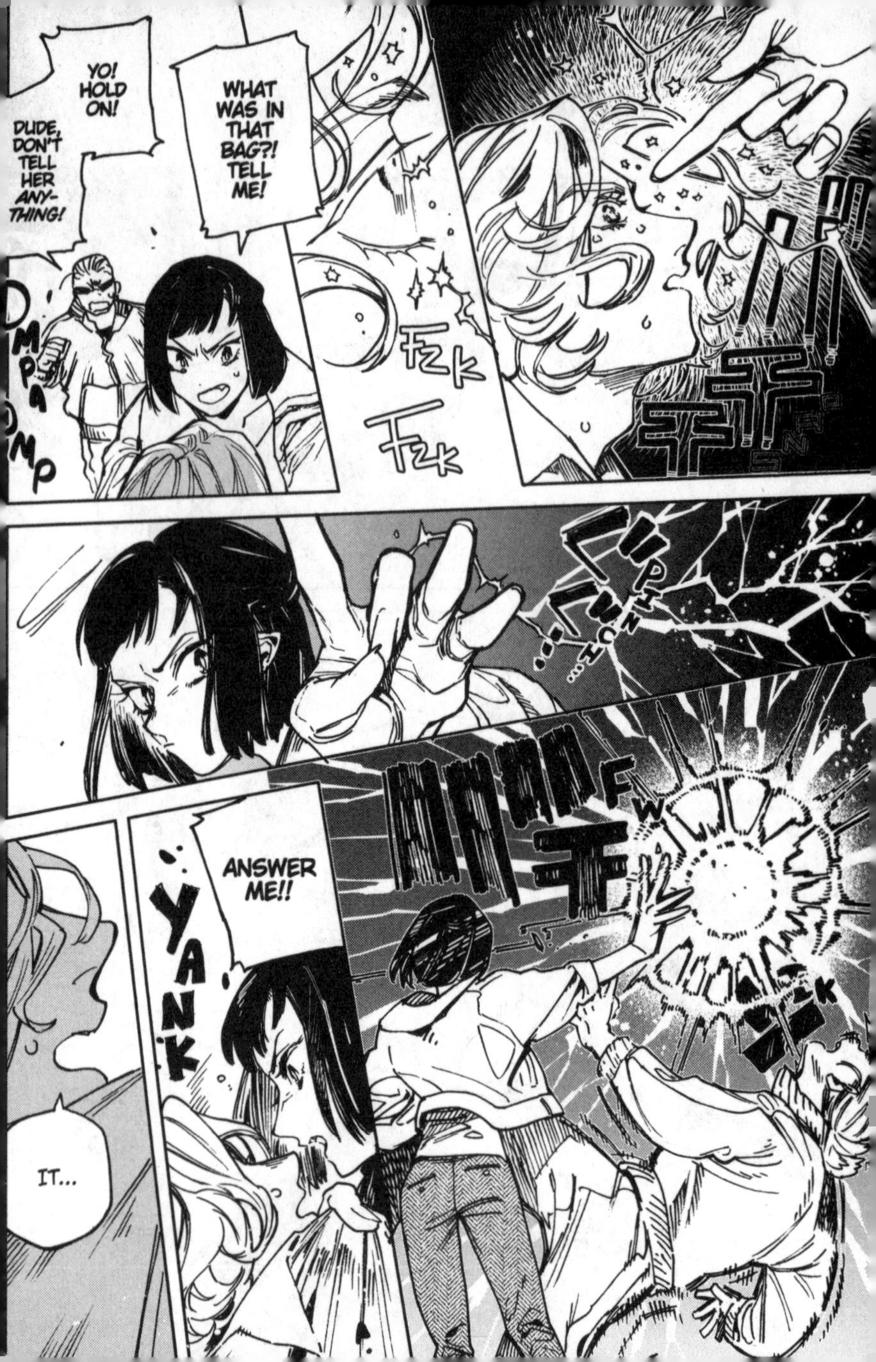
Fzk
Fzk
WHAT WAS IN THAT BAG?! TELL ME!
YO! HOLD ON!
DUDE, DON'T TELL HER ANYTHING!
PINCH...
ANSWER ME!!
YANK
IT...

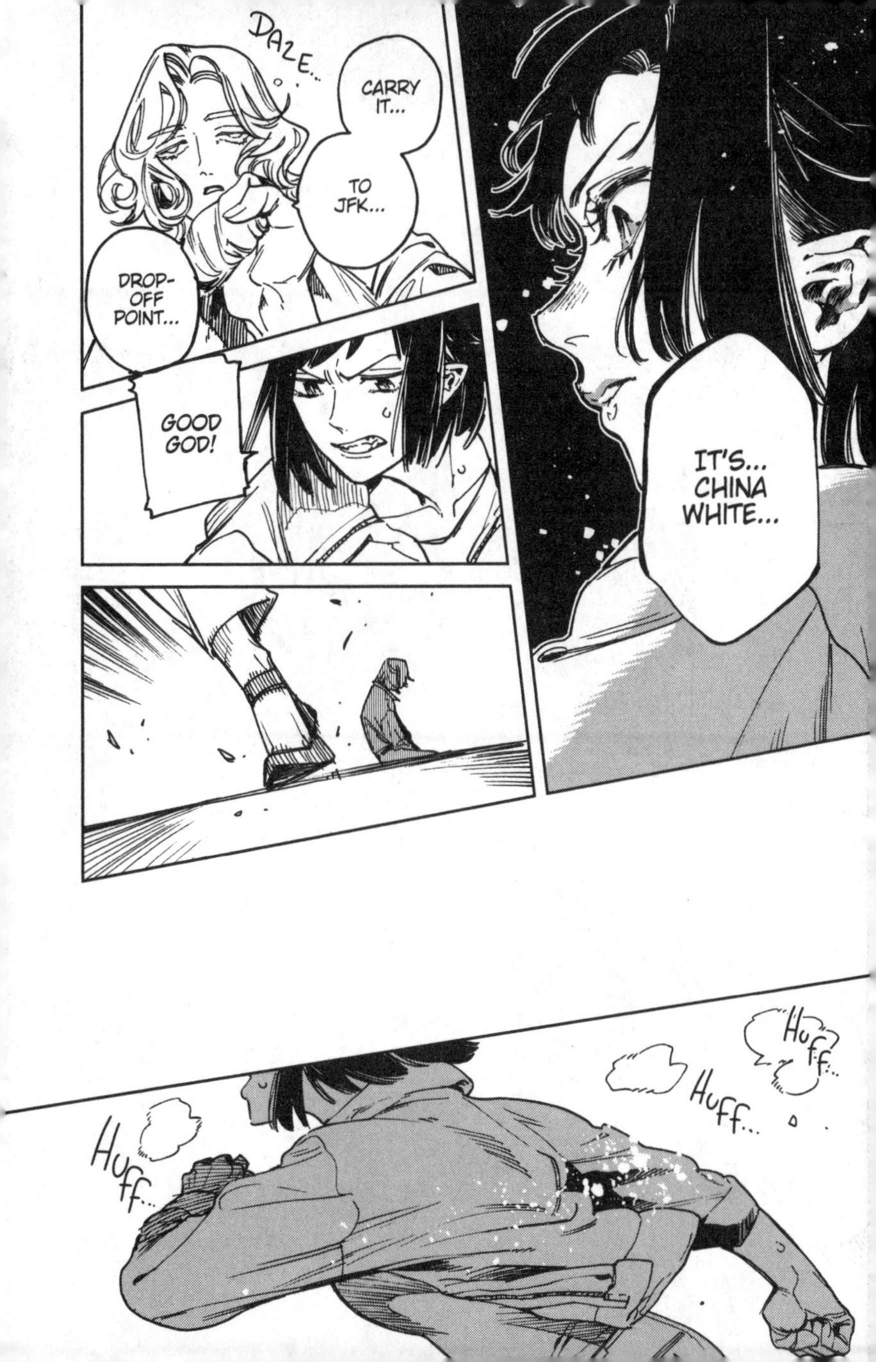
IT'S... CHINA WHITE...
DAZE...
CARRY IT...
TO JFK...
DROP-OFF POINT...
GOOD GOD!
HUFF...
HUFF...
HUFF...

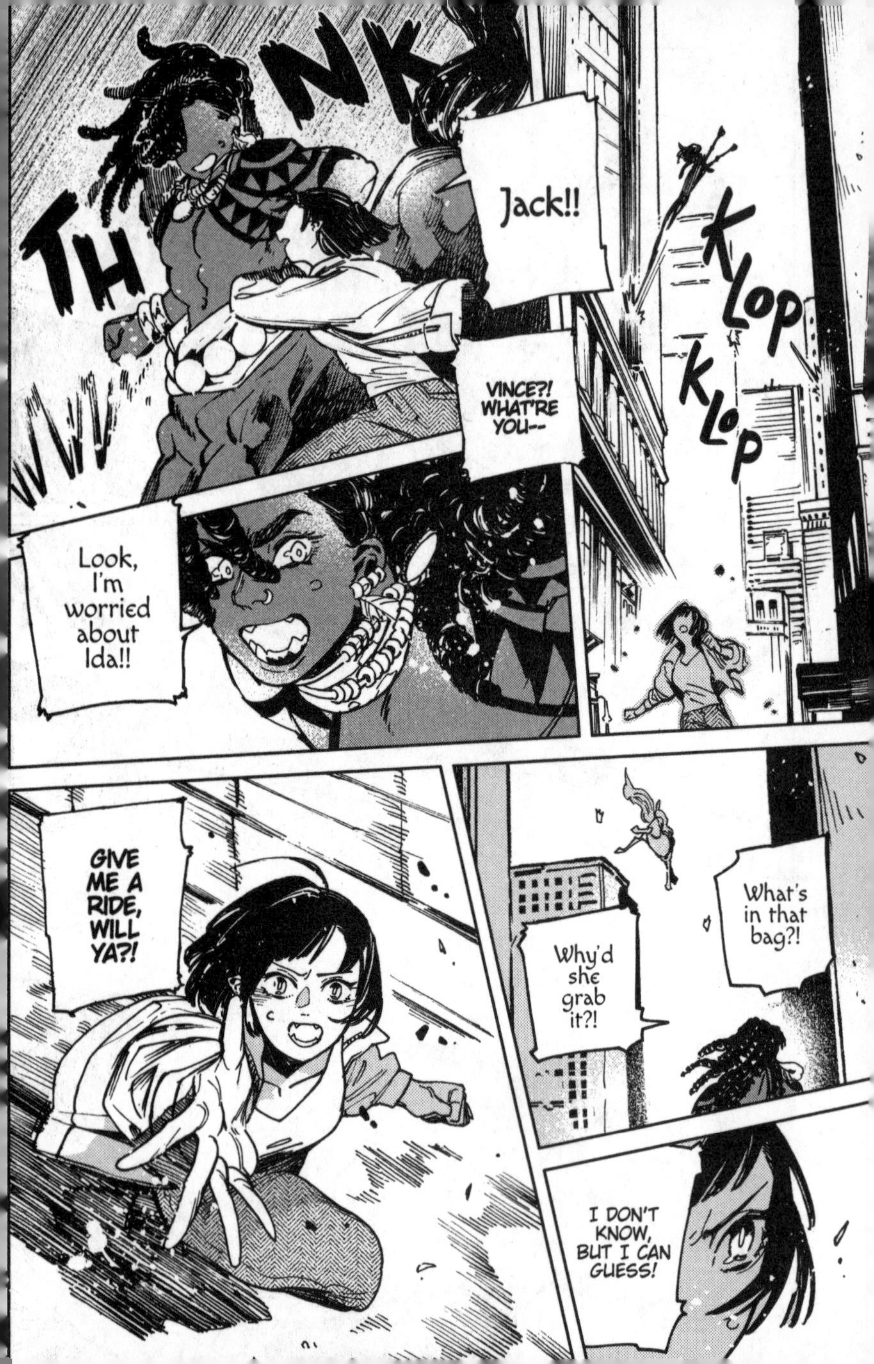
KLOP
KLOP
THNK
Jack!!
VINCE?! WHAT'RE YOU--
Look, I'm worried about Ida!!
What's in that bag?!
Why'd she grab it?!
I DON'T KNOW, BUT I CAN GUESS!
GIVE ME A RIDE, WILL YA?!

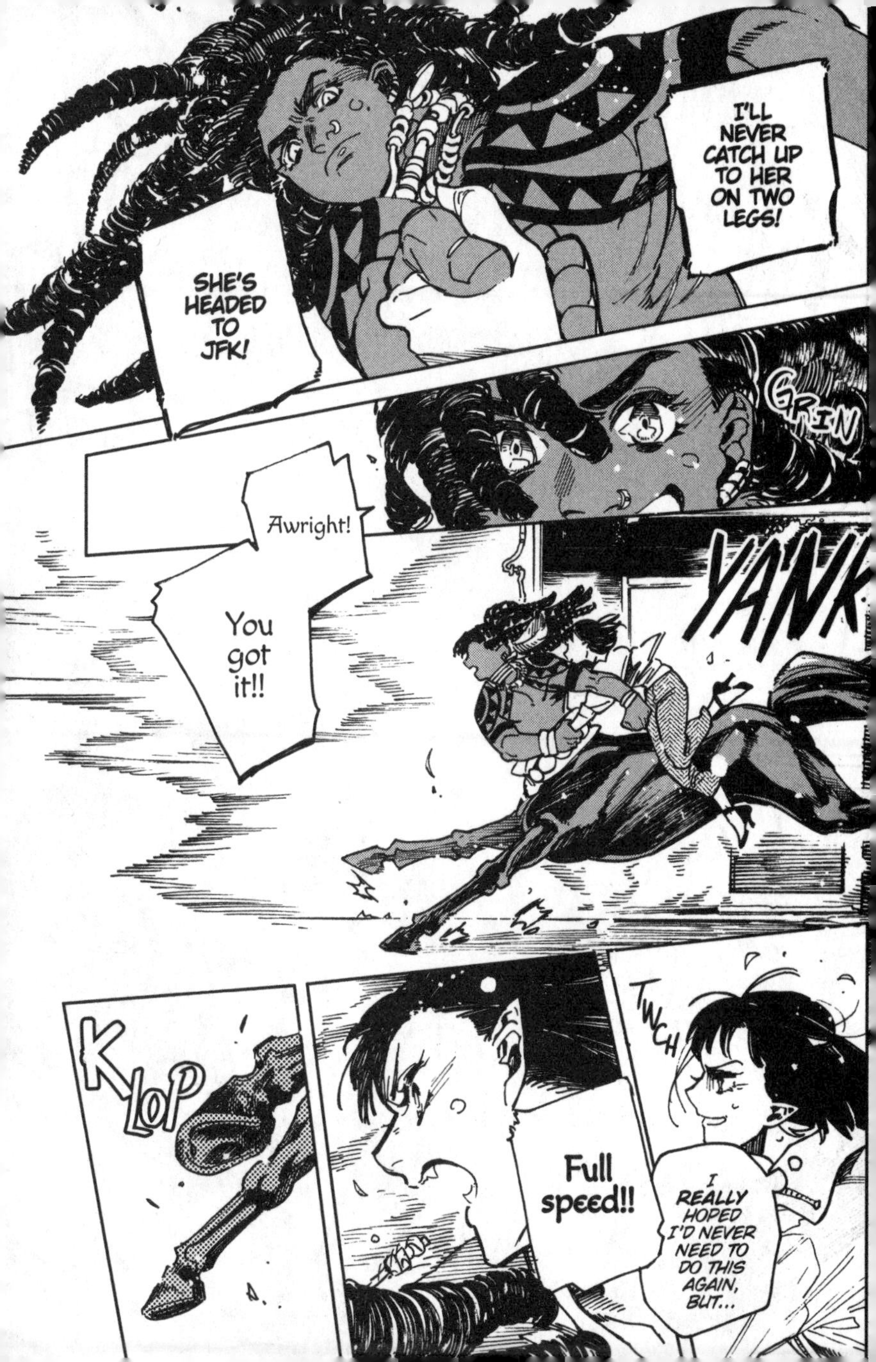
I'LL NEVER CATCH UP TO HER ON TWO LEGS!
SHE'S HEADED TO JFK!
GRIN
Awright!
YANK
You got it!!
TWCH
I REALLY HOPED I'D NEVER NEED TO DO THIS AGAIN, BUT...
Full speed!!
KLOP

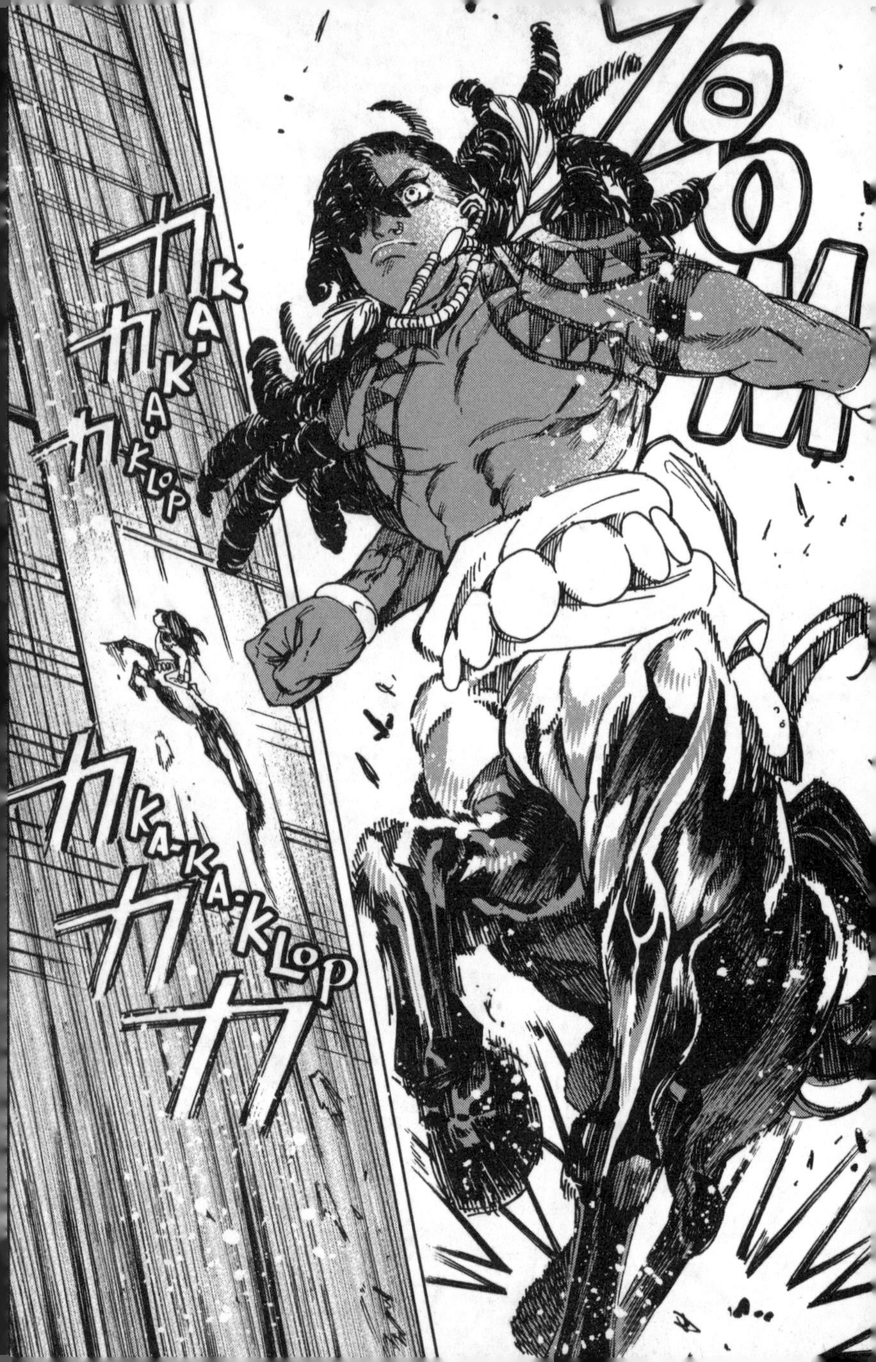
VOOM
カカカ KA-KA-KLOP
カカカカ KA-KA-KA-KLOP

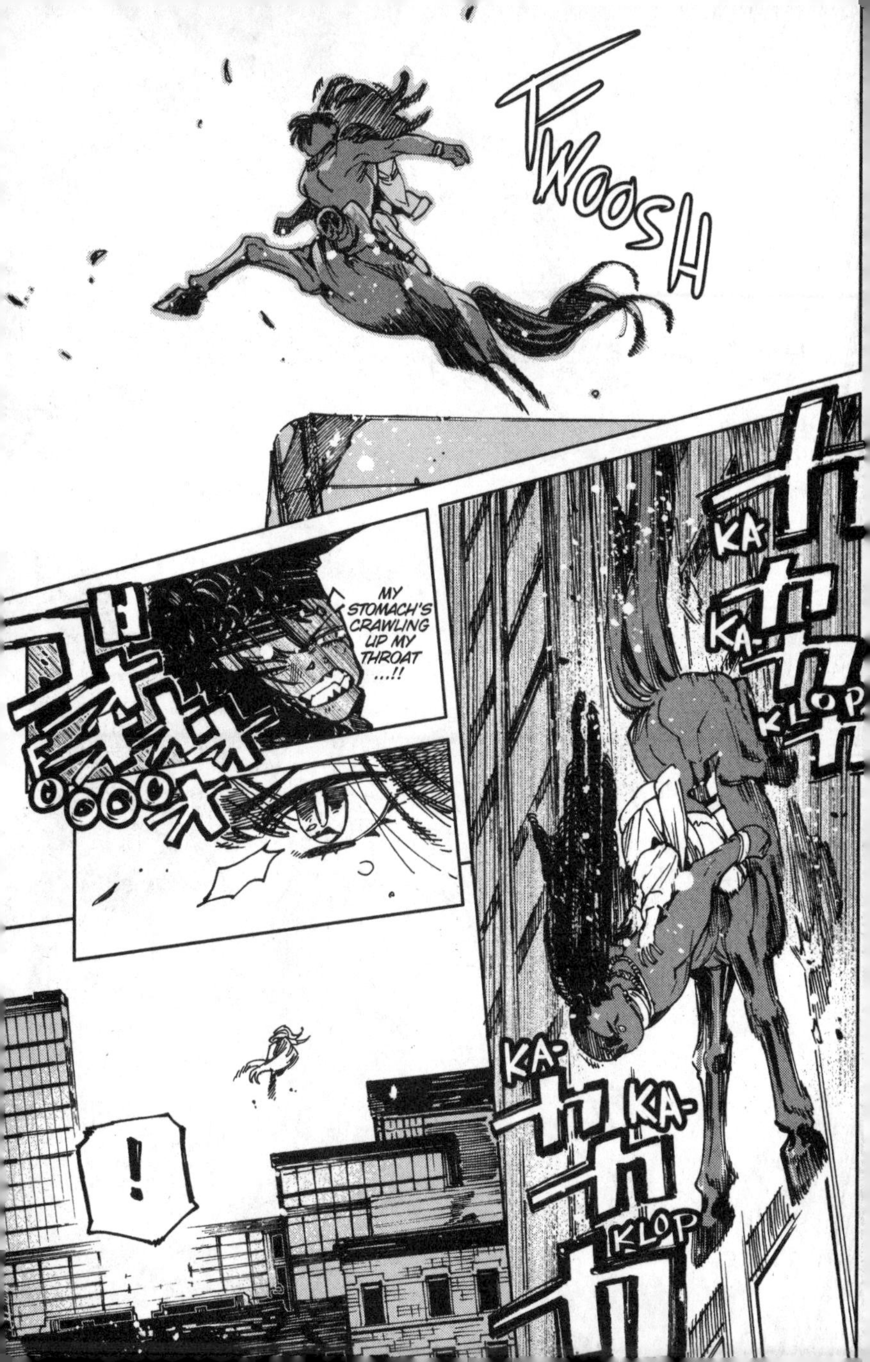
FWOOSH
KA-KA-KLOP
KA-KA-KLOP
MY STOMACH'S CRAWLING UP MY THROAT ...!!
FOOOO
!

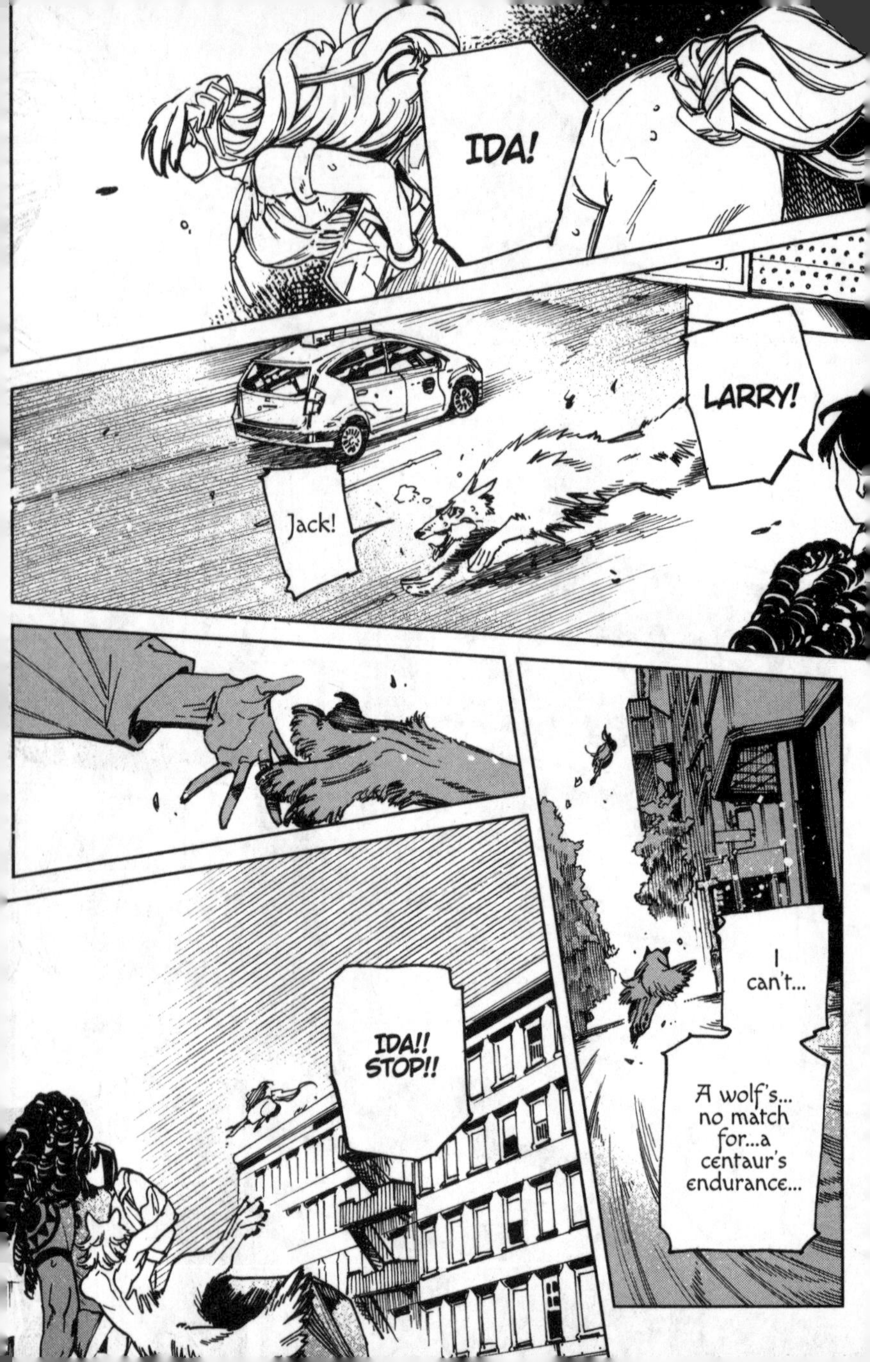
IDA!
LARRY!
Jack!
I can't...
A wolf's... no match for...a centaur's endurance...
IDA!! STOP!!

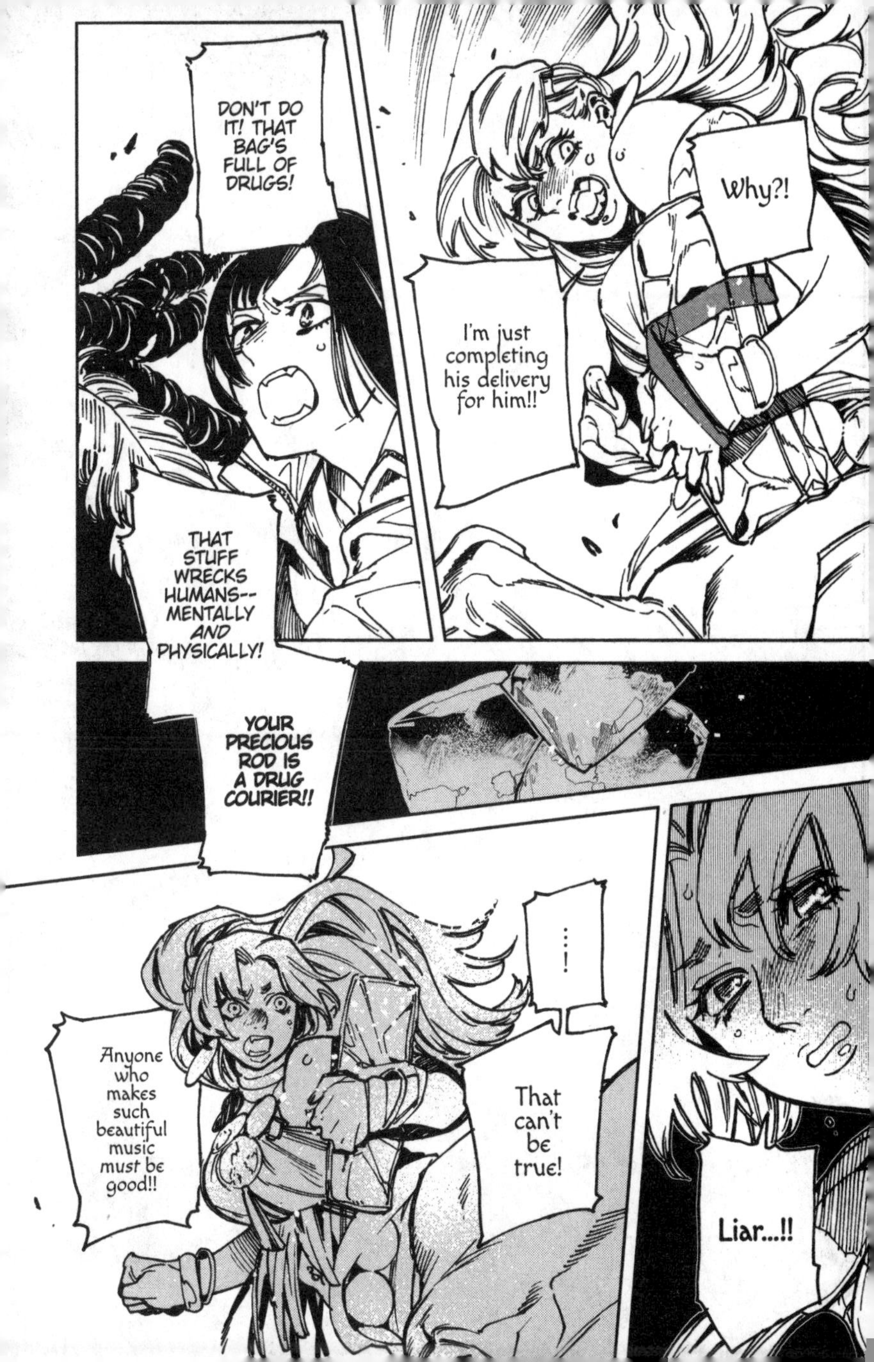
Why?!
I'm just completing his delivery for him!!
DON'T DO IT! THAT BAG'S FULL OF DRUGS!
THAT STUFF WRECKS HUMANS--MENTALLY AND PHYSICALLY!
YOUR PRECIOUS ROD IS A DRUG COURIER!!
Liar...!!
...!
That can't be true!
Anyone who makes such beautiful music must be good!!

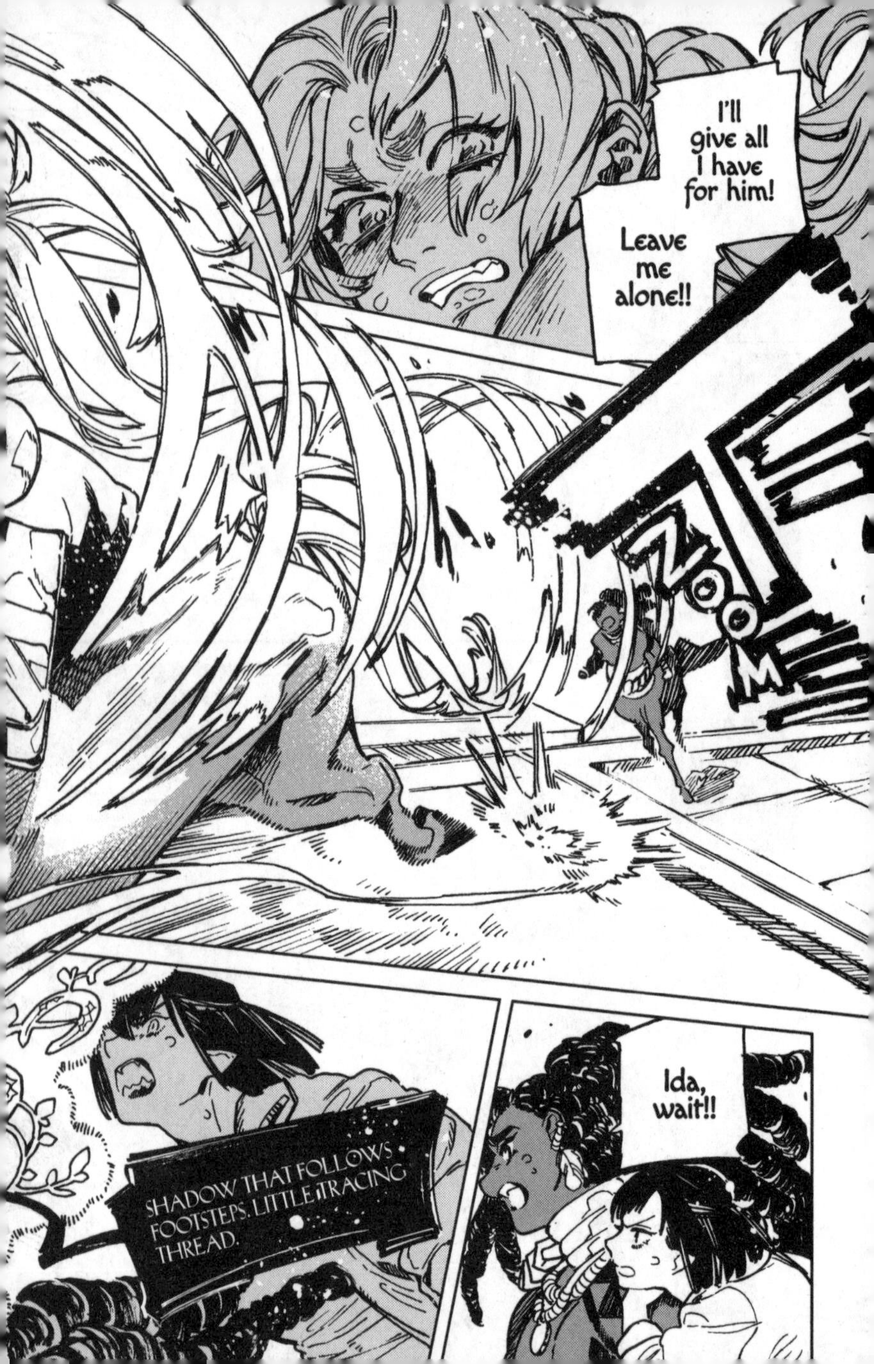
I'll give all I have for him!
Leave me alone!!
ZOOOM
Ida, wait!!
SHADOW THAT FOLLOWS FOOTSTEPS. LITTLE TRACING THREAD.

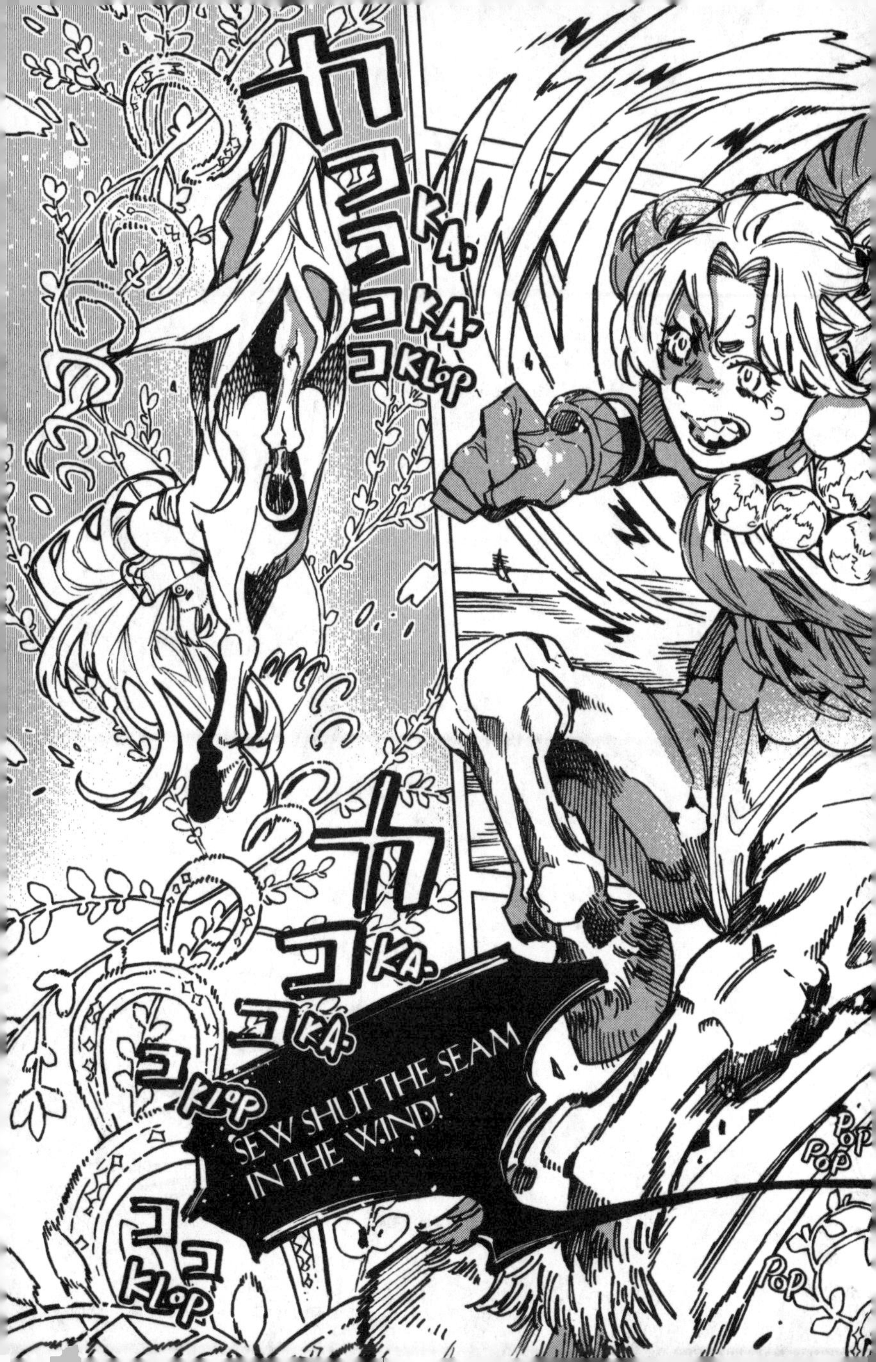

カコ KA-
コ KA-
コ KLOP
カコ KA-
コ KA-
コ KLOP
SEW SHUT THE SEAM IN THE WIND!
POP POP
コ コ KLOP
POP

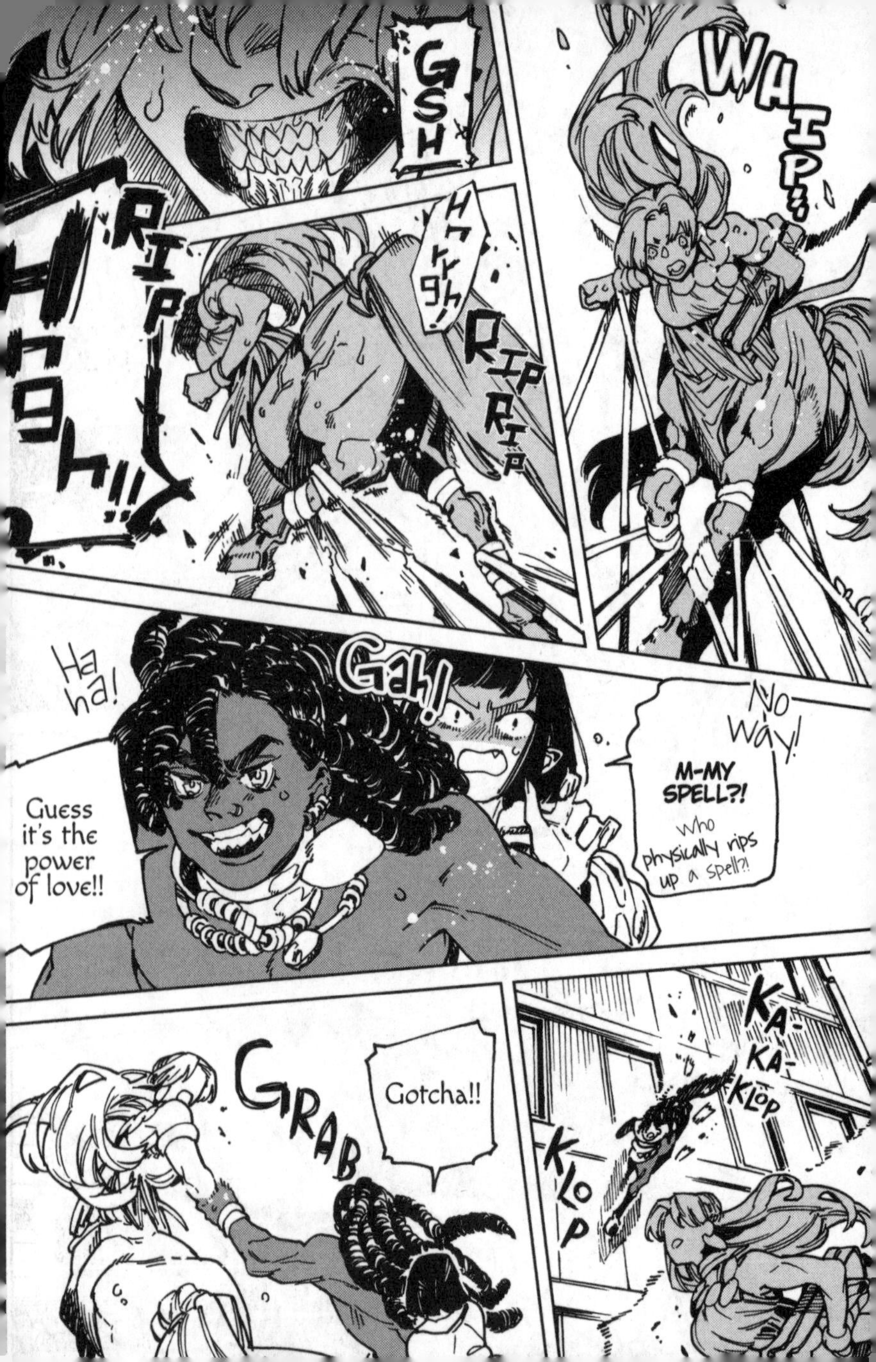
WHAIP!!
GSH
Hnnngh!
RIP RIP RIP
RIP
Hnngh!!
No way!
M-MY SPELL?!
Who physically rips up a spell?!
Gah!
Ha ha!
Guess it's the power of love!!
KA-KA-KLOP
KLOP
Gotcha!!
GRAB

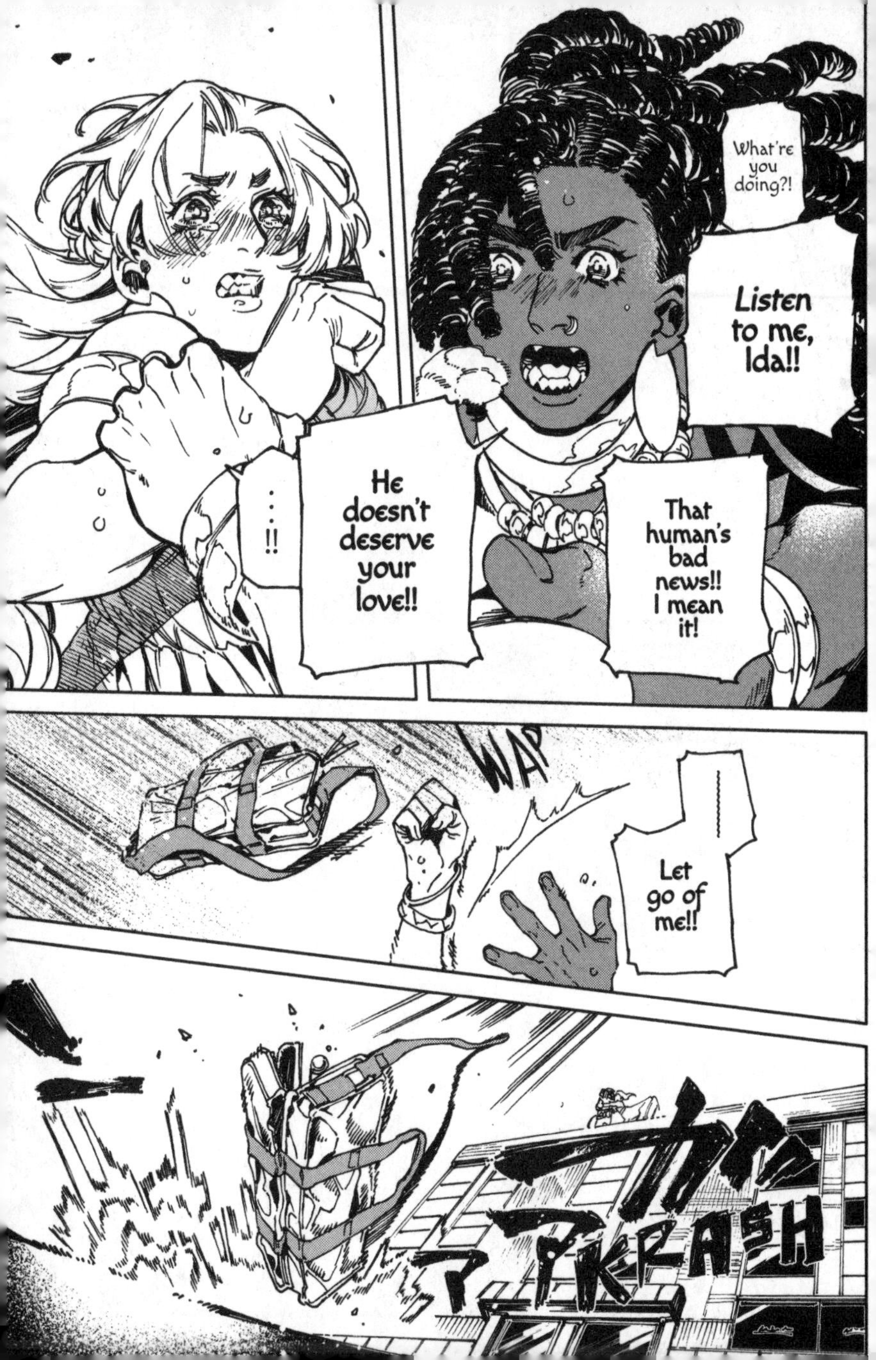
What're you doing?!
Listen to me, Ida!!
That human's bad news!! I mean it!
He doesn't deserve your love!!
...!!
——
Let go of me!!
WAP
KRASH

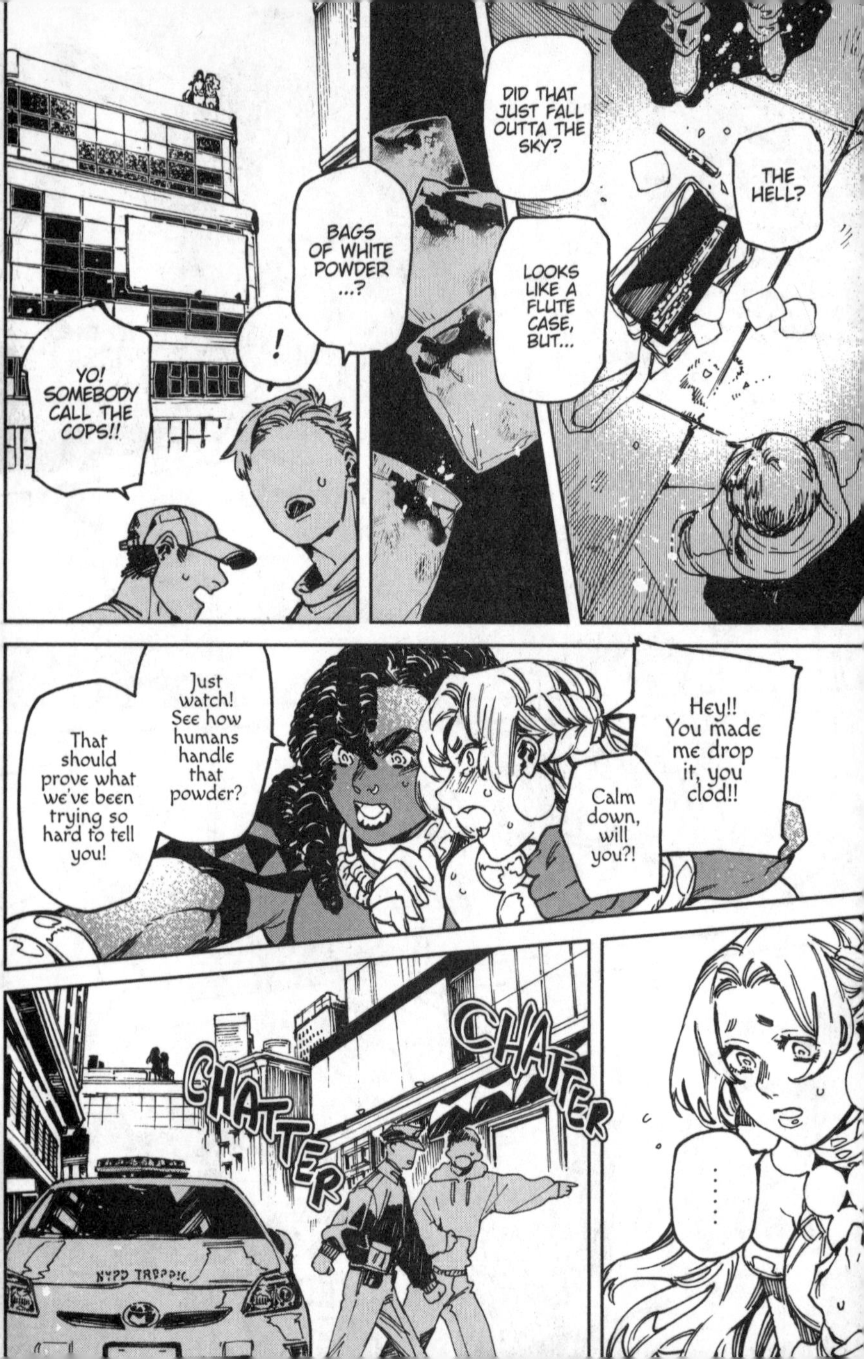
THE HELL?
LOOKS LIKE A FLUTE CASE, BUT...
DID THAT JUST FALL OUTTA THE SKY?
BAGS OF WHITE POWDER ...?
!
YO! SOMEBODY CALL THE COPS!!
Hey!! You made me drop it, you clod!!
Calm down, will you?!
Just watch! See how humans handle that powder?
That should prove what we've been trying so hard to tell you!
......
CHATTER
CHATTER

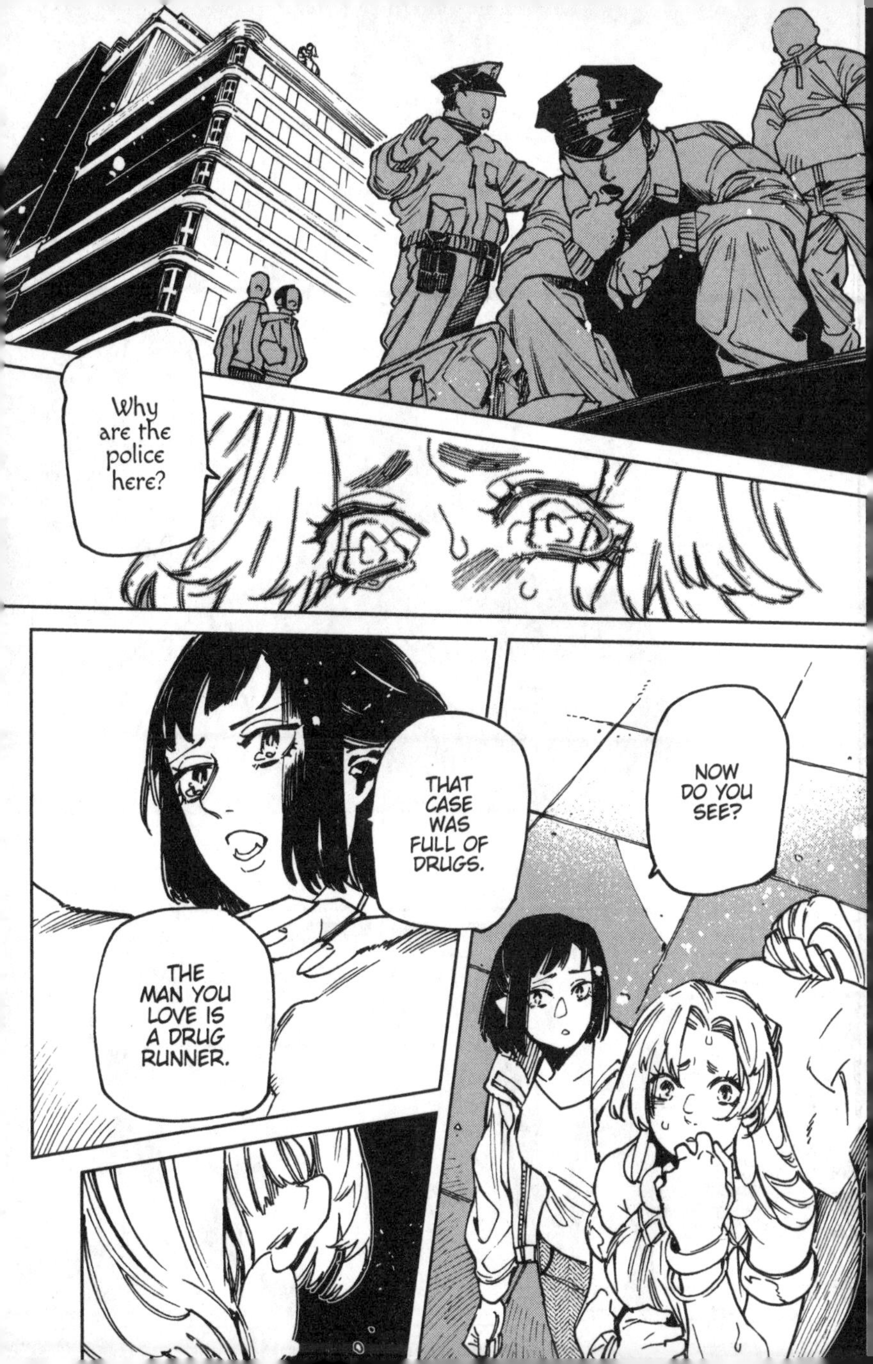
Why are the police here?
NOW DO YOU SEE?
THAT CASE WAS FULL OF DRUGS.
THE MAN YOU LOVE IS A DRUG RUNNER.

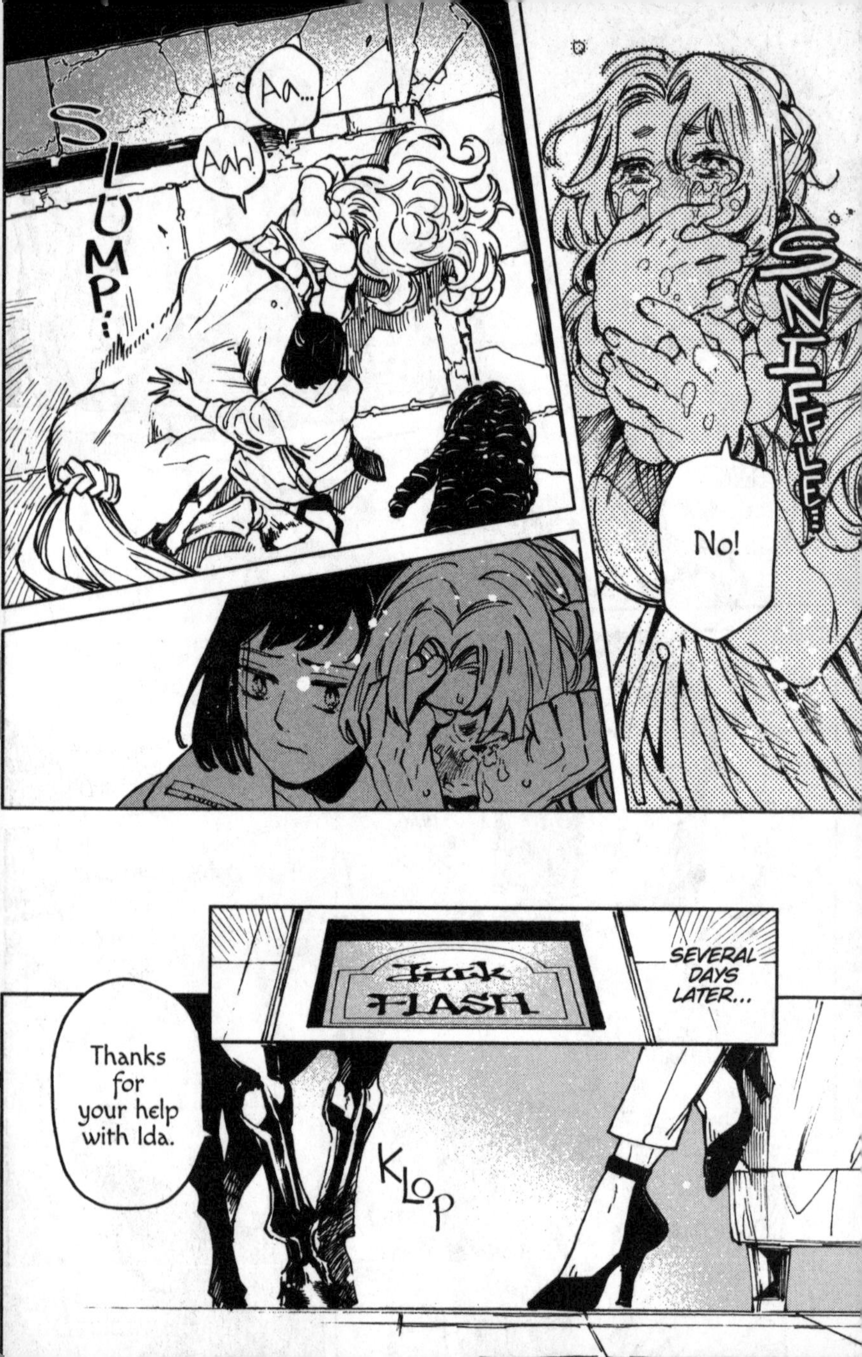
SNIFFLE...
No!
Aa...
Aah!
SLUMP!
Jack FLASH
SEVERAL DAYS LATER...
KLOP
Thanks for your help with Ida.

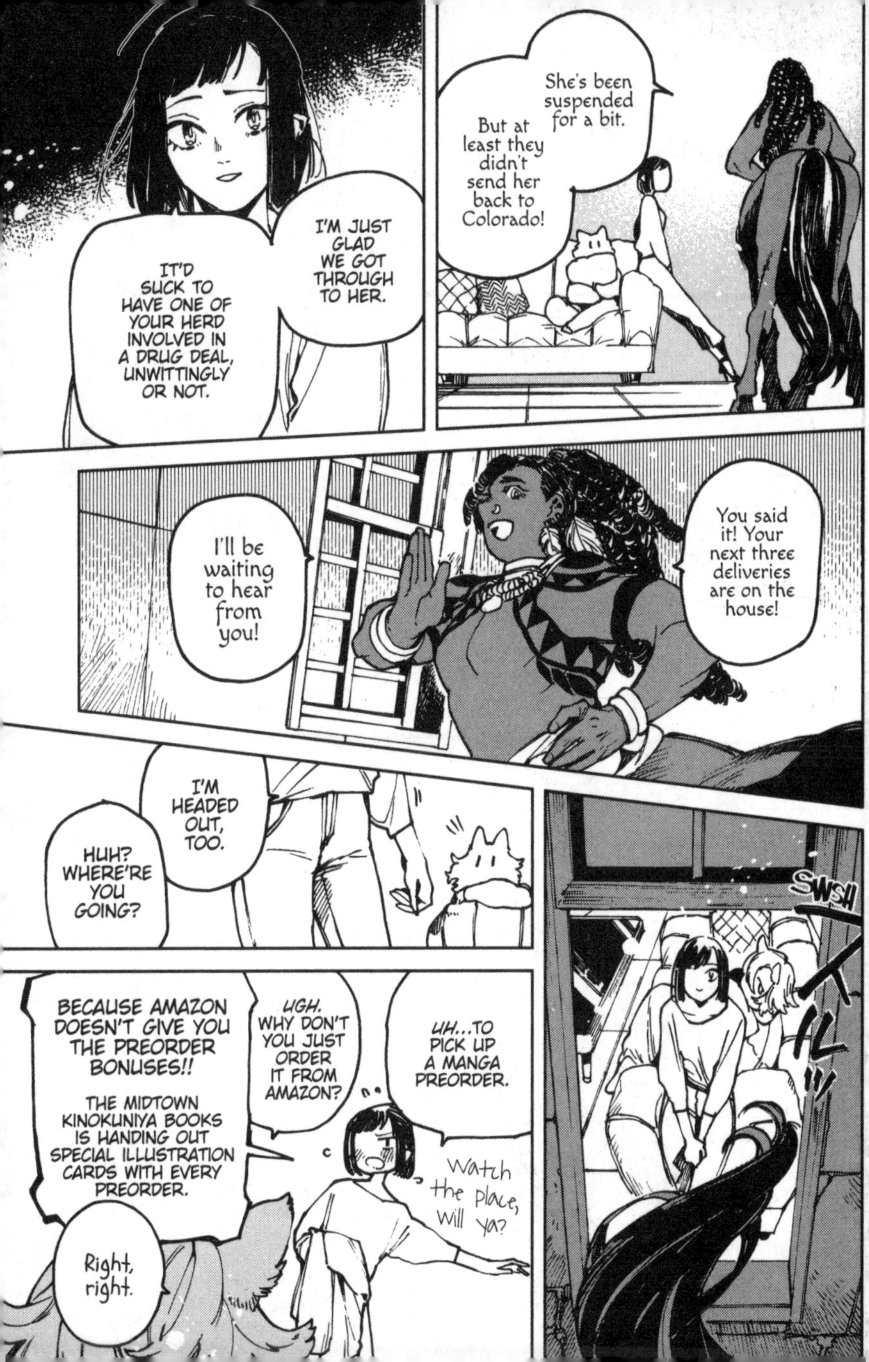
She's been suspended for a bit.
But at least they didn't send her back to Colorado!
I'M JUST GLAD WE GOT THROUGH TO HER.
IT'D SUCK TO HAVE ONE OF YOUR HERD INVOLVED IN A DRUG DEAL, UNWITTINGLY OR NOT.
You said it! Your next three deliveries are on the house!
I'll be waiting to hear from you!
SWSH
I'M HEADED OUT, TOO.
HUH? WHERE'RE YOU GOING?
UH...TO PICK UP A MANGA PREORDER.
UGH. WHY DON'T YOU JUST ORDER IT FROM AMAZON?
BECAUSE AMAZON DOESN'T GIVE YOU THE PREORDER BONUSES!!
THE MIDTOWN KINOKUNIYA BOOKS IS HANDING OUT SPECIAL ILLUSTRATION CARDS WITH EVERY PREORDER.
Watch the place, will ya?
Right, right.

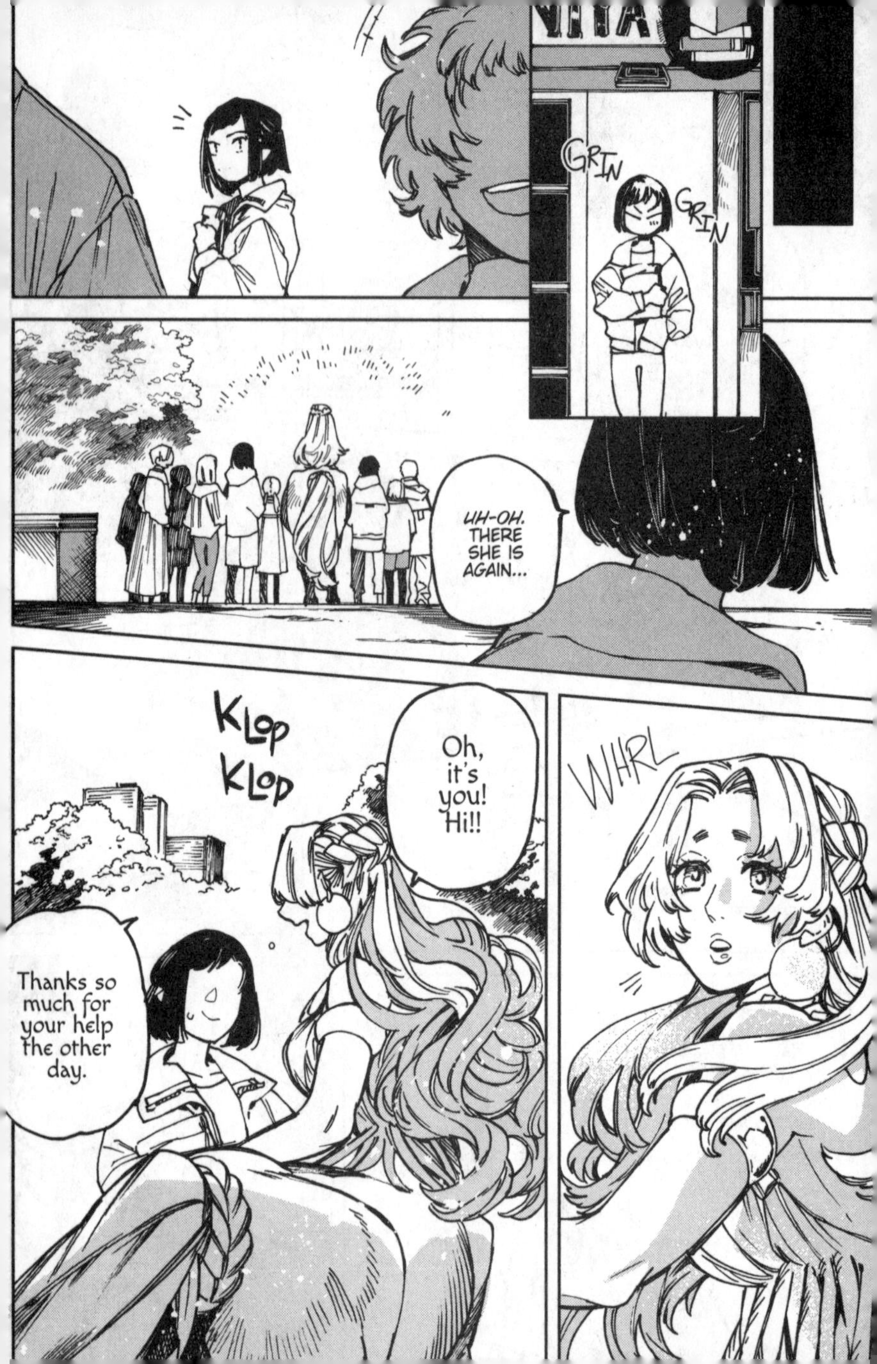
GRIN
GRIN
UH-OH. THERE SHE IS AGAIN...
WHRL
Oh, it's you! Hi!!
KLOP
KLOP
Thanks so much for your help the other day.

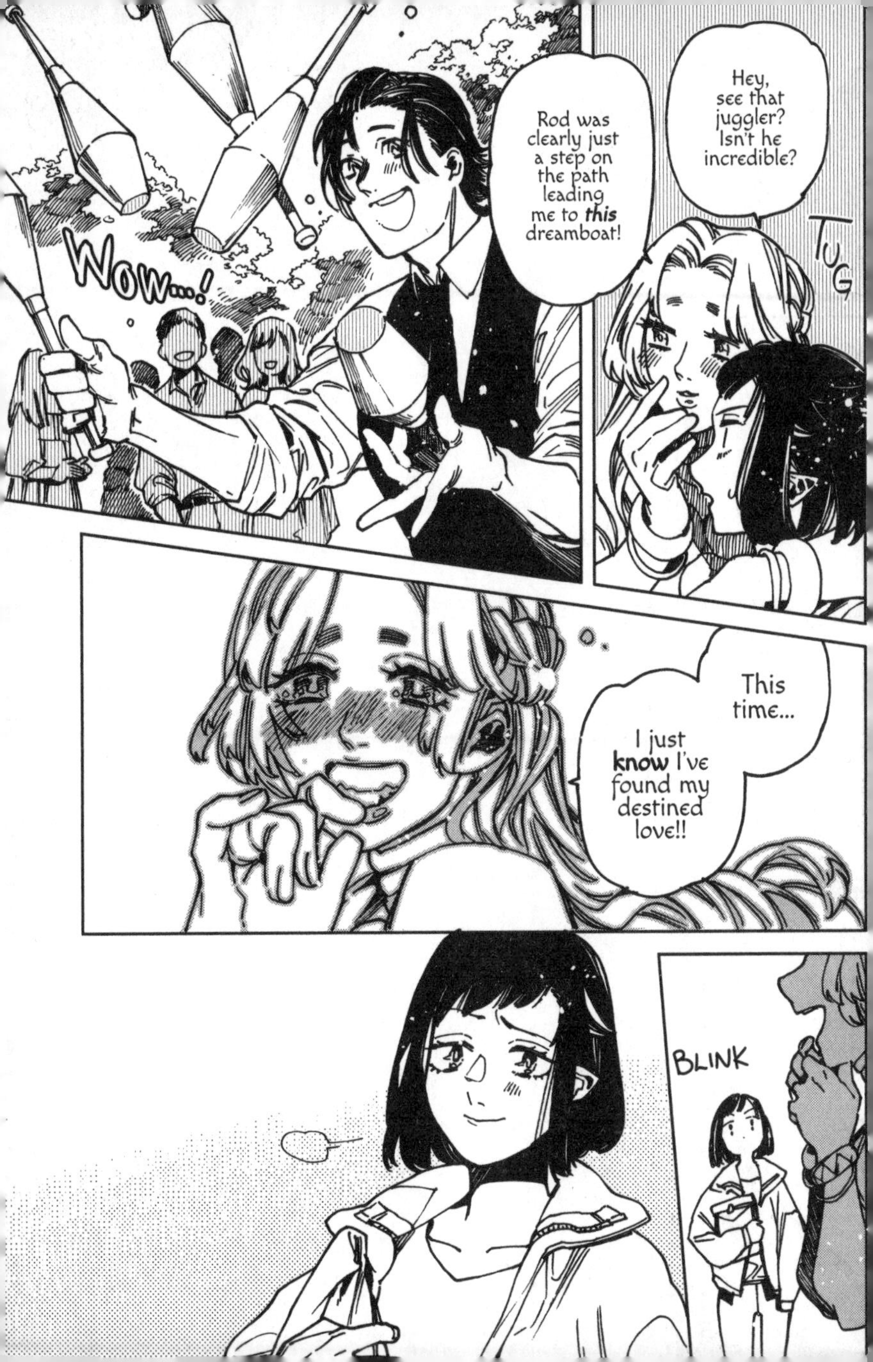
Hey, see that juggler? Isn't he incredible?
TUG
Rod was clearly just a step on the path leading me to **this** dreamboat!
Wow...!
This time...
I just **know** I've found my destined love!!
BLINK

The Ancient Magus' Bride

JACK FLASH AND THE FAERIE CASE FILES

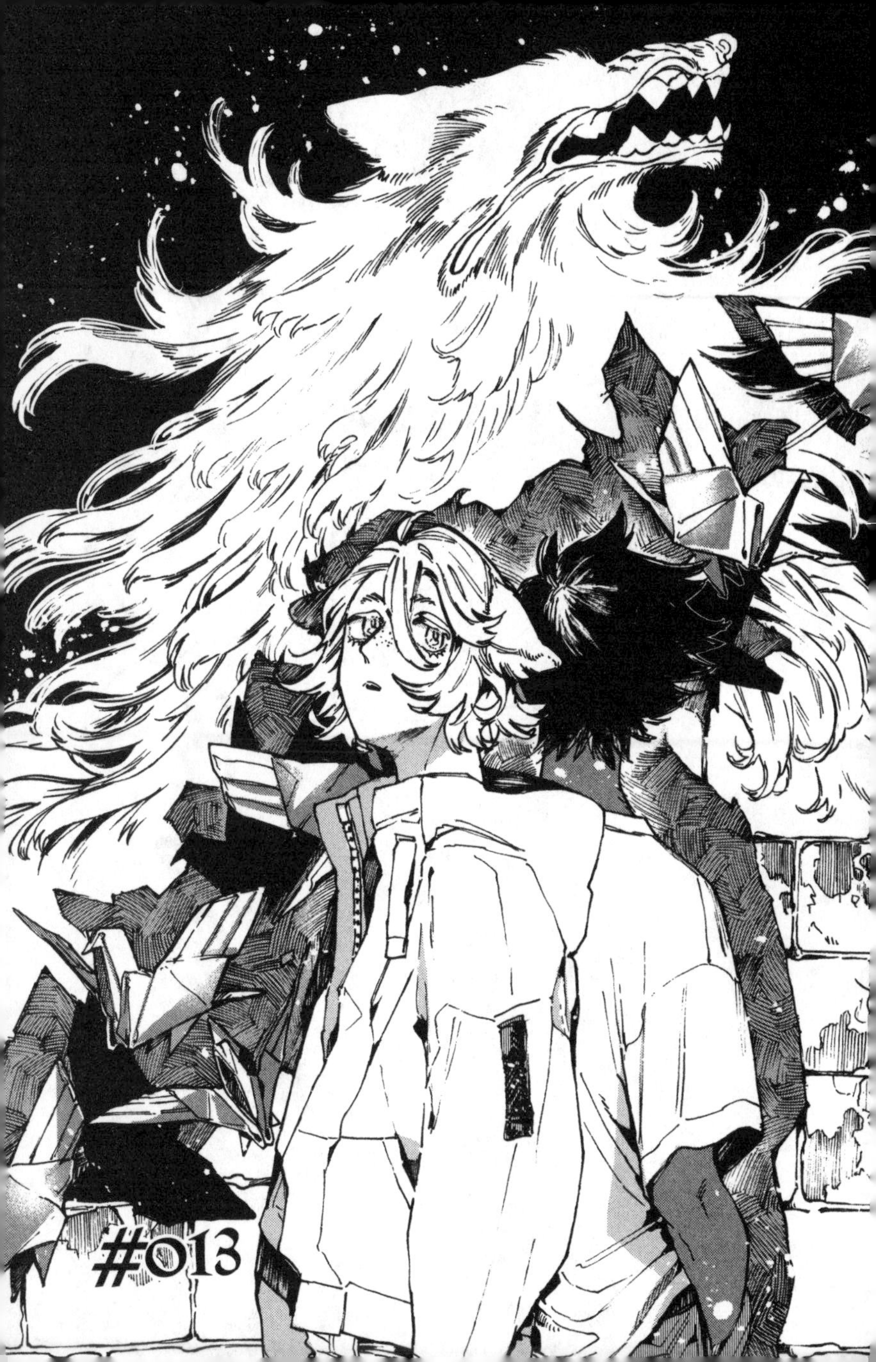
#013

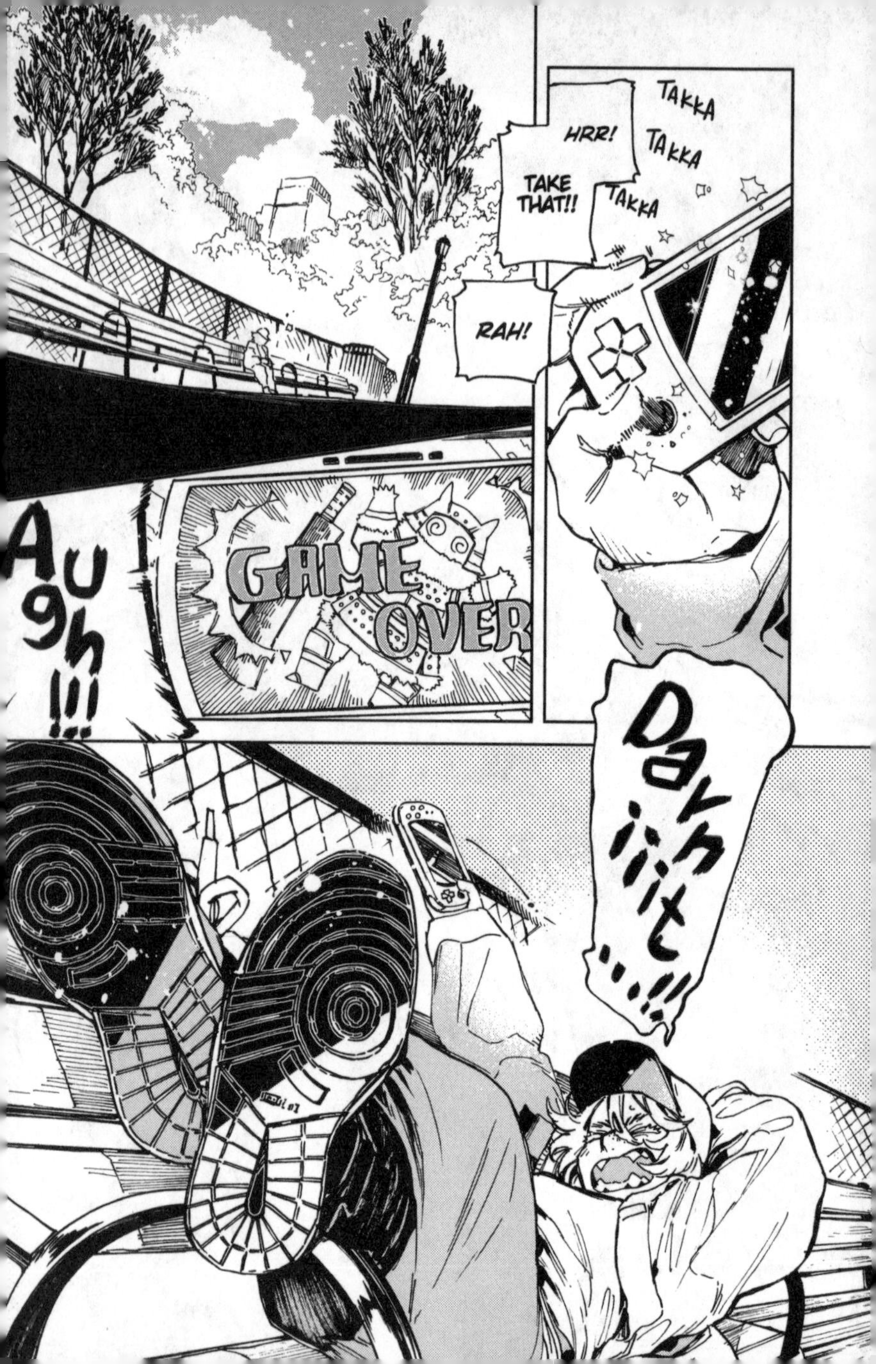
TAKKA
TAKKA
TAKKA
HRR!
TAKE THAT!!
RAH!
GAME OVER
Augh!!!
Damn it...!!!

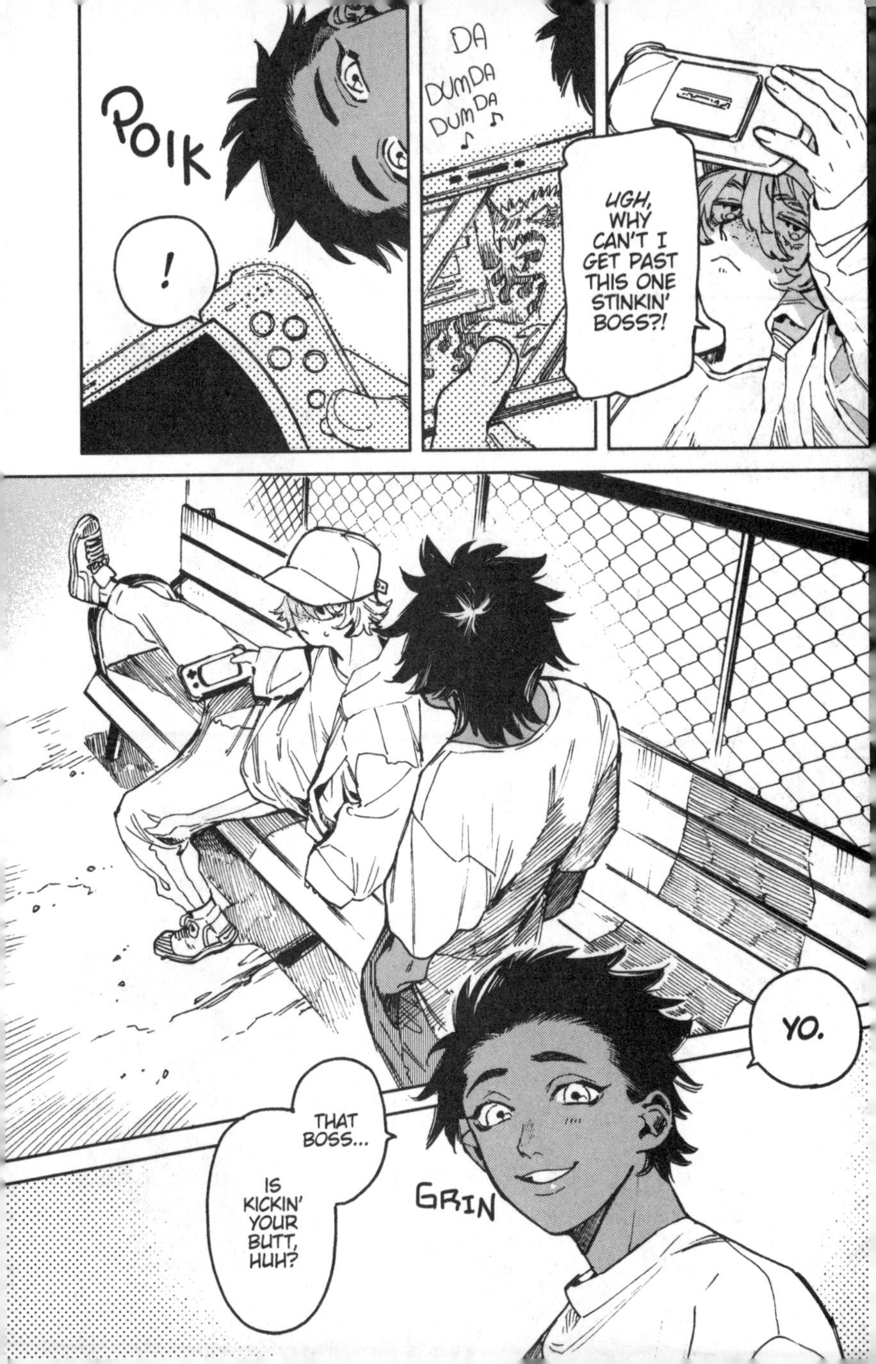
UGH, WHY CAN'T I GET PAST THIS ONE STINKIN' BOSS?!
DA DUMDA DUMDA ♪ ♪
POIK
!
YO.
THAT BOSS...
IS KICKIN' YOUR BUTT, HUH?
GRIN

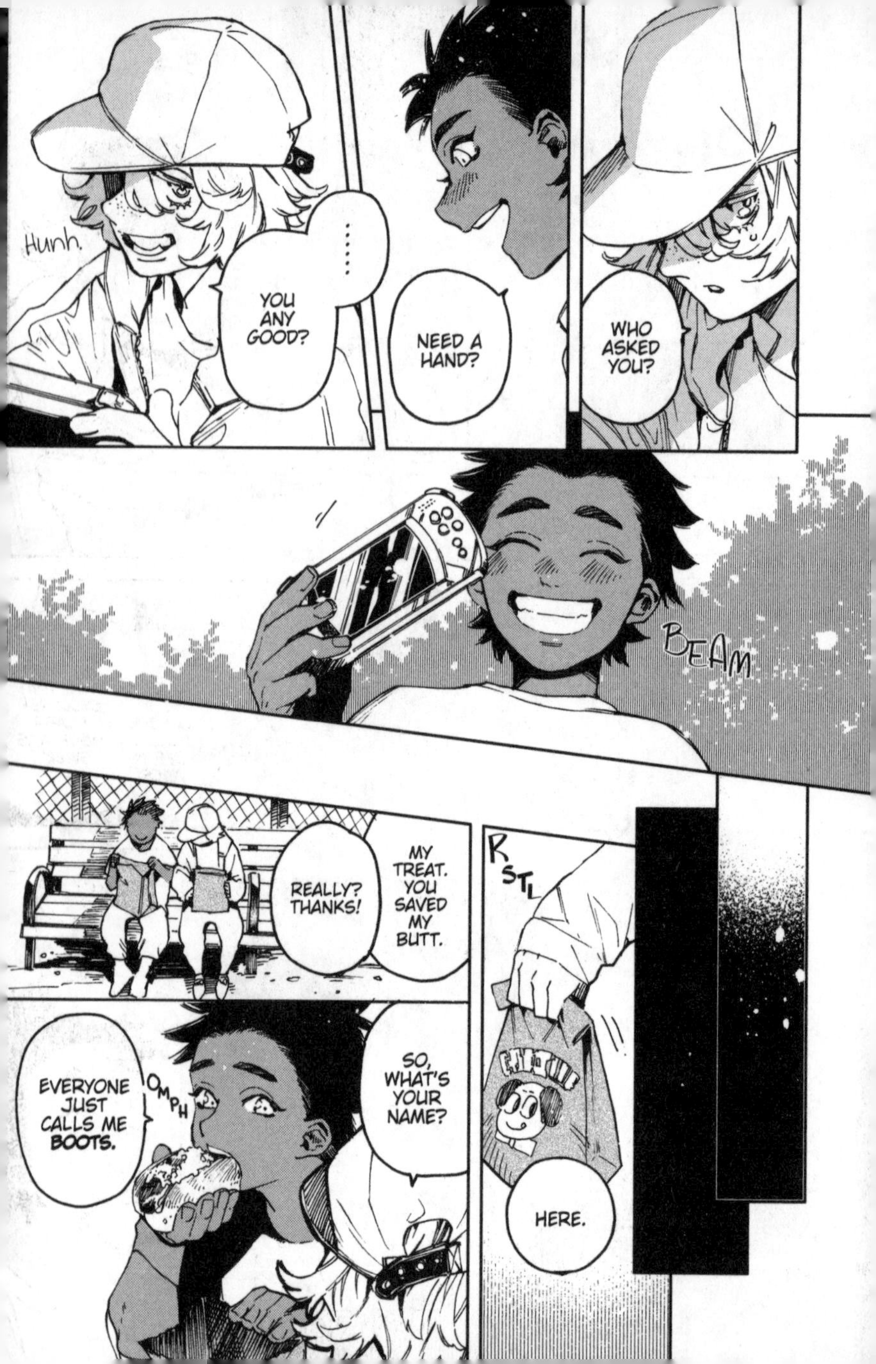
WHO ASKED YOU?
NEED A HAND?
......
YOU ANY GOOD?
Hunh.
BEAM
RSTL
HERE.
MY TREAT. YOU SAVED MY BUTT.
REALLY? THANKS!
SO, WHAT'S YOUR NAME?
OMPH
EVERYONE JUST CALLS ME **BOOTS**.

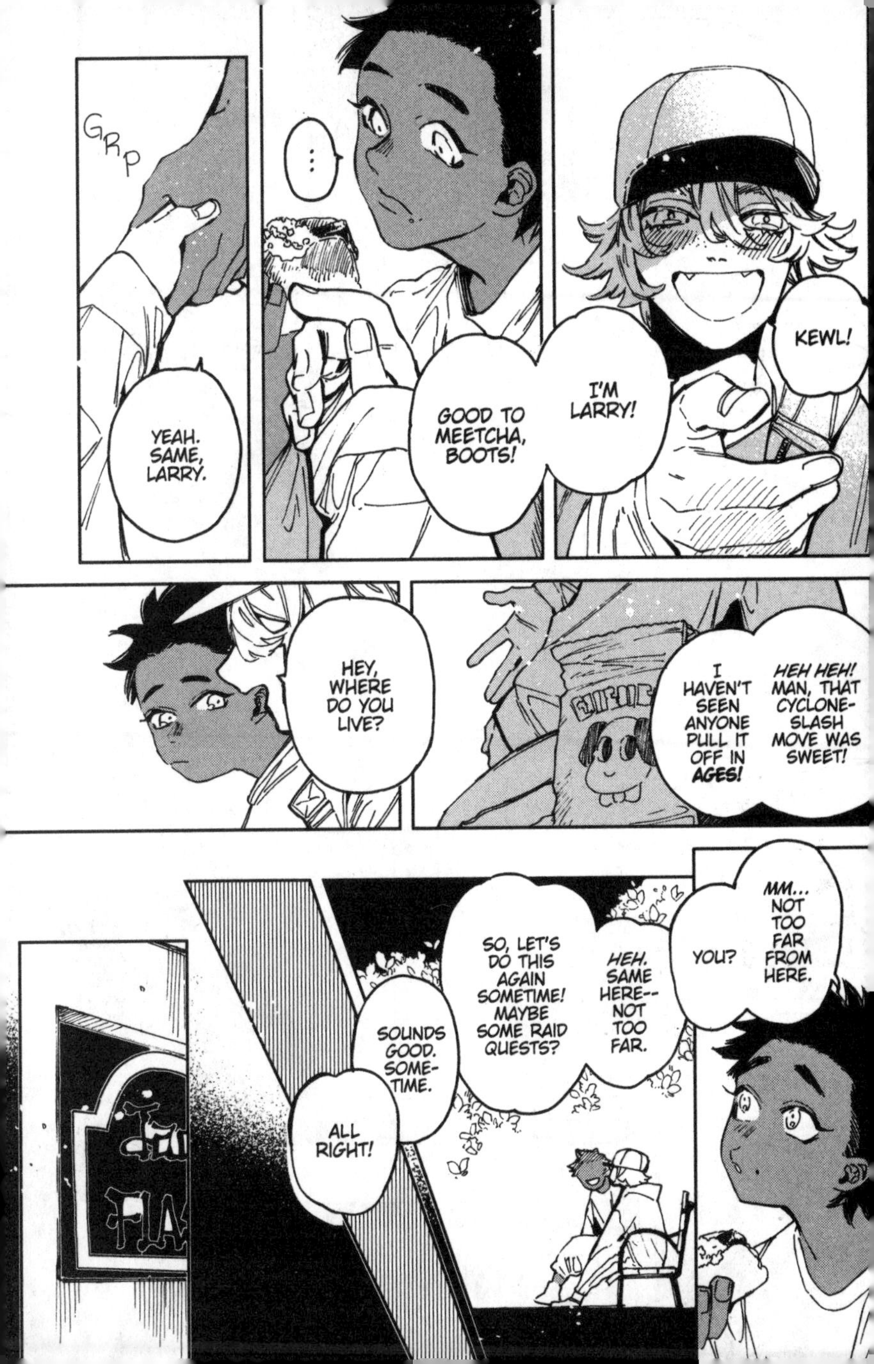
KEWL!
I'M LARRY!
GOOD TO MEETCHA, BOOTS!
...
GRP
YEAH. SAME, LARRY.
HEH HEH! MAN, THAT CYCLONE-SLASH MOVE WAS SWEET!
I HAVEN'T SEEN ANYONE PULL IT OFF IN AGES!
HEY, WHERE DO YOU LIVE?
MM... NOT TOO FAR FROM HERE.
YOU?
HEH. SAME HERE-- NOT TOO FAR.
SO, LET'S DO THIS AGAIN SOMETIME! MAYBE SOME RAID QUESTS?
SOUNDS GOOD. SOME-TIME.
ALL RIGHT!

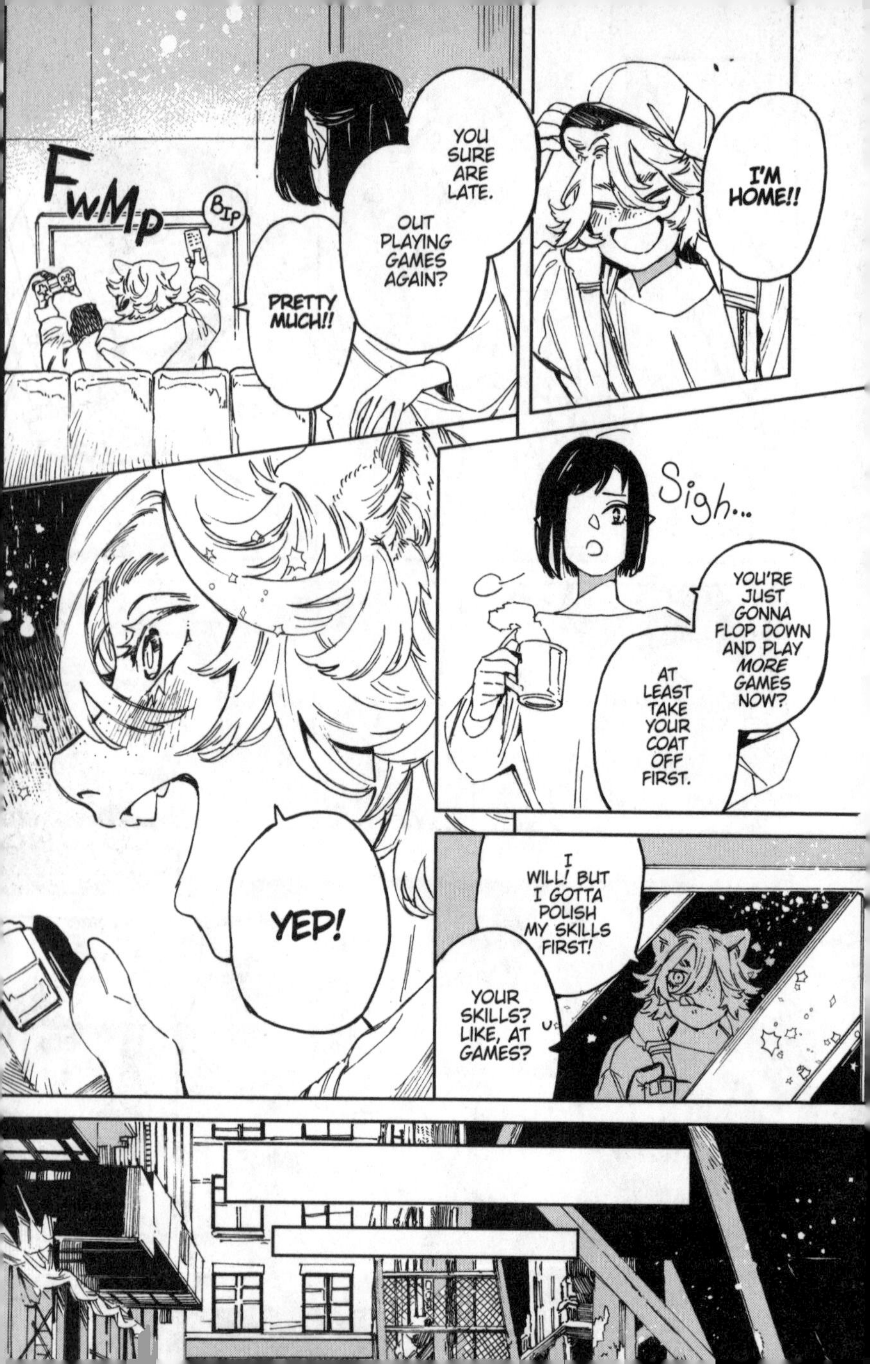
I'M HOME!!
YOU SURE ARE LATE.
OUT PLAYING GAMES AGAIN?
BIP
FWMP
PRETTY MUCH!!
Sigh...
YOU'RE JUST GONNA FLOP DOWN AND PLAY *MORE* GAMES NOW?
AT LEAST TAKE YOUR COAT OFF FIRST.
I WILL! BUT I GOTTA POLISH MY SKILLS FIRST!
YOUR SKILLS? LIKE, AT GAMES?
YEP!

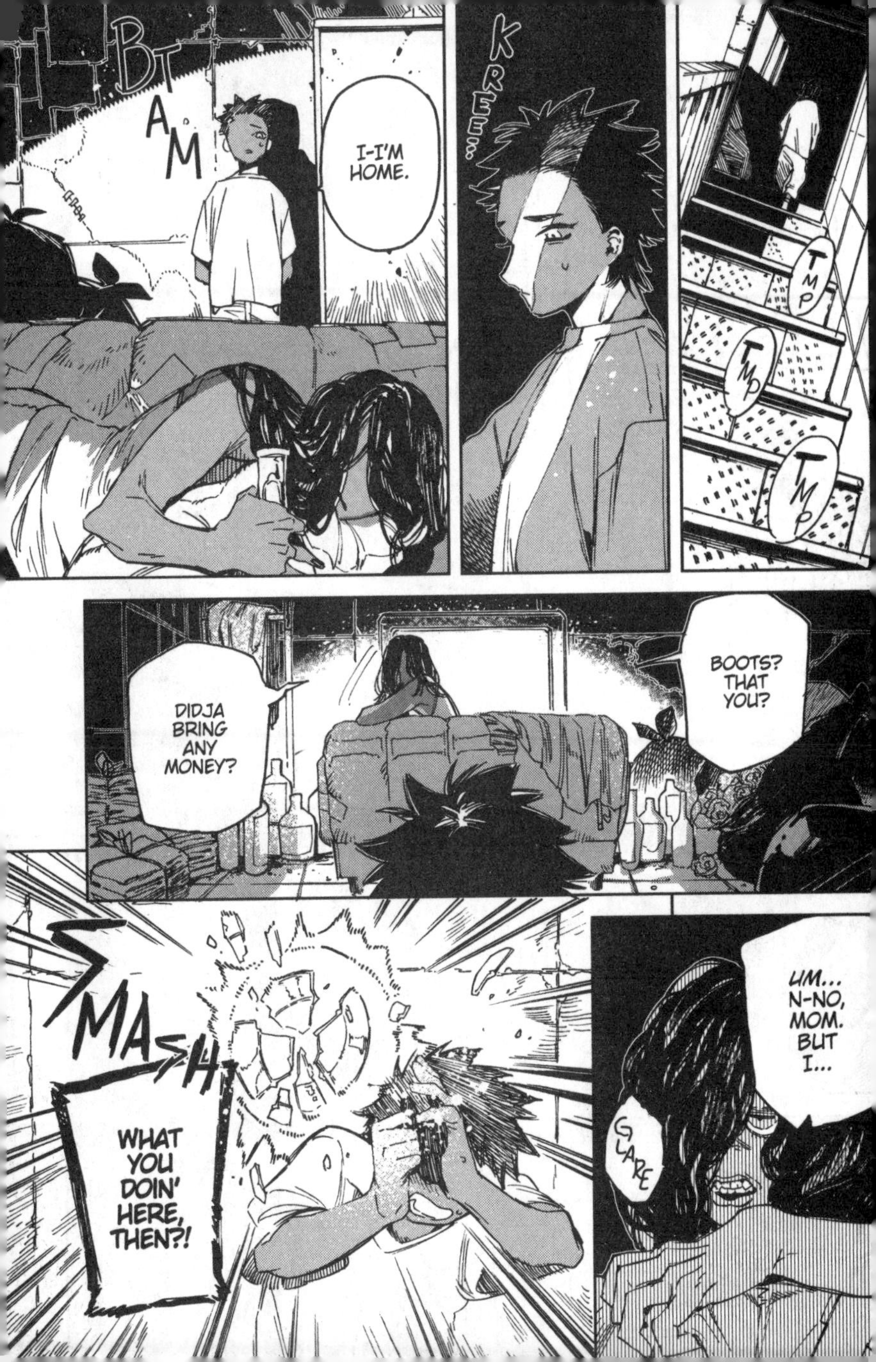
TMP
TMP
TMP
KREE...
BTAM
I-I'M HOME.
BOOTS? THAT YOU?
DIDJA BRING ANY MONEY?
UM... N-NO, MOM. BUT I...
GLARE
SMASH
WHAT YOU DOIN' HERE, THEN?!

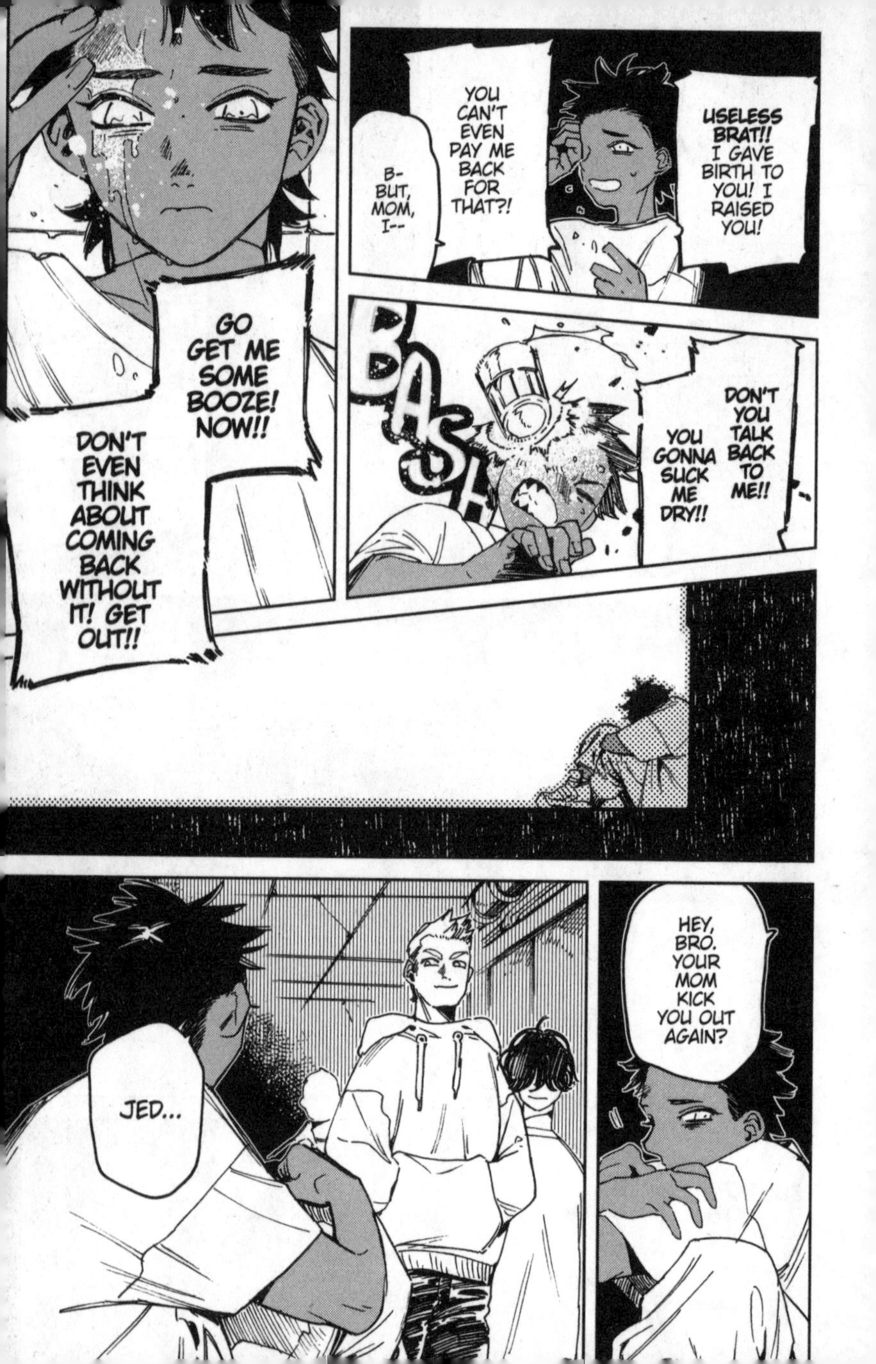
USELESS BRAT!! I GAVE BIRTH TO YOU! I RAISED YOU!
YOU CAN'T EVEN PAY ME BACK FOR THAT?!
B-BUT, MOM, I--
BASH
DON'T YOU TALK BACK TO ME!!
YOU GONNA SUCK ME DRY!!
GO GET ME SOME BOOZE! NOW!!
DON'T EVEN THINK ABOUT COMING BACK WITHOUT IT! GET OUT!!
HEY, BRO. YOUR MOM KICK YOU OUT AGAIN?
JED...

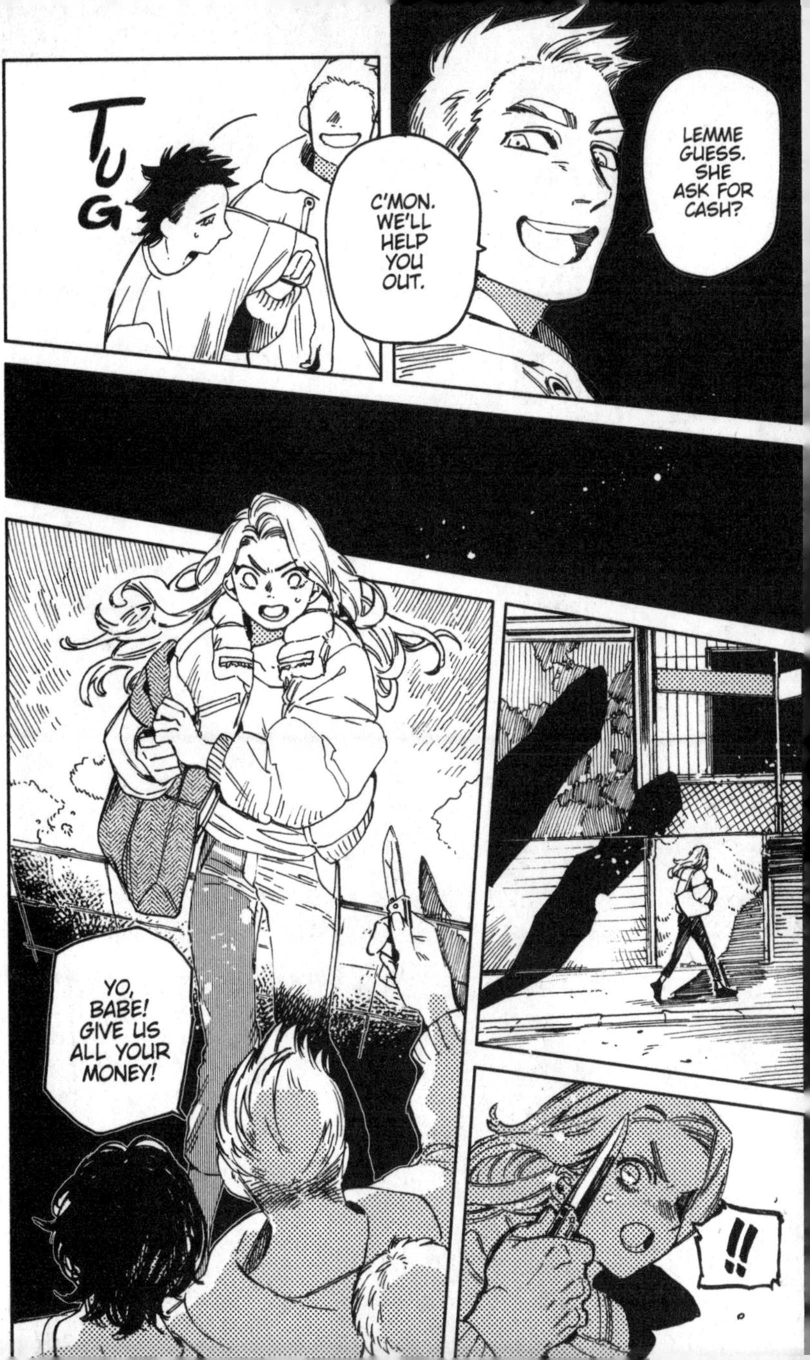

LEMME GUESS. SHE ASK FOR CASH?
C'MON. WE'LL HELP YOU OUT.
TUG
!!
YO, BABE! GIVE US ALL YOUR MONEY!

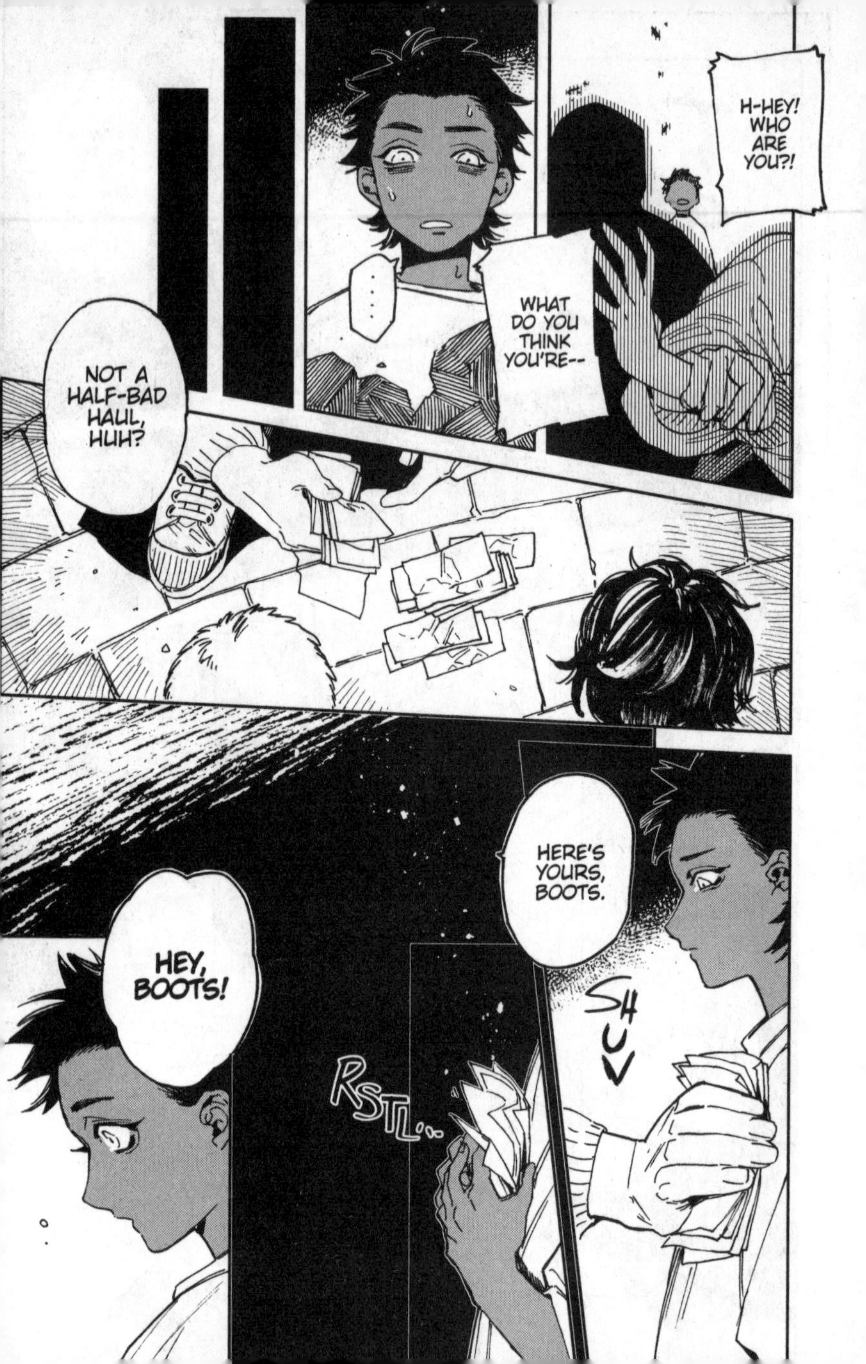
H-HEY! WHO ARE YOU?!
WHAT DO YOU THINK YOU'RE--
NOT A HALF-BAD HAUL, HUH?
HERE'S YOURS, BOOTS.
SHUV
RSTL...
HEY, BOOTS!

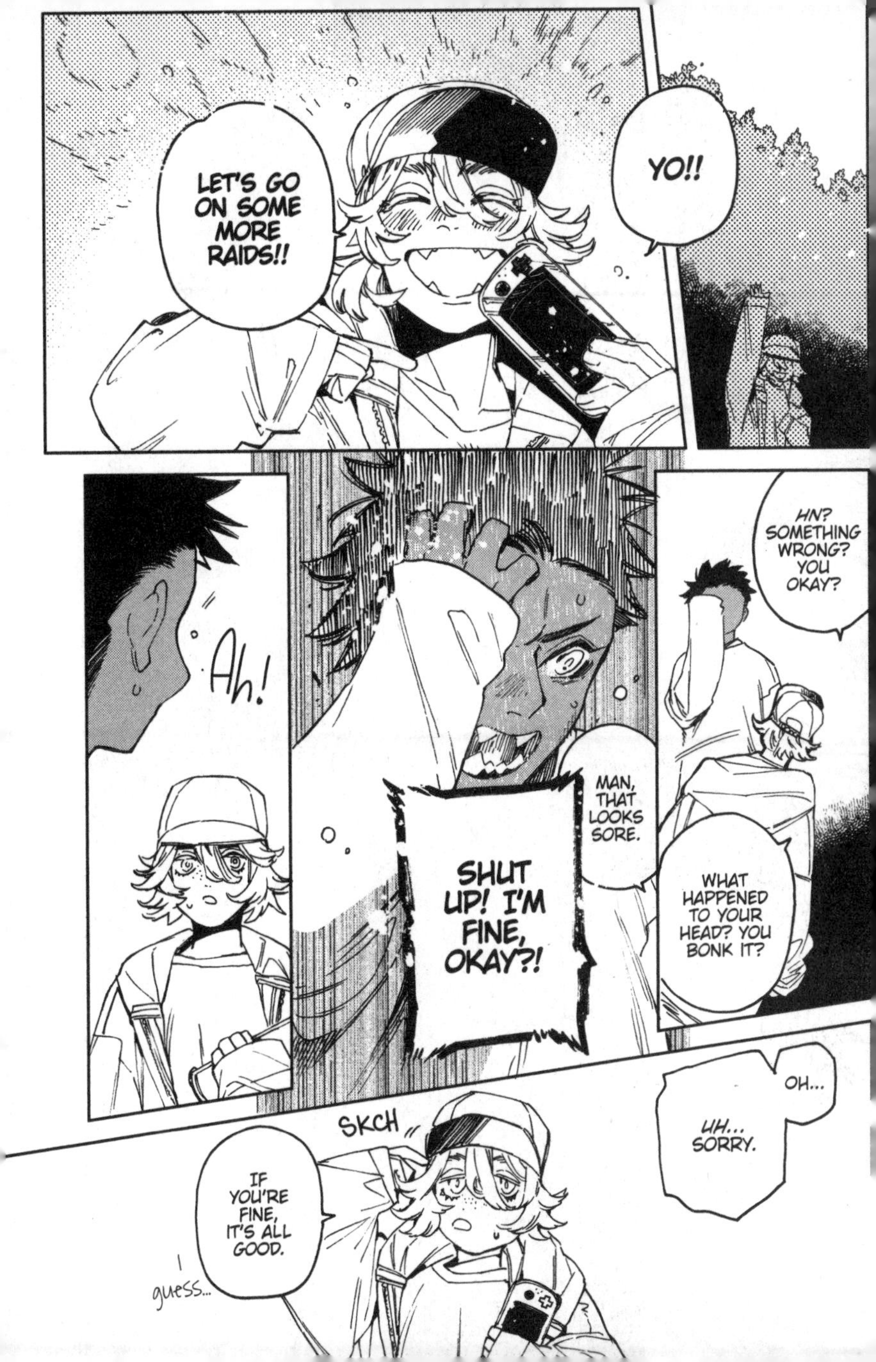
YO!!
LET'S GO ON SOME MORE RAIDS!!
HN? SOMETHING WRONG? YOU OKAY?
WHAT HAPPENED TO YOUR HEAD? YOU BONK IT?
MAN, THAT LOOKS SORE.
SHUT UP! I'M FINE, OKAY?!
Ah!
OH...
UH... SORRY.
SKCH
IF YOU'RE FINE, IT'S ALL GOOD.
I guess...

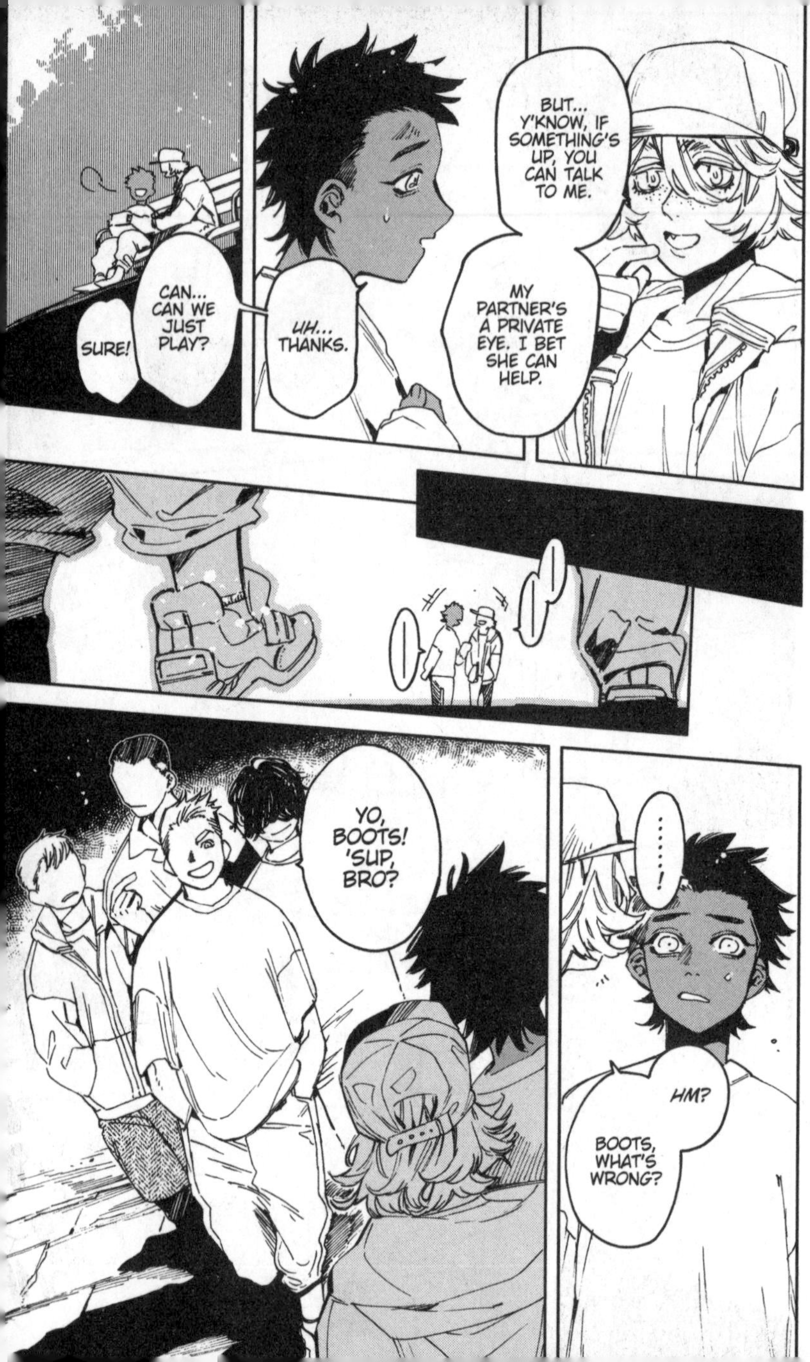
BUT... Y'KNOW, IF SOMETHING'S UP, YOU CAN TALK TO ME.
MY PARTNER'S A PRIVATE EYE. I BET SHE CAN HELP.
UH... THANKS.
CAN... CAN WE JUST PLAY?
SURE!
!
!
!
......!
HM?
BOOTS, WHAT'S WRONG?
YO, BOOTS! 'SUP, BRO?

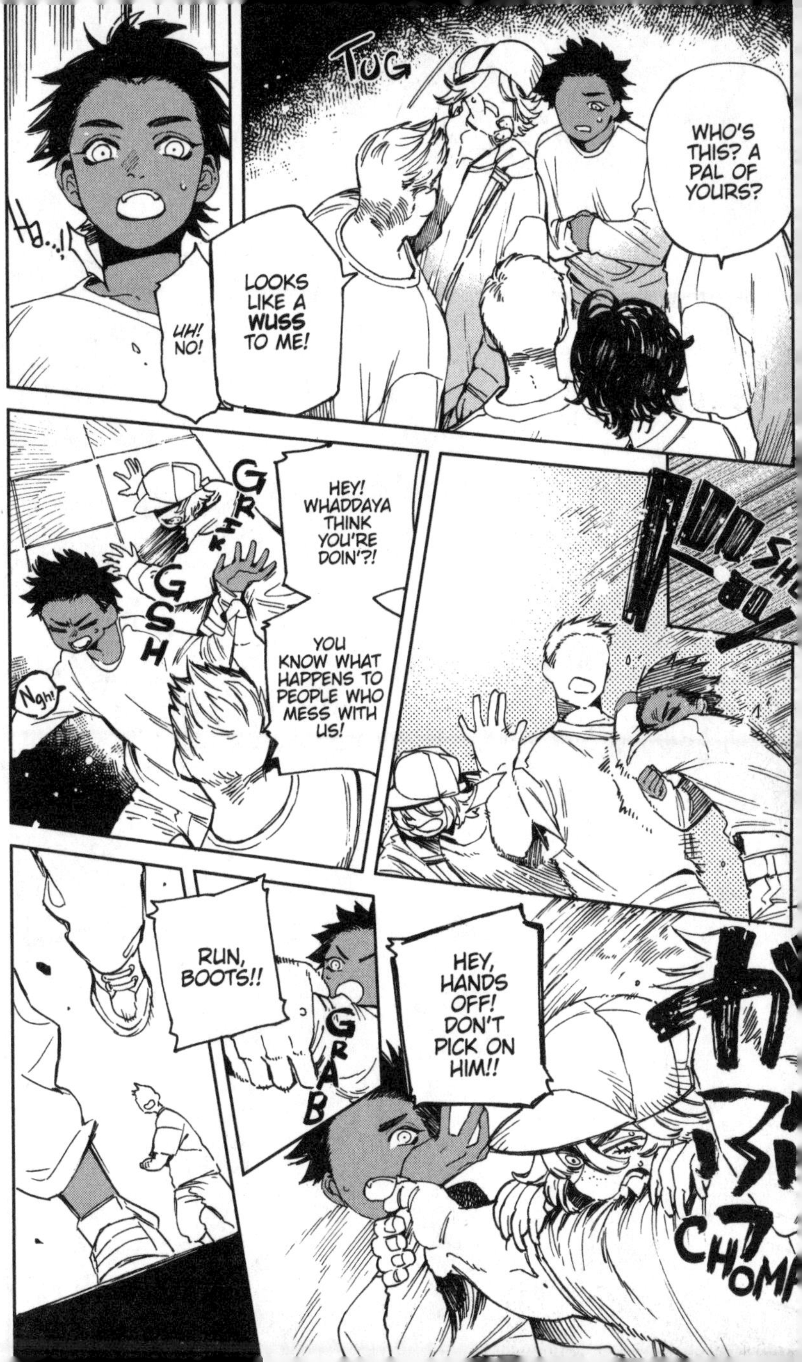
TUG
WHO'S THIS? A PAL OF YOURS?
LOOKS LIKE A WUSS TO ME!
UH! NO!
Ha...!
SHO
HEY! WHADDAYA THINK YOU'RE DOIN'?!
GRK
GSH
YOU KNOW WHAT HAPPENS TO PEOPLE WHO MESS WITH US!
Ngh!
HEY, HANDS OFF! DON'T PICK ON HIM!!
CHOM
RUN, BOOTS!!
GRAB

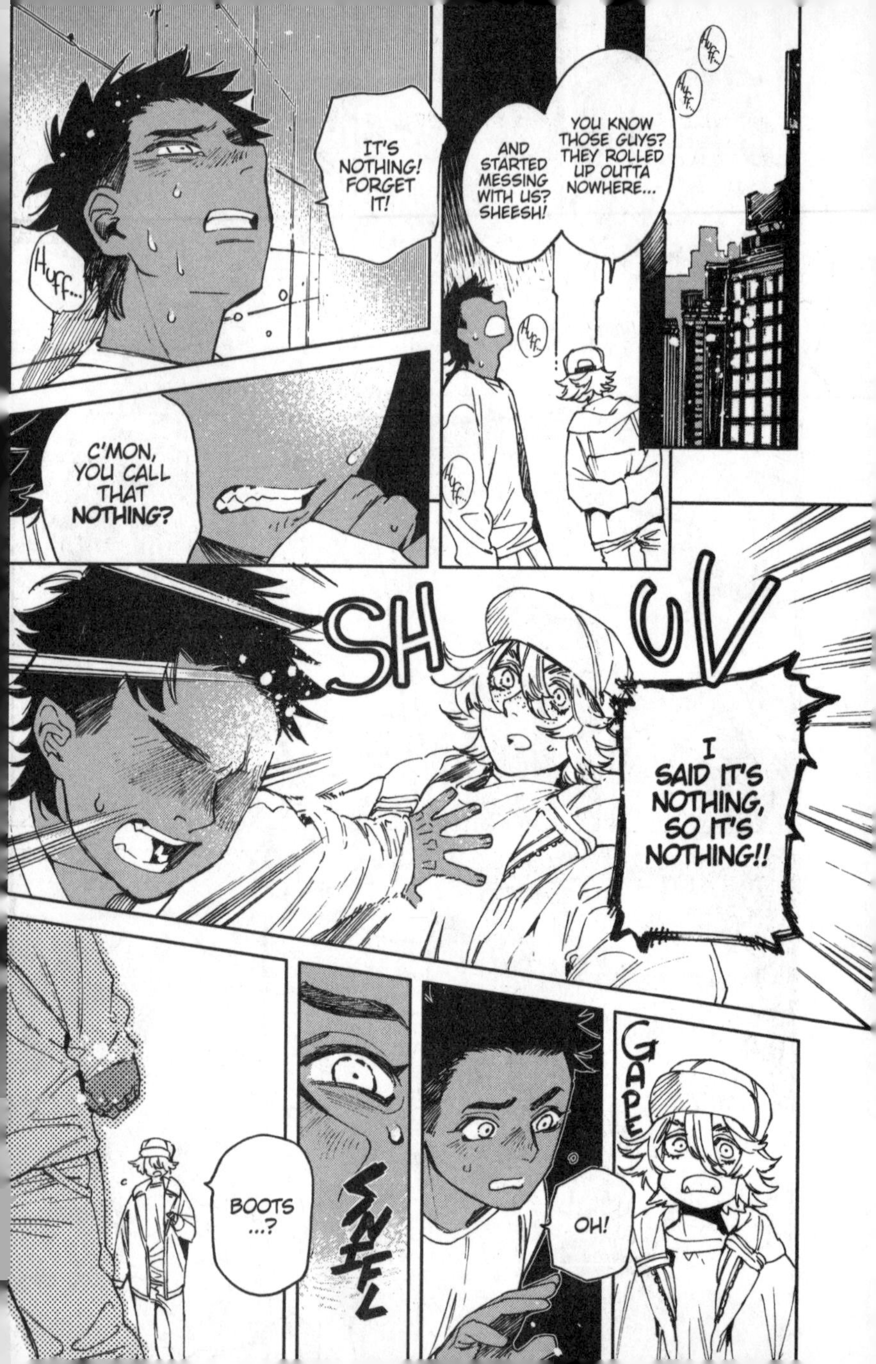
Huff...
Huff...
YOU KNOW THOSE GUYS? THEY ROLLED UP OUTTA NOWHERE...
AND STARTED MESSING WITH US? SHEESH!
Huff...
Huff...
Huff...
IT'S NOTHING! FORGET IT!
C'MON, YOU CALL THAT NOTHING?
SHUV
I SAID IT'S NOTHING, SO IT'S NOTHING!!
GAPE
OH!
SNIFL
BOOTS ...?

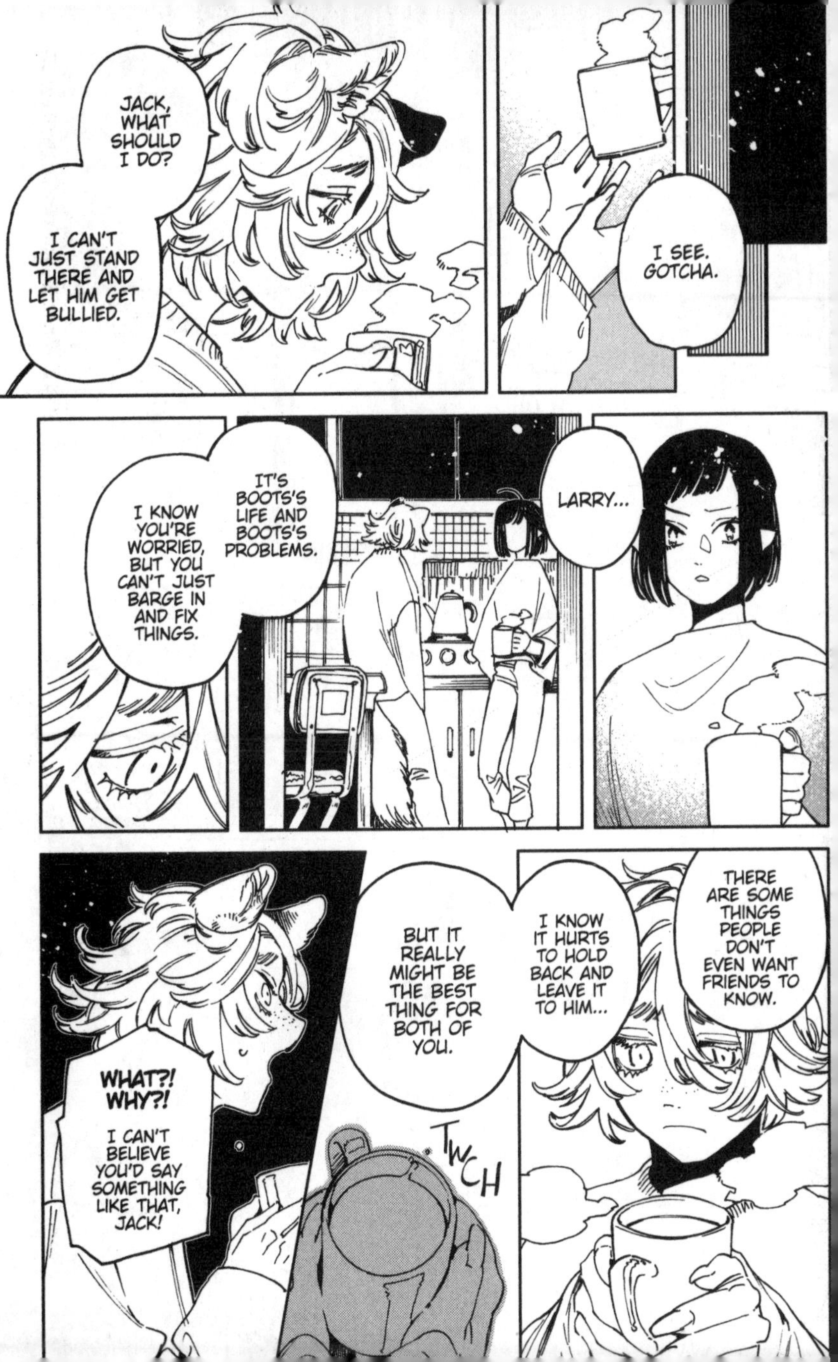
I SEE. GOTCHA.
JACK, WHAT SHOULD I DO?
I CAN'T JUST STAND THERE AND LET HIM GET BULLIED.
LARRY...
IT'S BOOTS'S LIFE AND BOOTS'S PROBLEMS.
I KNOW YOU'RE WORRIED, BUT YOU CAN'T JUST BARGE IN AND FIX THINGS.
THERE ARE SOME THINGS PEOPLE DON'T EVEN WANT FRIENDS TO KNOW.
I KNOW IT HURTS TO HOLD BACK AND LEAVE IT TO HIM...
BUT IT REALLY MIGHT BE THE BEST THING FOR BOTH OF YOU.
TWCH
WHAT?! WHY?!
I CAN'T BELIEVE YOU'D SAY SOMETHING LIKE THAT, JACK!

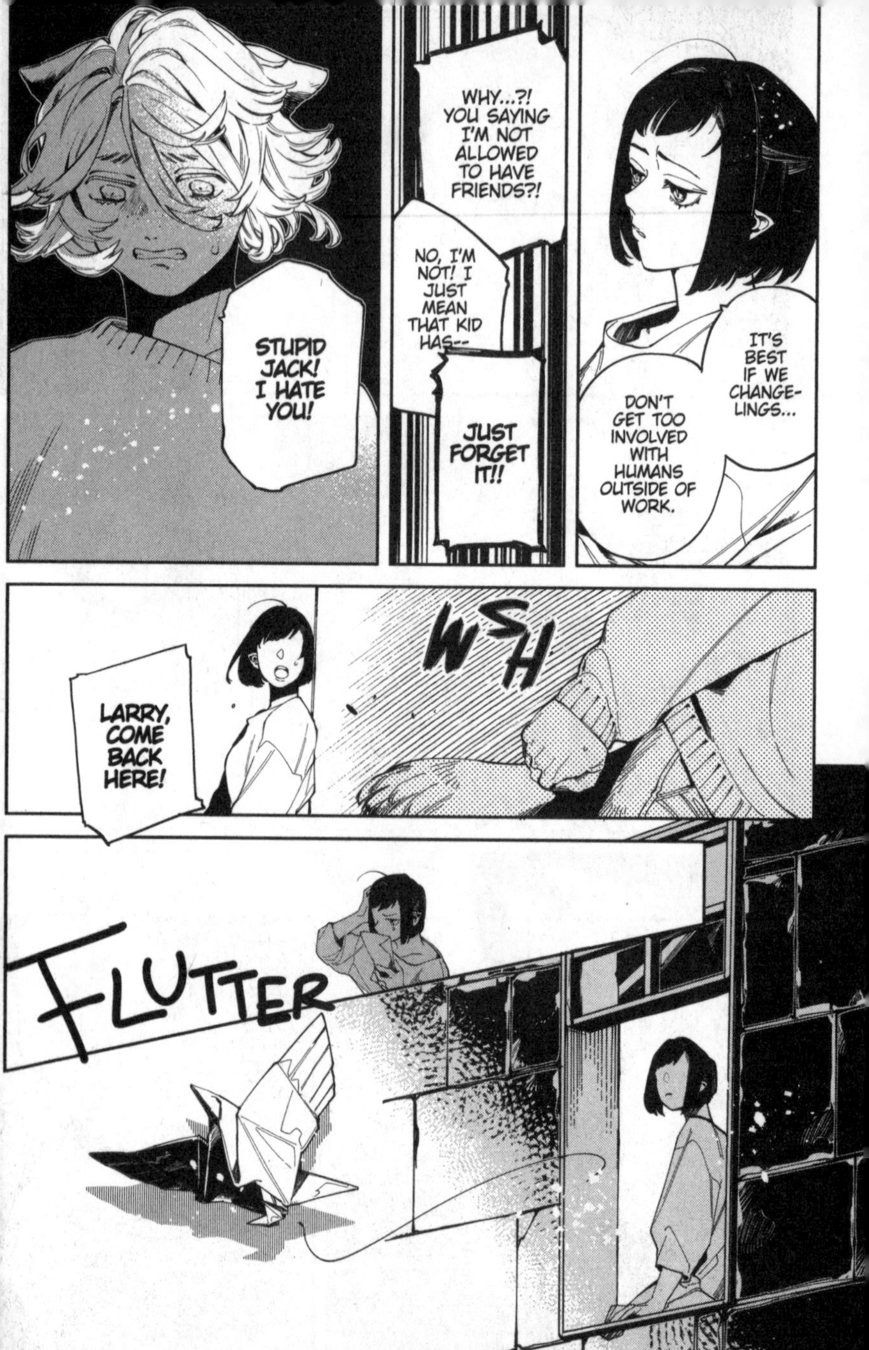
IT'S BEST IF WE CHANGELINGS...
DON'T GET TOO INVOLVED WITH HUMANS OUTSIDE OF WORK.
WHY...?! YOU SAYING I'M NOT ALLOWED TO HAVE FRIENDS?!
NO, I'M NOT! I JUST MEAN THAT KID HAS--
JUST FORGET IT!!
STUPID JACK! I HATE YOU!
WSH
LARRY, COME BACK HERE!
FLUTTER

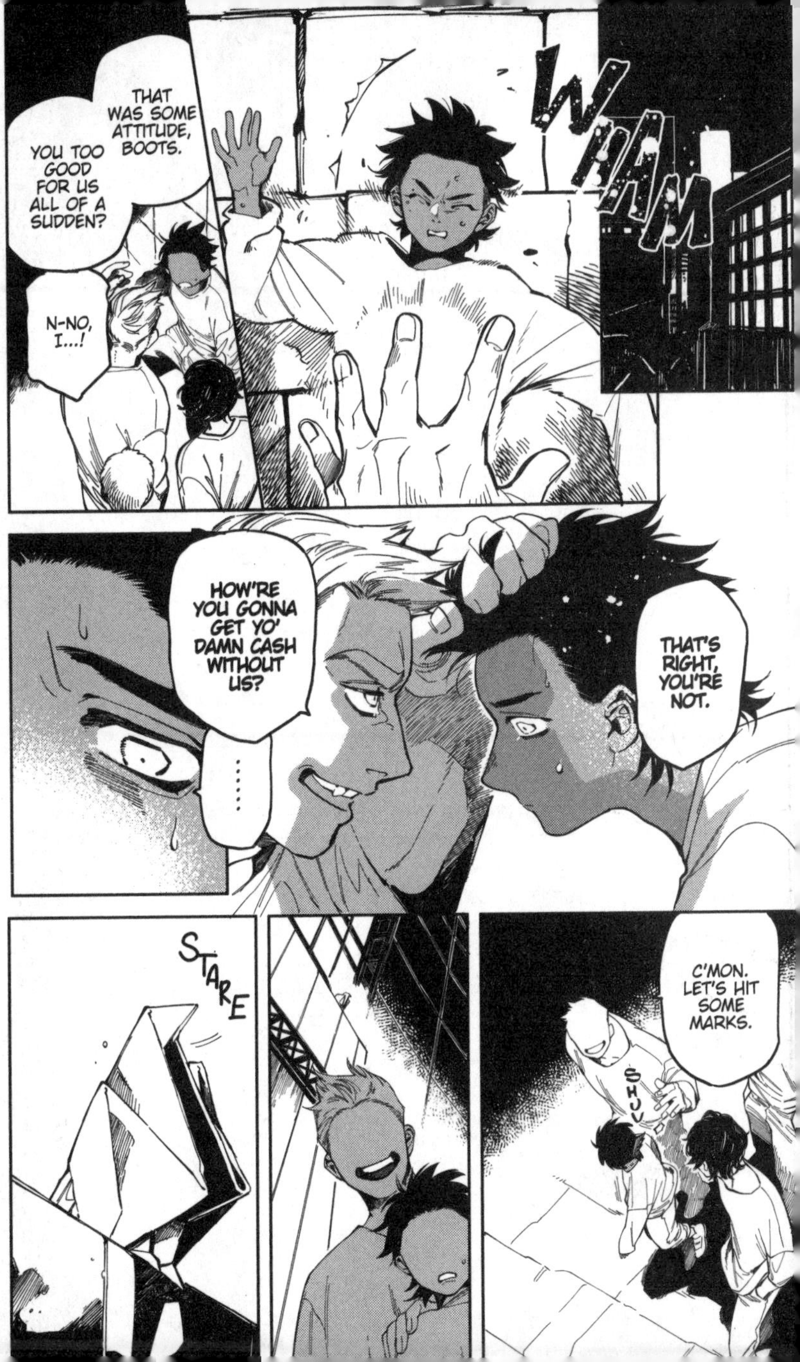
WHAM
THAT WAS SOME ATTITUDE, BOOTS.
YOU TOO GOOD FOR US ALL OF A SUDDEN?
N-NO, I...!
HOW'RE YOU GONNA GET YO' DAMN CASH WITHOUT US?
......
THAT'S RIGHT, YOU'RE NOT.
C'MON. LET'S HIT SOME MARKS.
SHUV
STARE

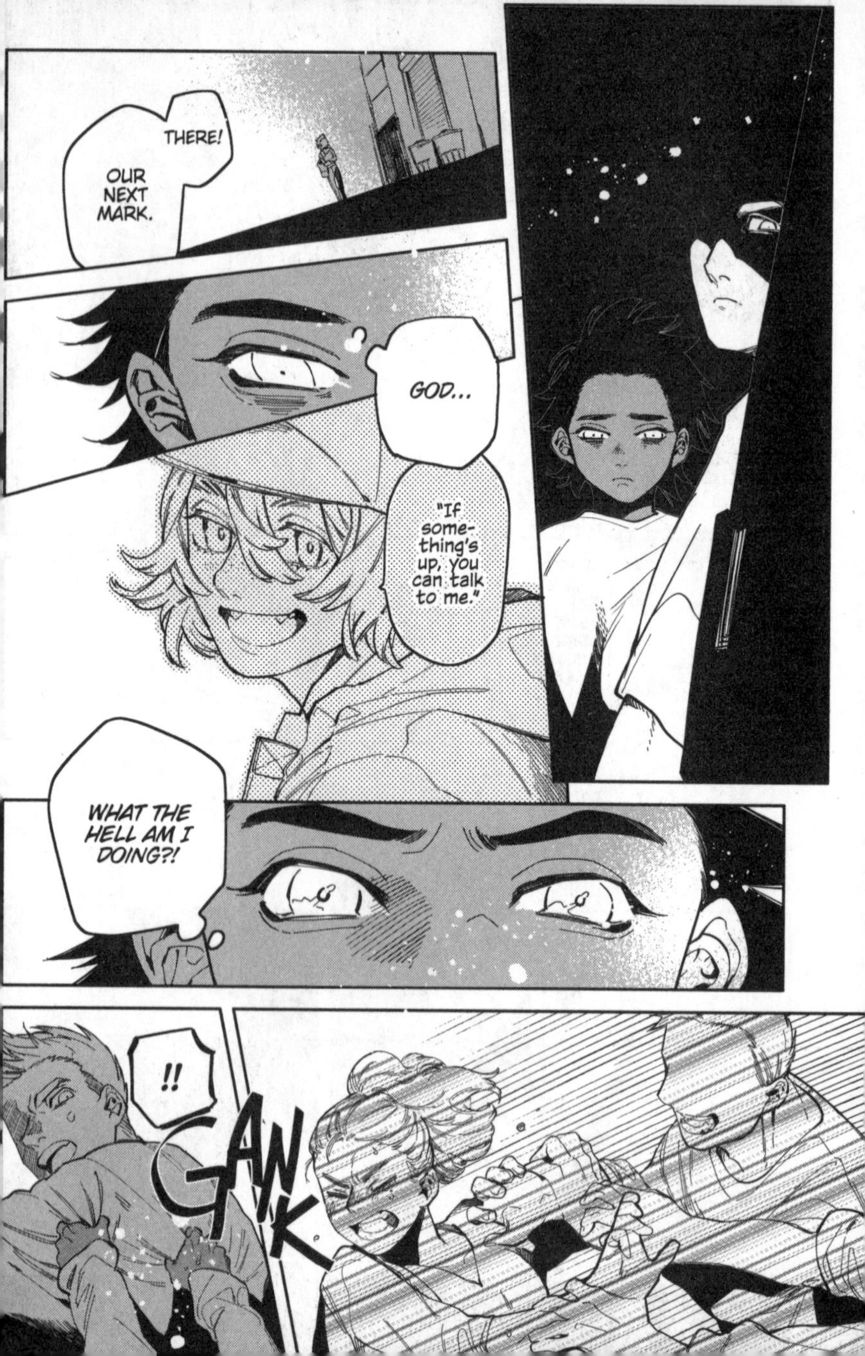
THERE! OUR NEXT MARK.
GOD...
"If something's up, you can talk to me."
WHAT THE HELL AM I DOING?!
GANK
!!

BOOTS, YOU LITTLE PUNK!!

YOU JUST BOUGHT YO'SELF A WHOLE WORLD OF TROUBLE!!

WSH

YeOW!!!

SHIT! THE PIGS'RE COMIN' ALREADY!

I...I JUST...!

SCATTER!!

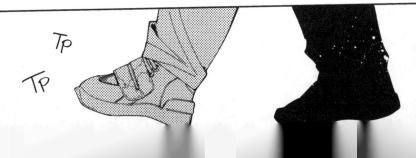

TP

TP

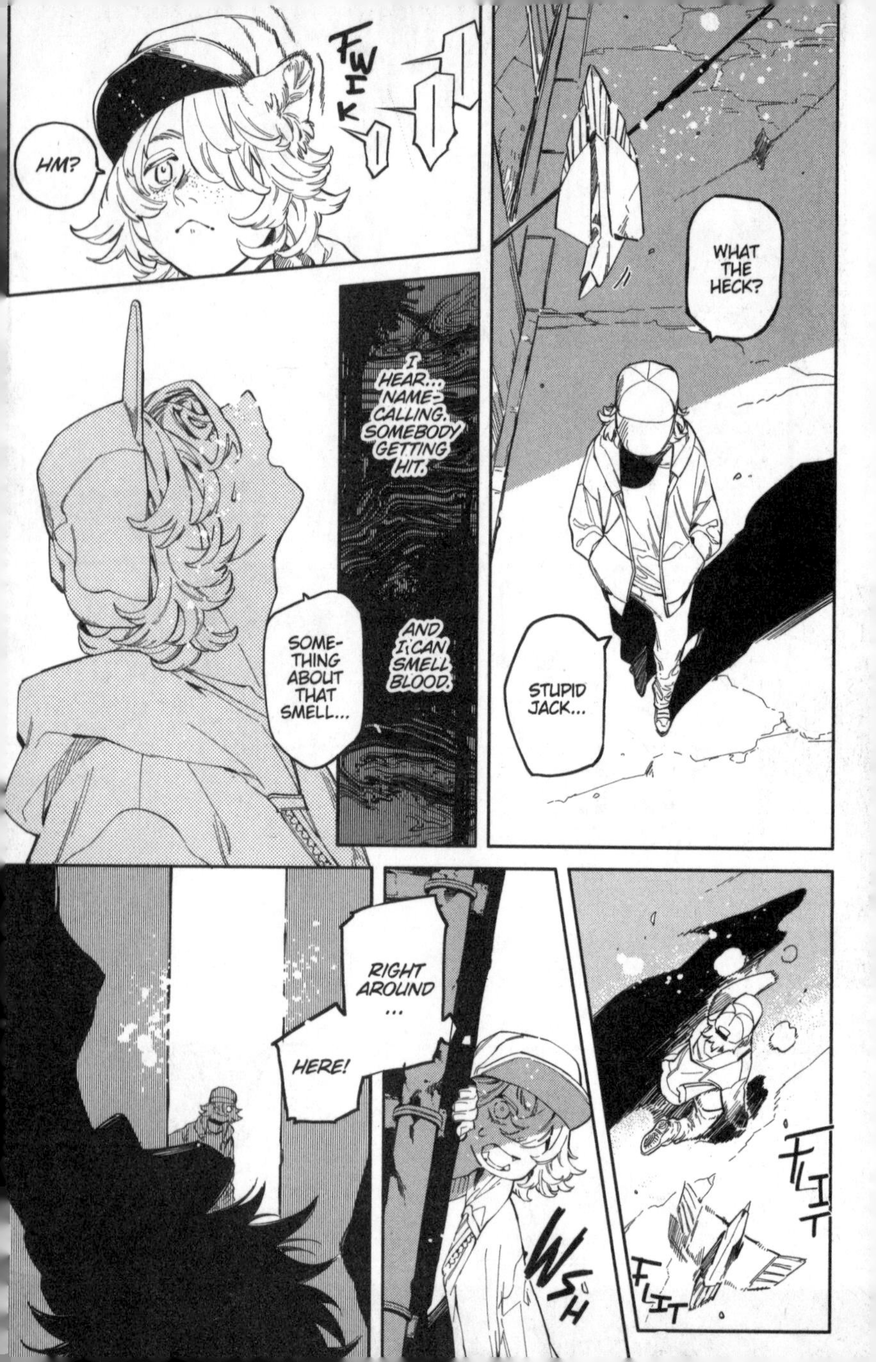
WHAT THE HECK?
STUPID JACK...
FWIK
HM?
I HEAR... NAME-CALLING. SOMEBODY GETTING HIT.
AND I CAN SMELL BLOOD.
SOME-THING ABOUT THAT SMELL...
FLIT
FLIT
RIGHT AROUND...
HERE!
WSH

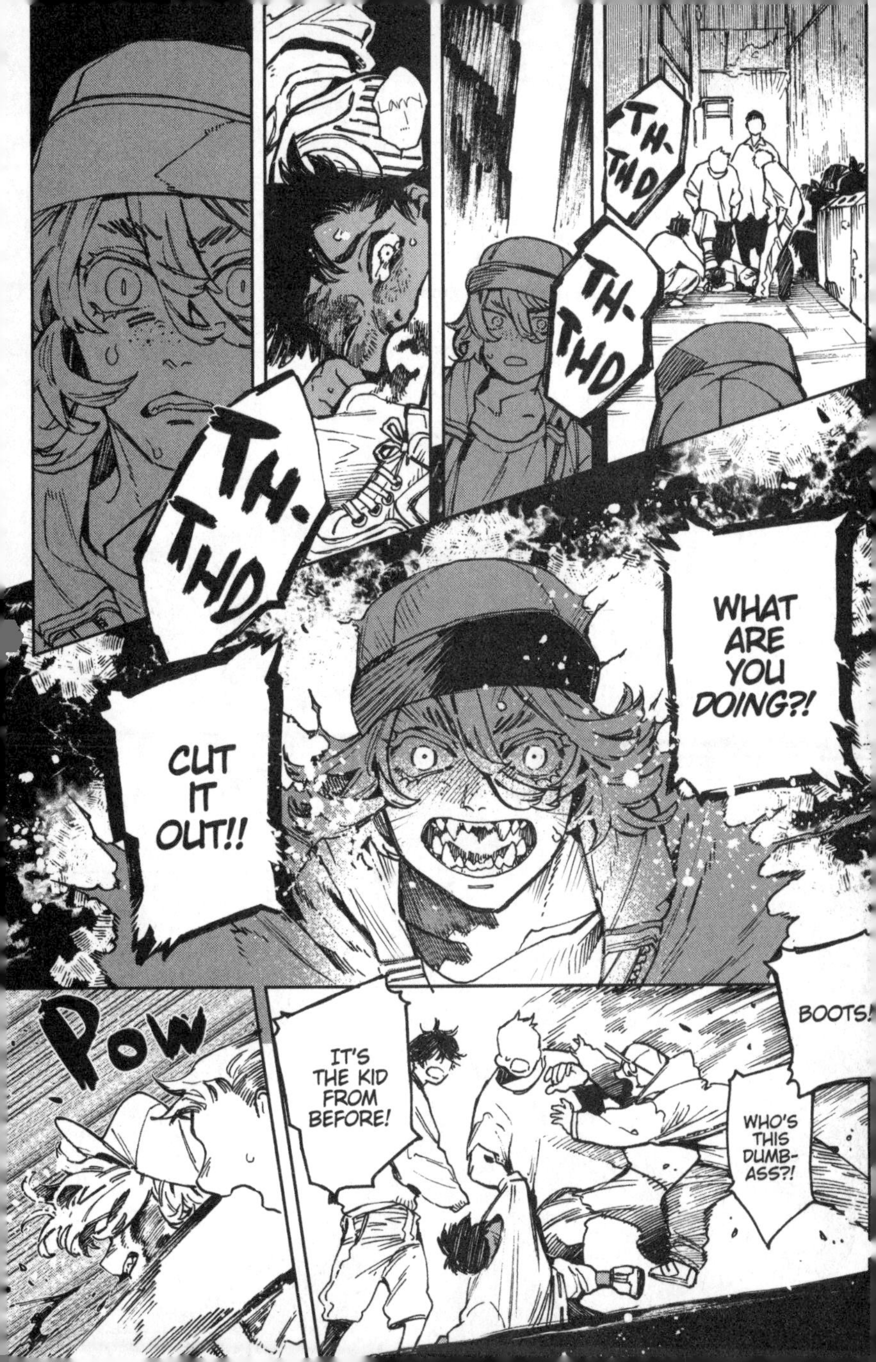
TH-THD
TH-THD
Larry...
TH-THD
WHAT ARE YOU DOING?!
CUT IT OUT!!
BOOTS!
WHO'S THIS DUMB-ASS?!
IT'S THE KID FROM BEFORE!
POW

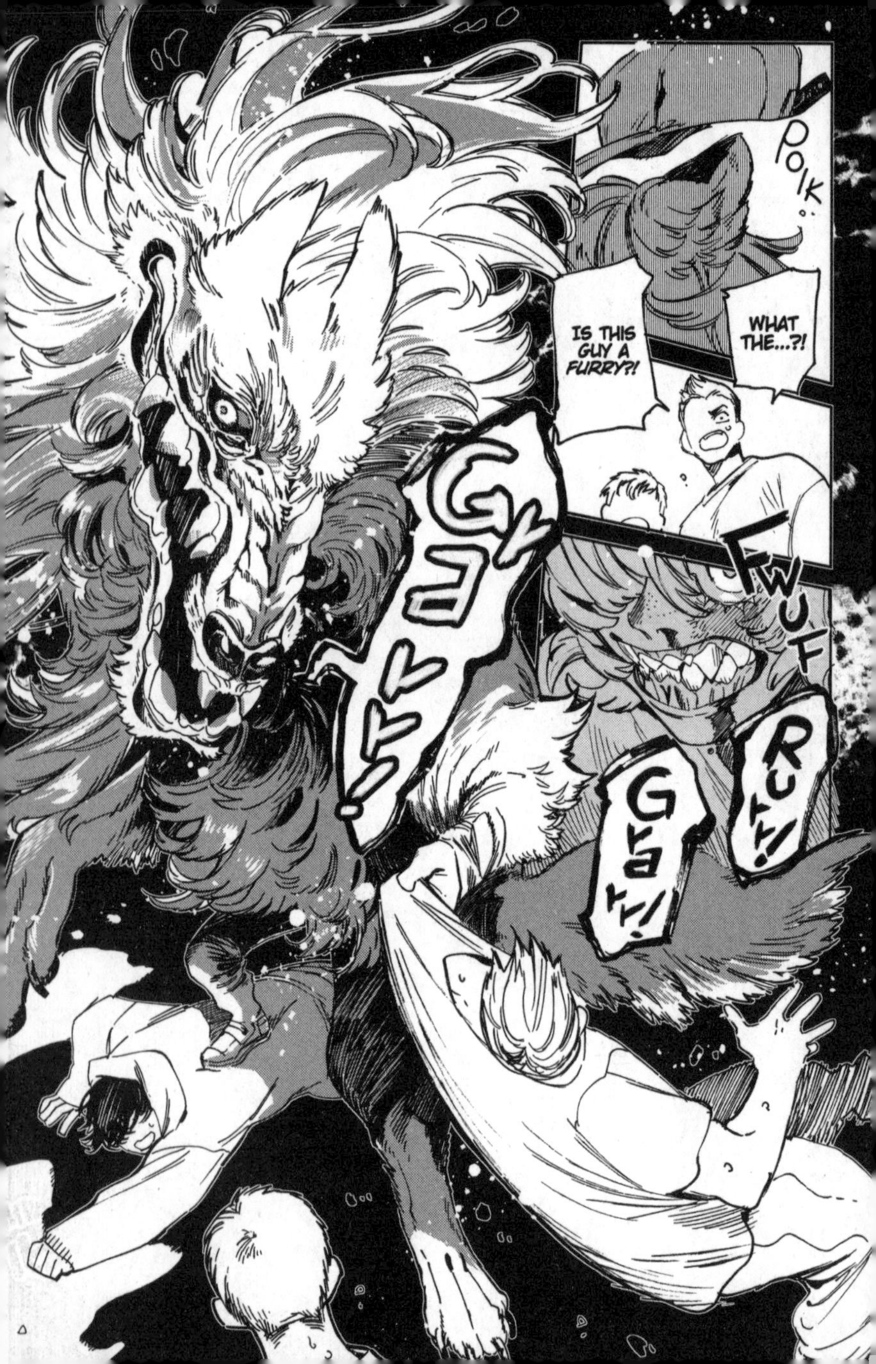
POIK
WHAT THE...?!
IS THIS GUY A FURRY?!
FWUF

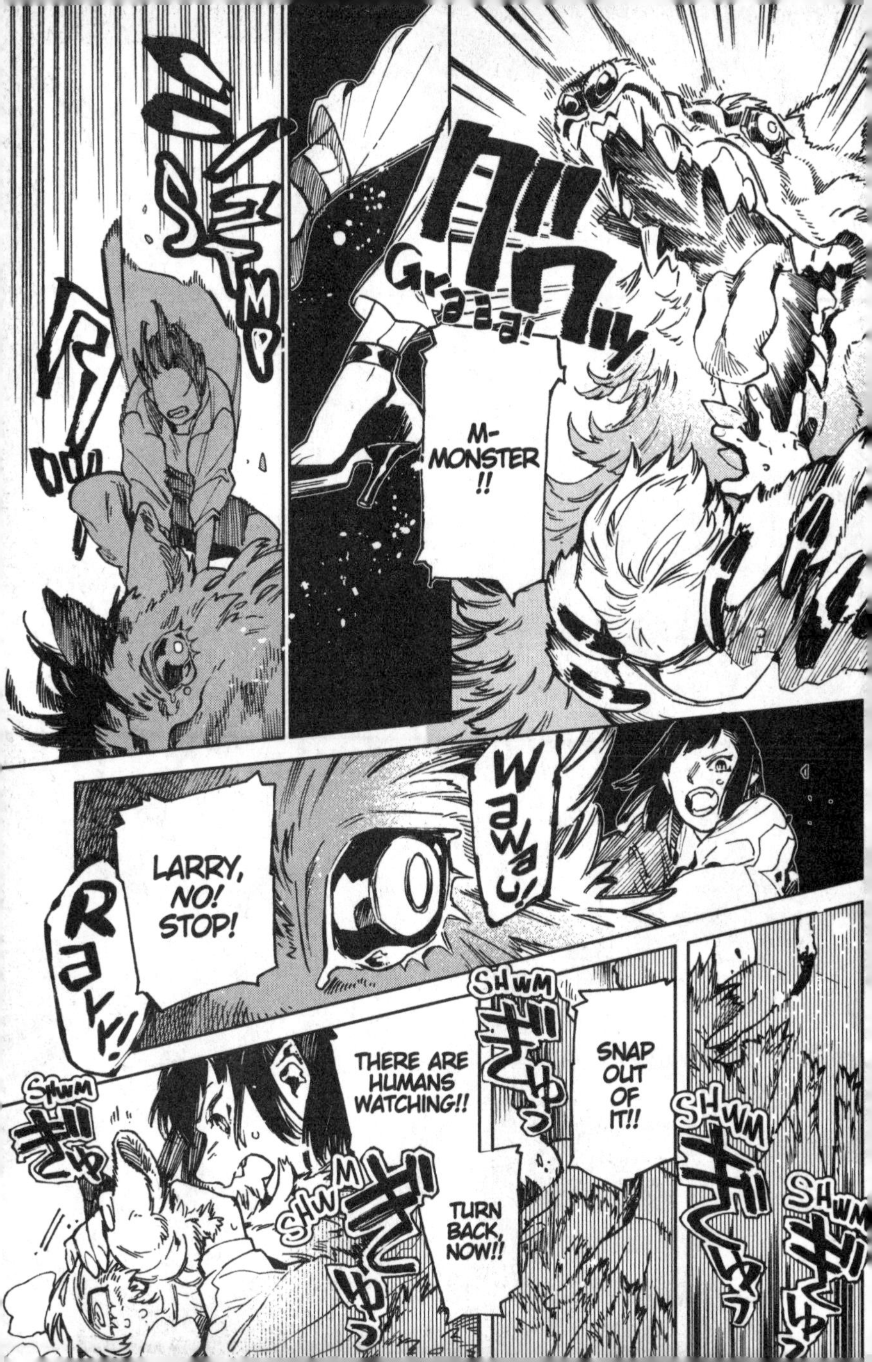
Graaaa!
M-MONSTER!!
Wawau!
LARRY, NO! STOP!
SHWM
SHWM
SNAP OUT OF IT!!
SHWM
THERE ARE HUMANS WATCHING!!
TURN BACK, NOW!!
SHWM
SHWM

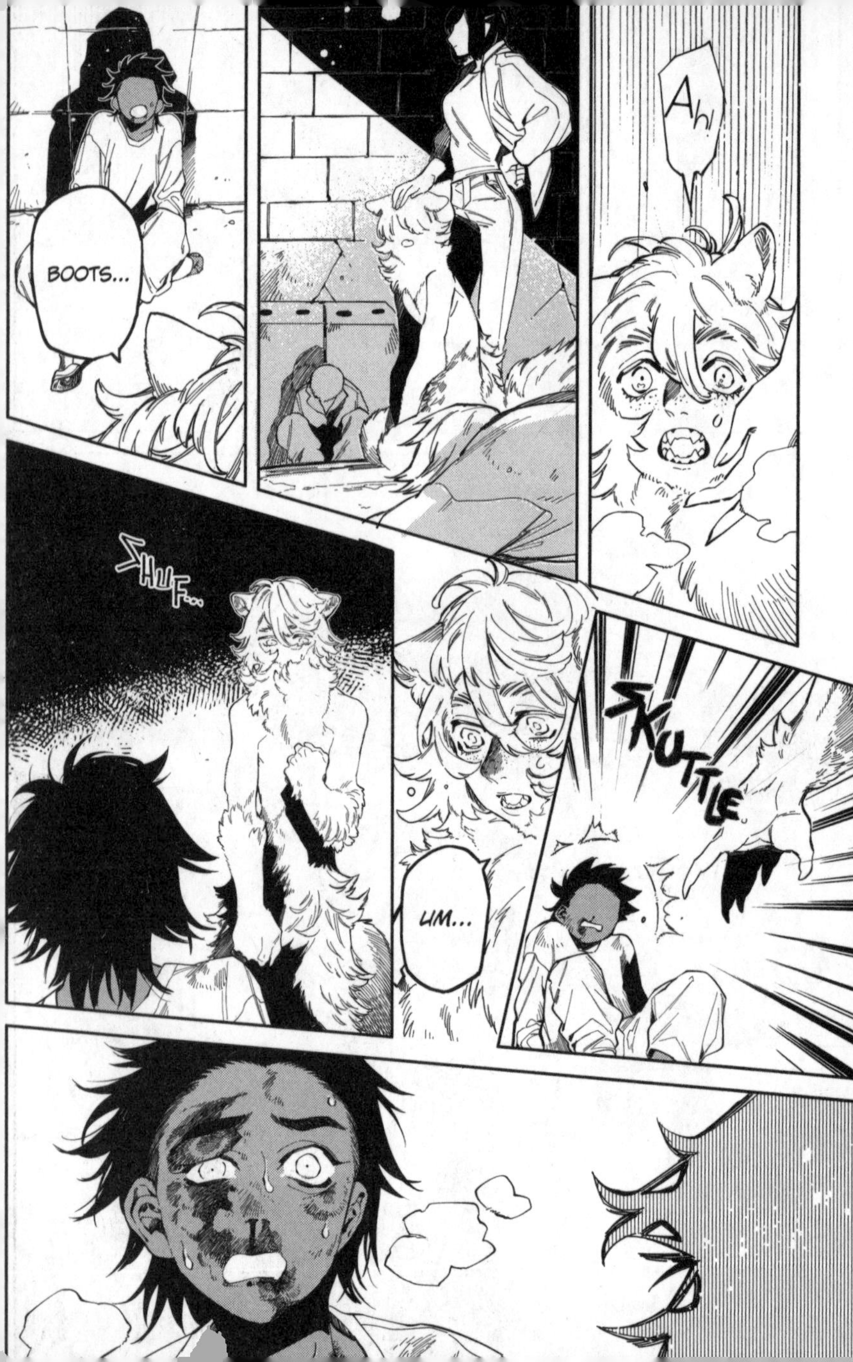
Ah!
BOOTS...
SKUTTLE
UM...
SHUF...

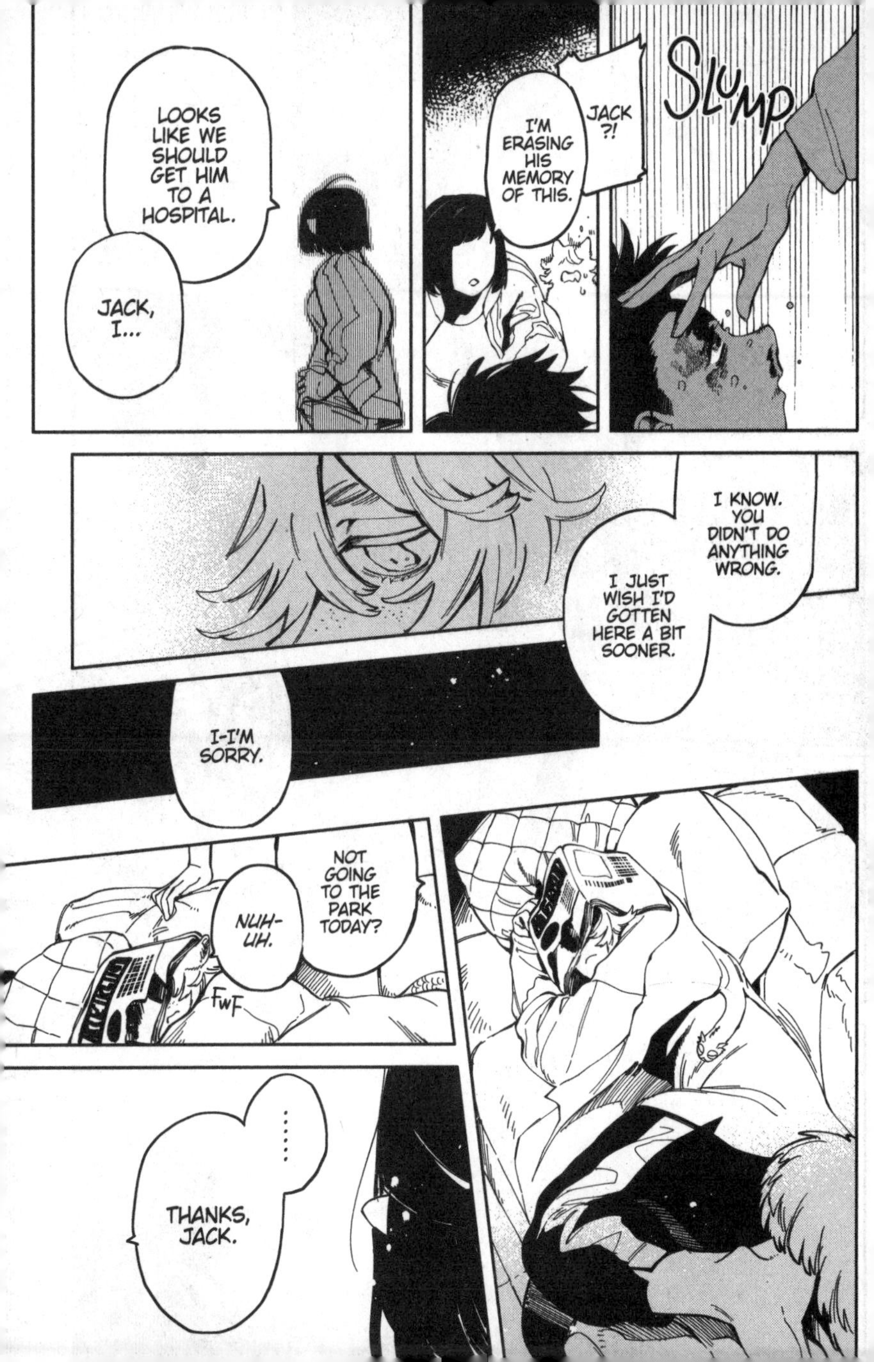
SLUMP
JACK?!
I'M ERASING HIS MEMORY OF THIS.
LOOKS LIKE WE SHOULD GET HIM TO A HOSPITAL.
JACK, I...
I KNOW. YOU DIDN'T DO ANYTHING WRONG.
I JUST WISH I'D GOTTEN HERE A BIT SOONER.
I-I'M SORRY.
NOT GOING TO THE PARK TODAY?
NUH-UH.
FWF
......
THANKS, JACK.

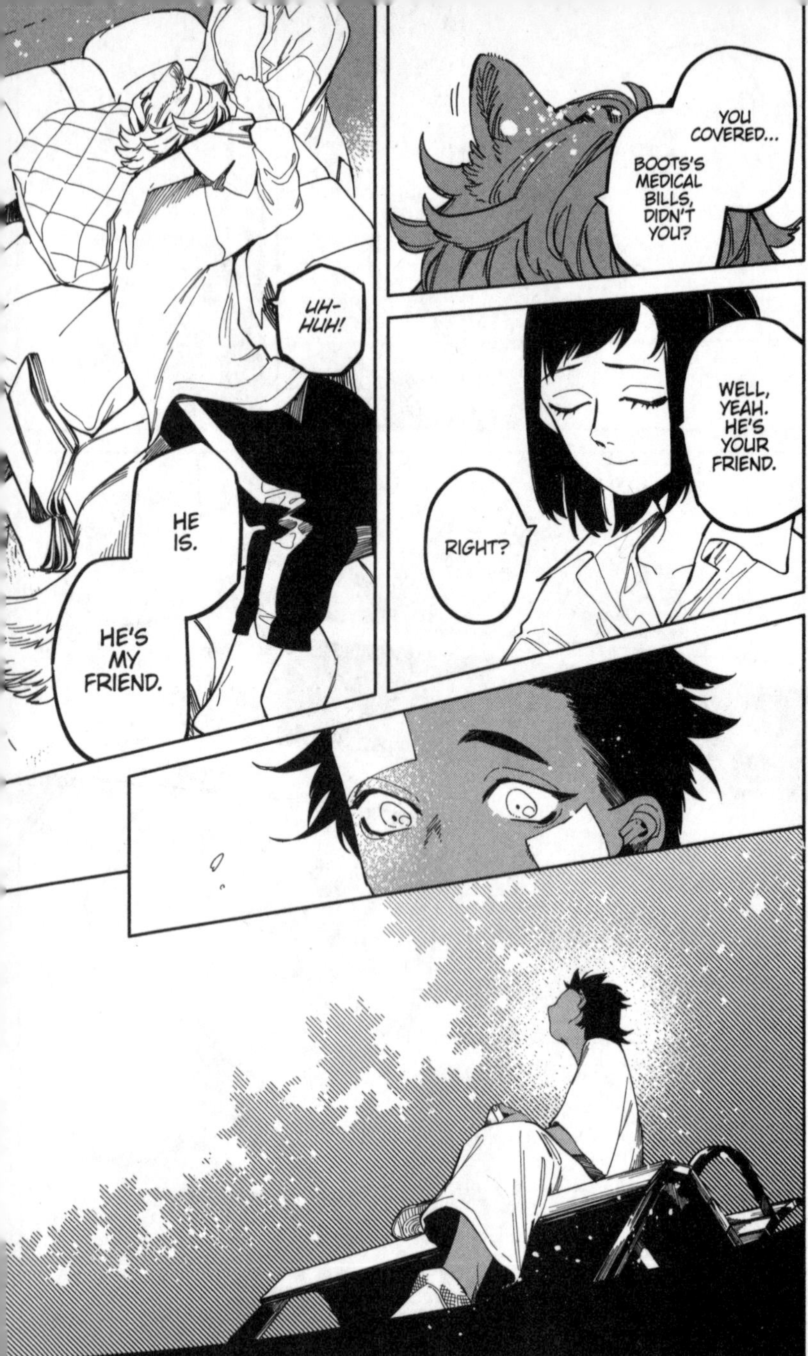
YOU COVERED...
BOOTS'S MEDICAL BILLS, DIDN'T YOU?
WELL, YEAH. HE'S YOUR FRIEND.
RIGHT?
UH-HUH!
HE IS.
HE'S MY FRIEND.

The Ancient
Magus' Bride

JACK FLASH AND THE FAERIE CASE FILES

The Ancient Magus' Bride

JACK FLASH AND THE FAERIE CASE FILES

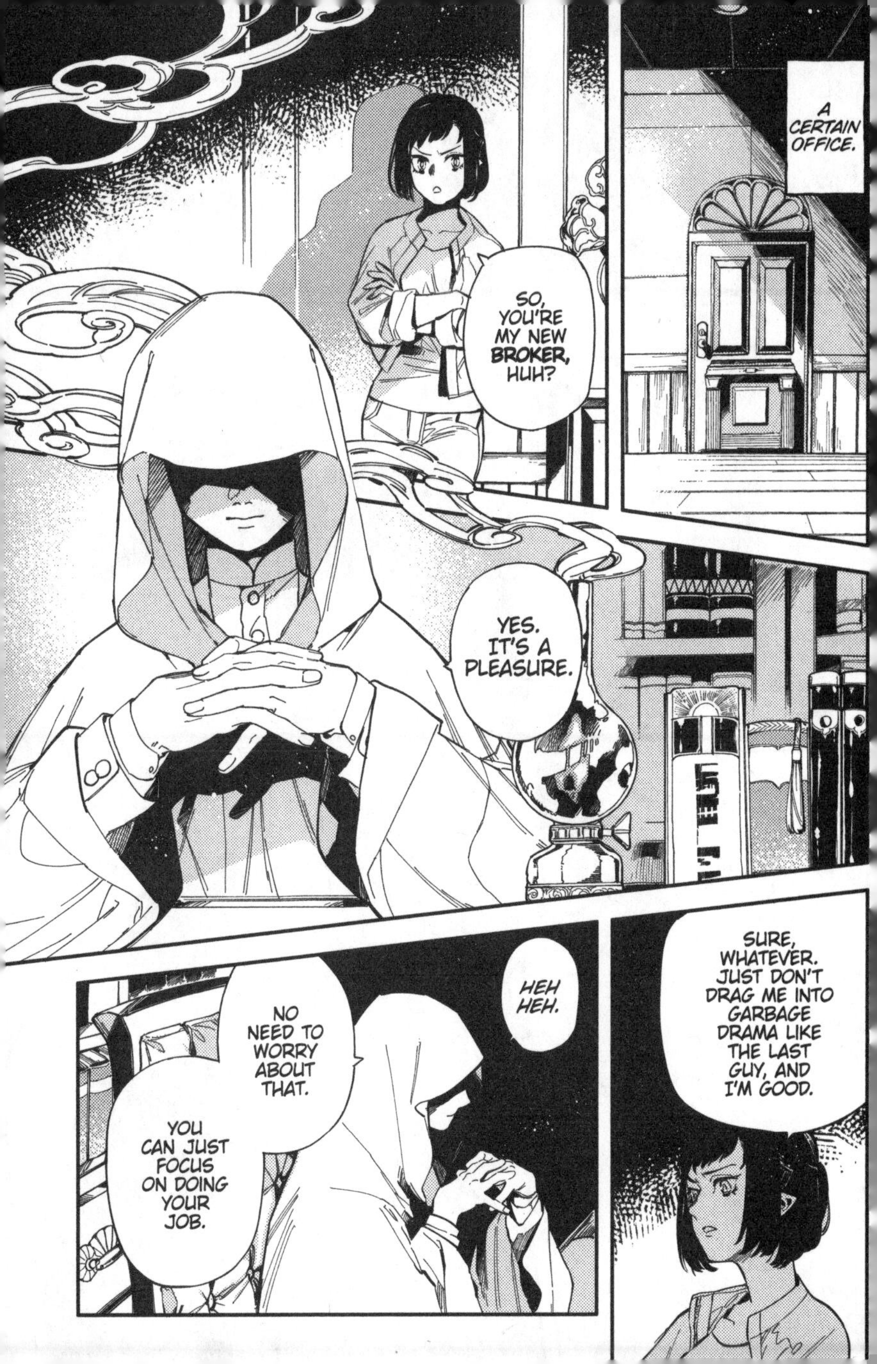
A CERTAIN OFFICE.
SO, YOU'RE MY NEW BROKER, HUH?
YES. IT'S A PLEASURE.
SURE, WHATEVER. JUST DON'T DRAG ME INTO GARBAGE DRAMA LIKE THE LAST GUY, AND I'M GOOD.
HEH HEH.
NO NEED TO WORRY ABOUT THAT.
YOU CAN JUST FOCUS ON DOING YOUR JOB.

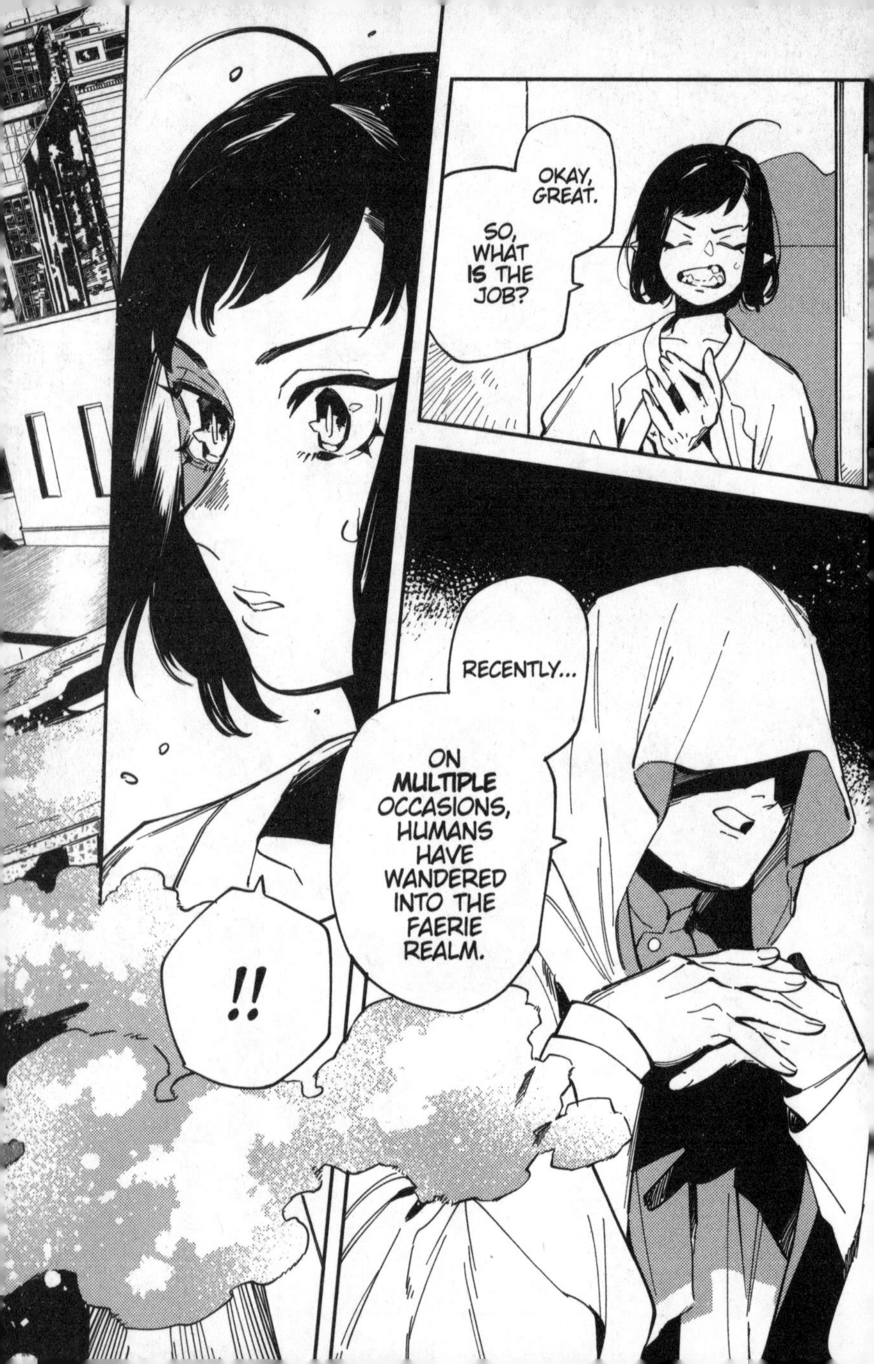
OKAY, GREAT.
SO, WHAT IS THE JOB?
RECENTLY...
ON MULTIPLE OCCASIONS, HUMANS HAVE WANDERED INTO THE FAERIE REALM.
!!

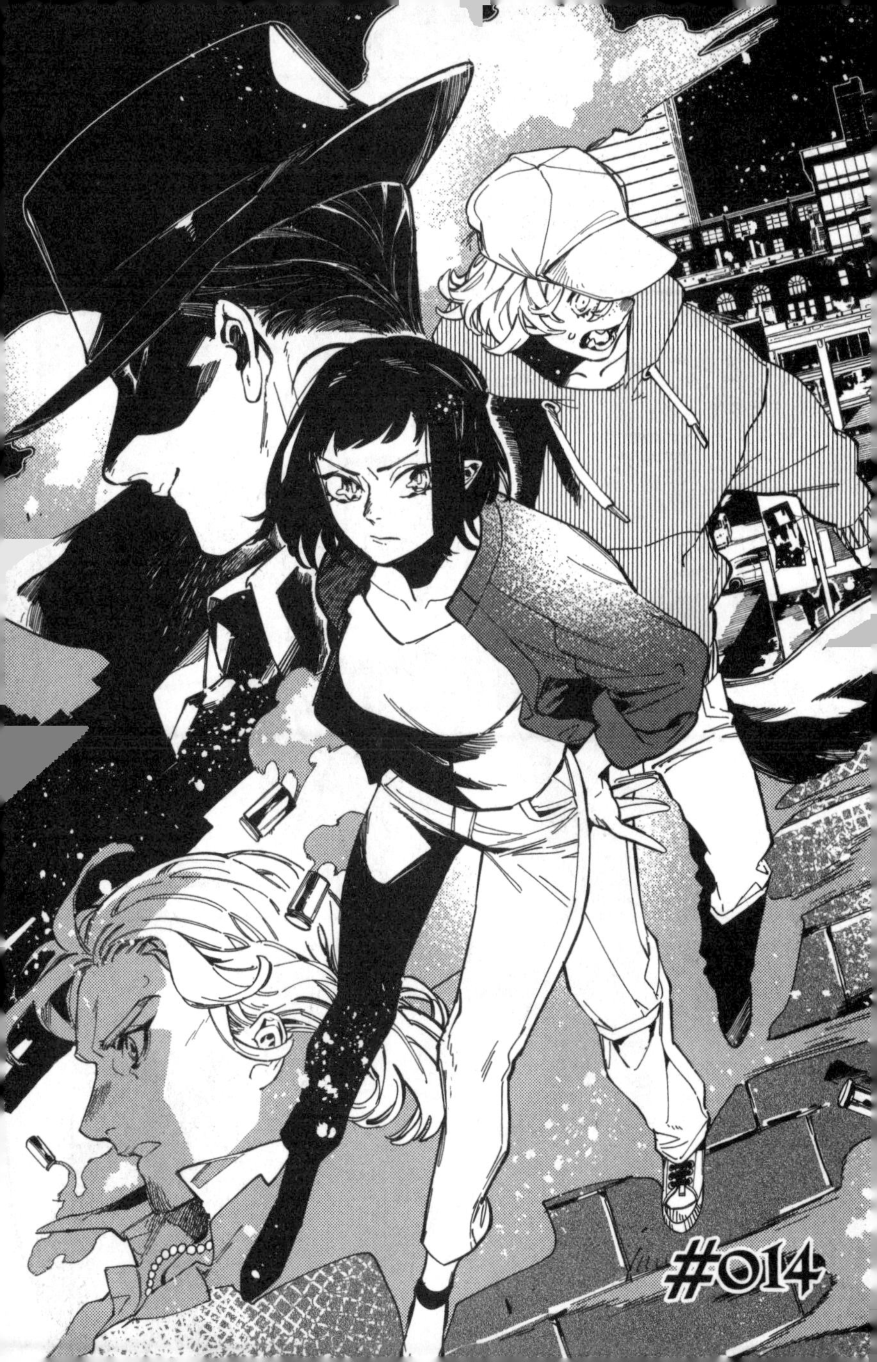
#014

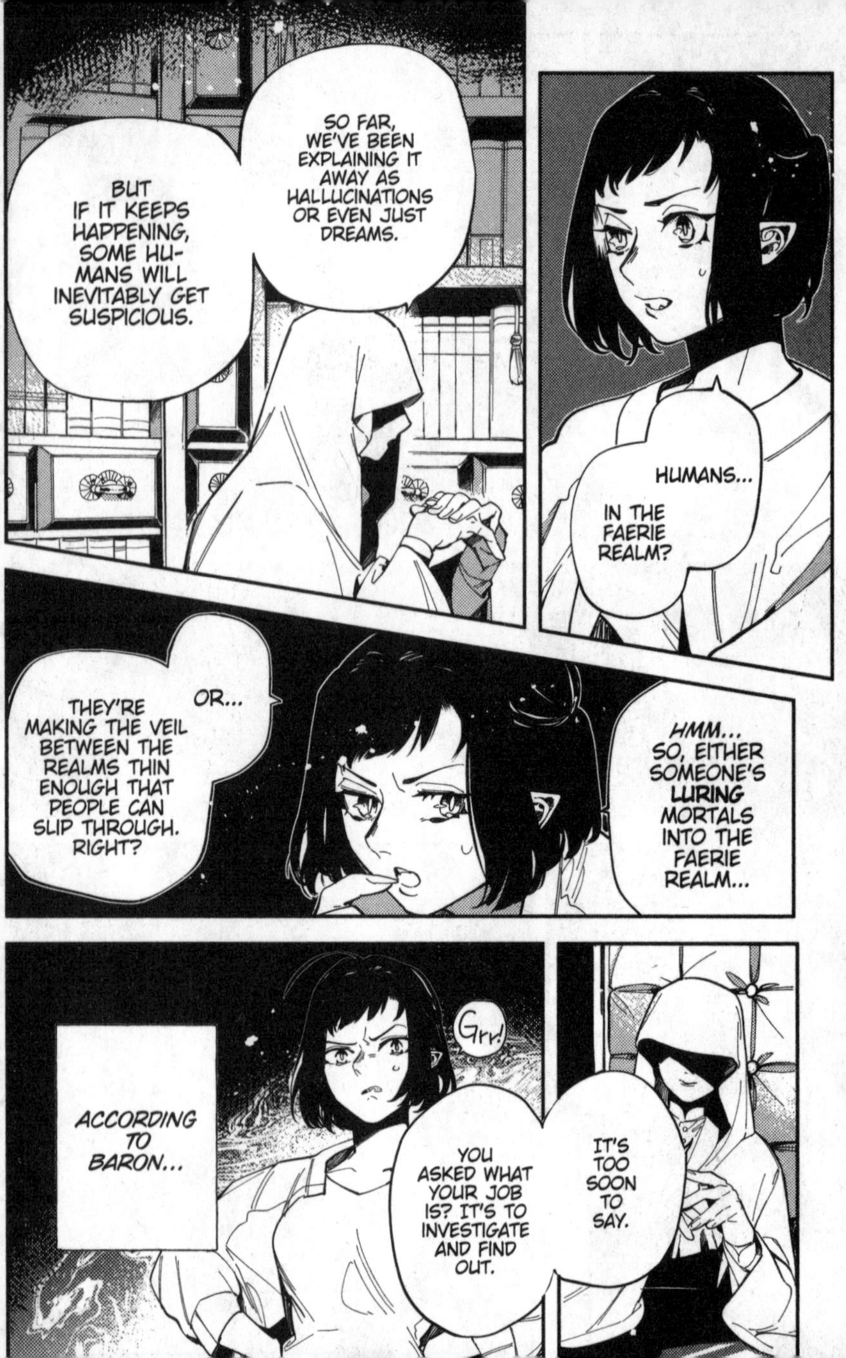
HUMANS...
IN THE FAERIE REALM?
SO FAR, WE'VE BEEN EXPLAINING IT AWAY AS HALLUCINATIONS OR EVEN JUST DREAMS.
BUT IF IT KEEPS HAPPENING, SOME HU-MANS WILL INEVITABLY GET SUSPICIOUS.
HMM... SO, EITHER SOMEONE'S **LURING** MORTALS INTO THE FAERIE REALM...
OR... THEY'RE MAKING THE VEIL BETWEEN THE REALMS THIN ENOUGH THAT PEOPLE CAN SLIP THROUGH. RIGHT?
IT'S TOO SOON TO SAY.
YOU ASKED WHAT YOUR JOB IS? IT'S TO INVESTIGATE AND FIND OUT.
Grr!
ACCORDING TO BARON...

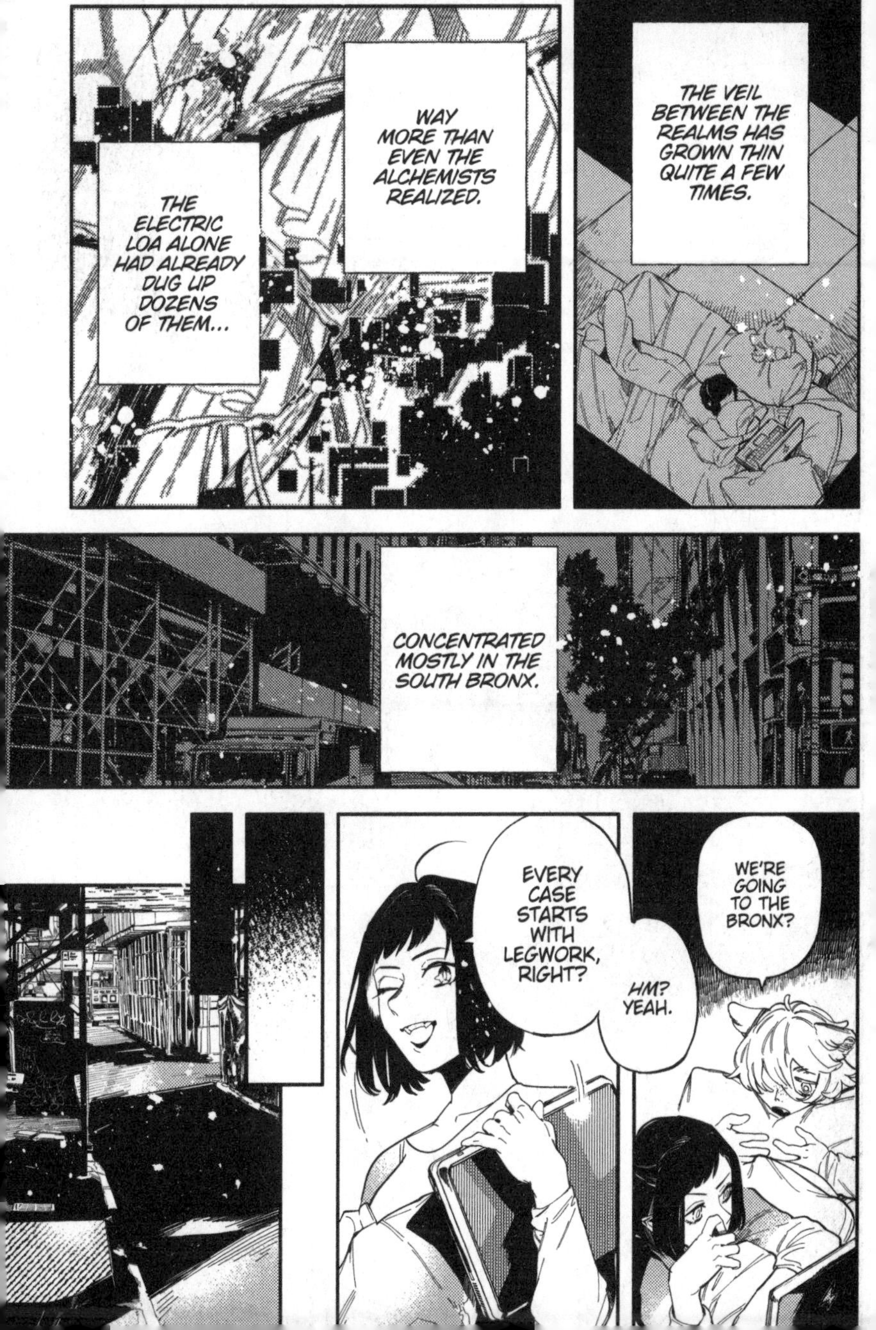
THE VEIL BETWEEN THE REALMS HAS GROWN THIN QUITE A FEW TIMES.
WAY MORE THAN EVEN THE ALCHEMISTS REALIZED.
THE ELECTRIC LOA ALONE HAD ALREADY DUG UP DOZENS OF THEM...
CONCENTRATED MOSTLY IN THE SOUTH BRONX.
WE'RE GOING TO THE BRONX?
HM? YEAH.
EVERY CASE STARTS WITH LEGWORK, RIGHT?

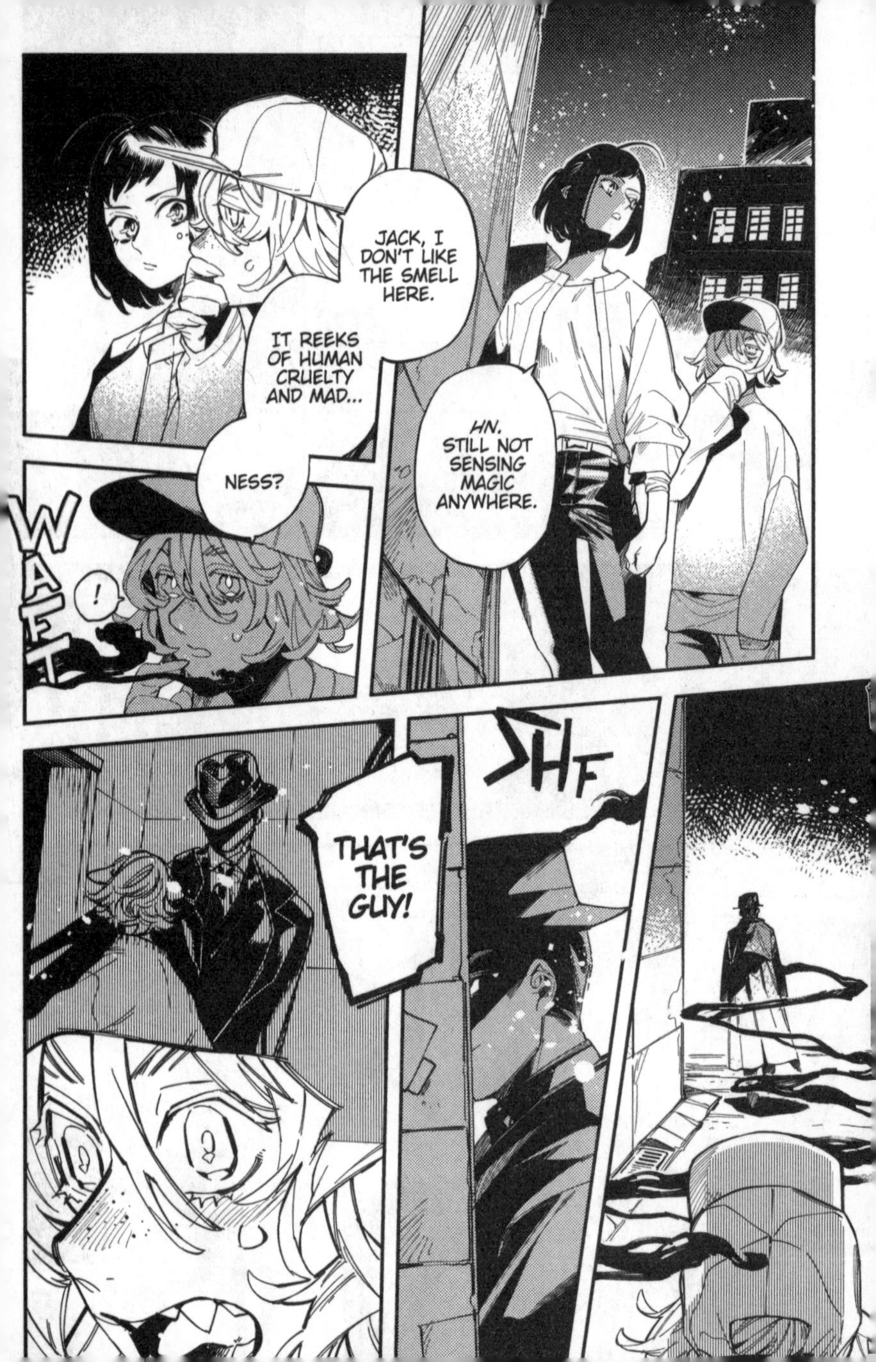
HN. STILL NOT SENSING MAGIC ANYWHERE.
JACK, I DON'T LIKE THE SMELL HERE.
IT REEKS OF HUMAN CRUELTY AND MAD...
NESS?
WAFT
!
SHF
THAT'S THE GUY!

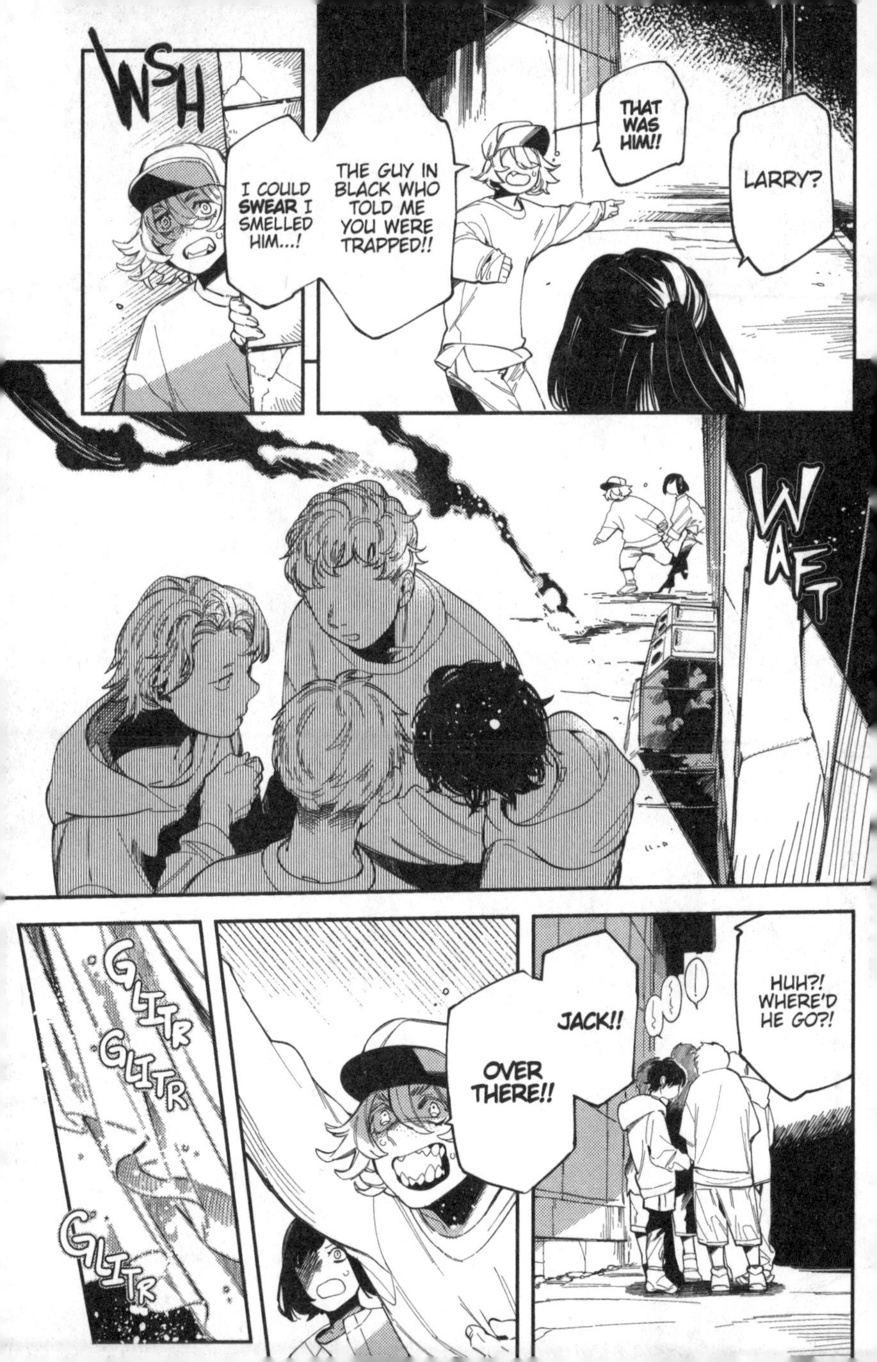
LARRY?
THAT WAS HIM!!
THE GUY IN BLACK WHO TOLD ME YOU WERE TRAPPED!!
WSH
I COULD **SWEAR** I SMELLED HIM...!
WAFT
HUH?! WHERE'D HE GO?!
!
JACK!!
OVER THERE!!
GLITR
GLITR
GLITR

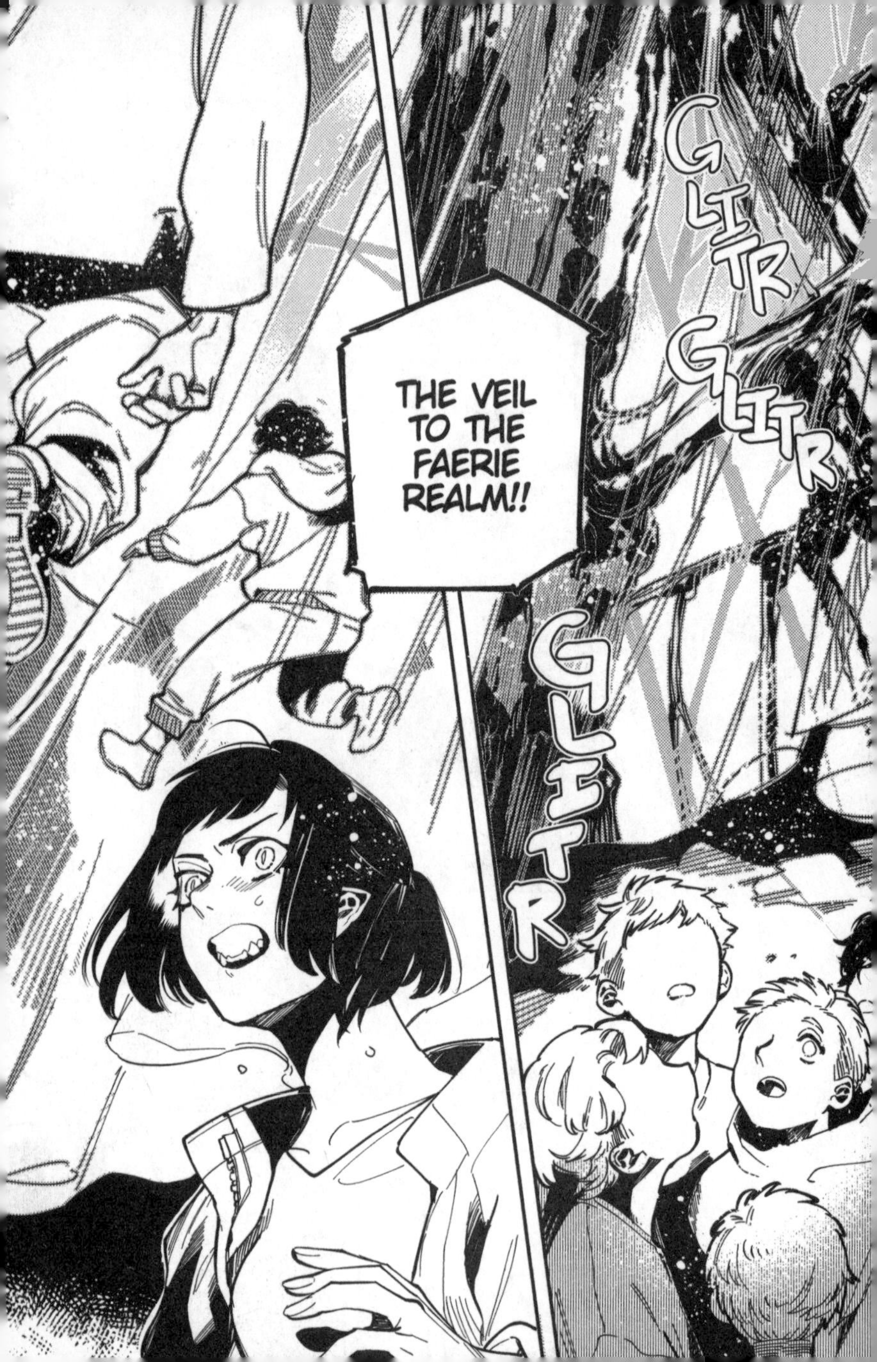
GLITR
GLITR
THE VEIL TO THE FAERIE REALM!!
GLITR

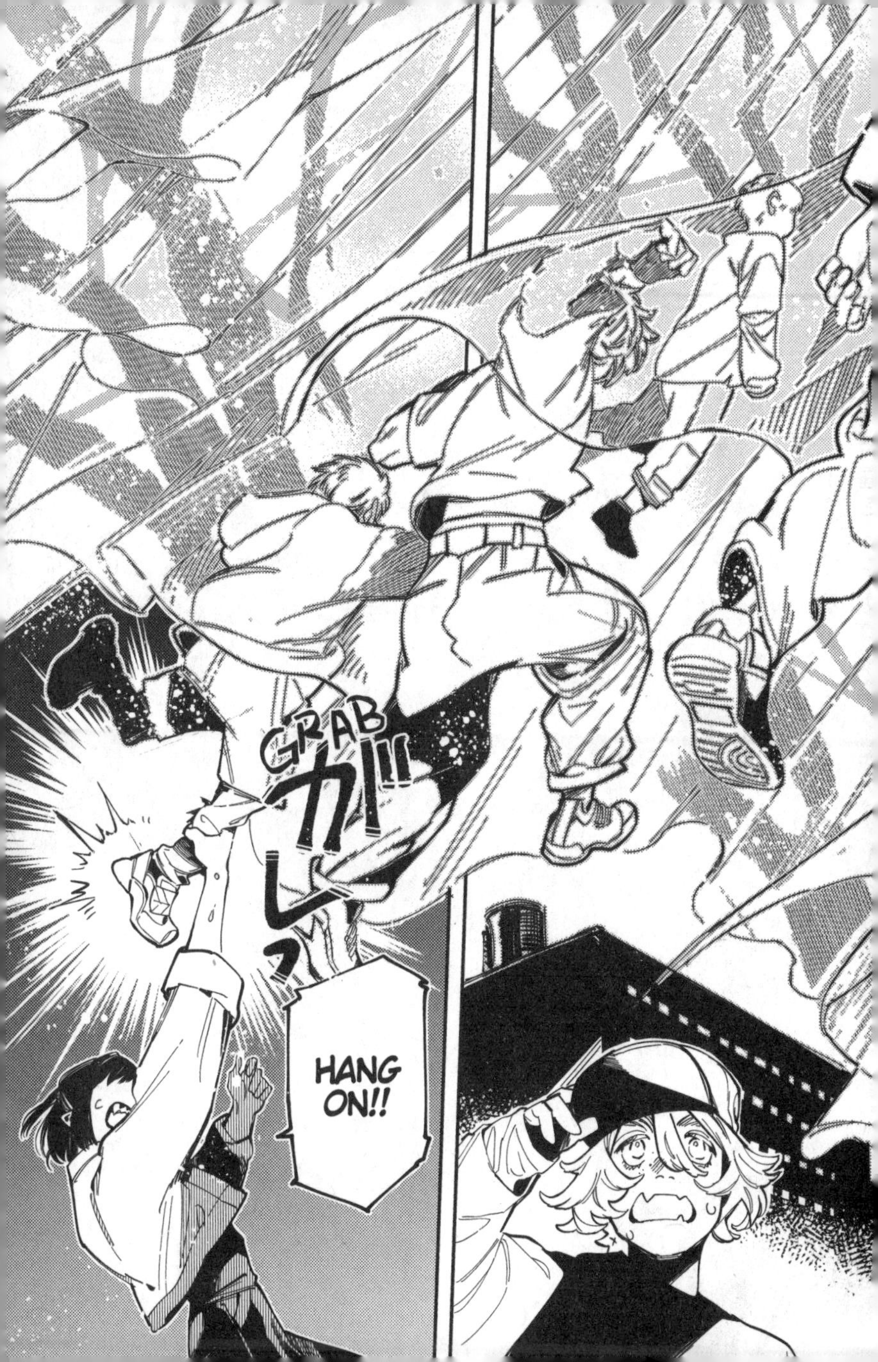
GRAB
HANG ON!!

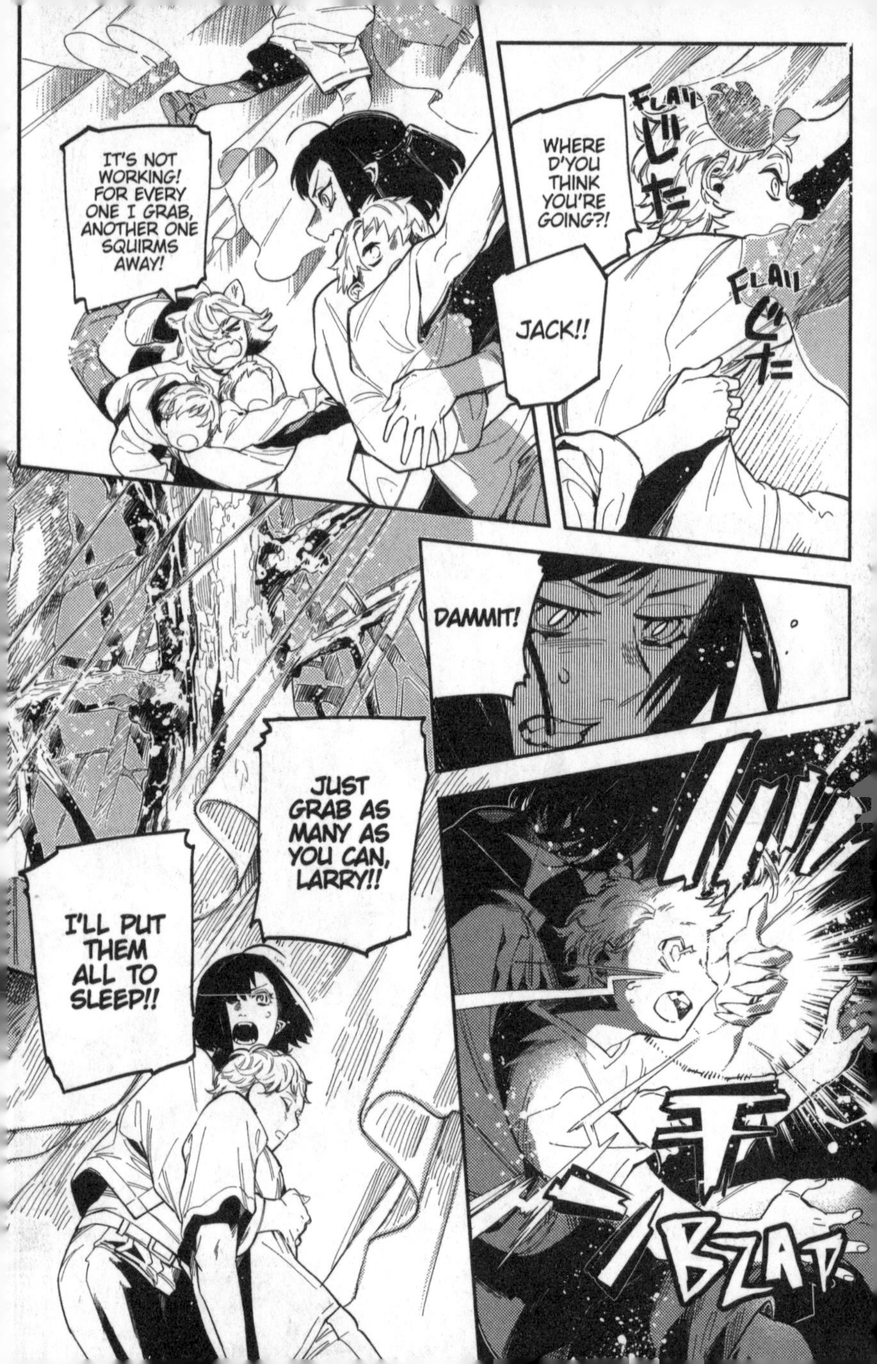
FLAIL
WHERE D'YOU THINK YOU'RE GOING?!
JACK!!
FLAIL
IT'S NOT WORKING! FOR EVERY ONE I GRAB, ANOTHER ONE SQUIRMS AWAY!
DAMMIT!
BZAT
JUST GRAB AS MANY AS YOU CAN, LARRY!!
I'LL PUT THEM ALL TO SLEEP!!

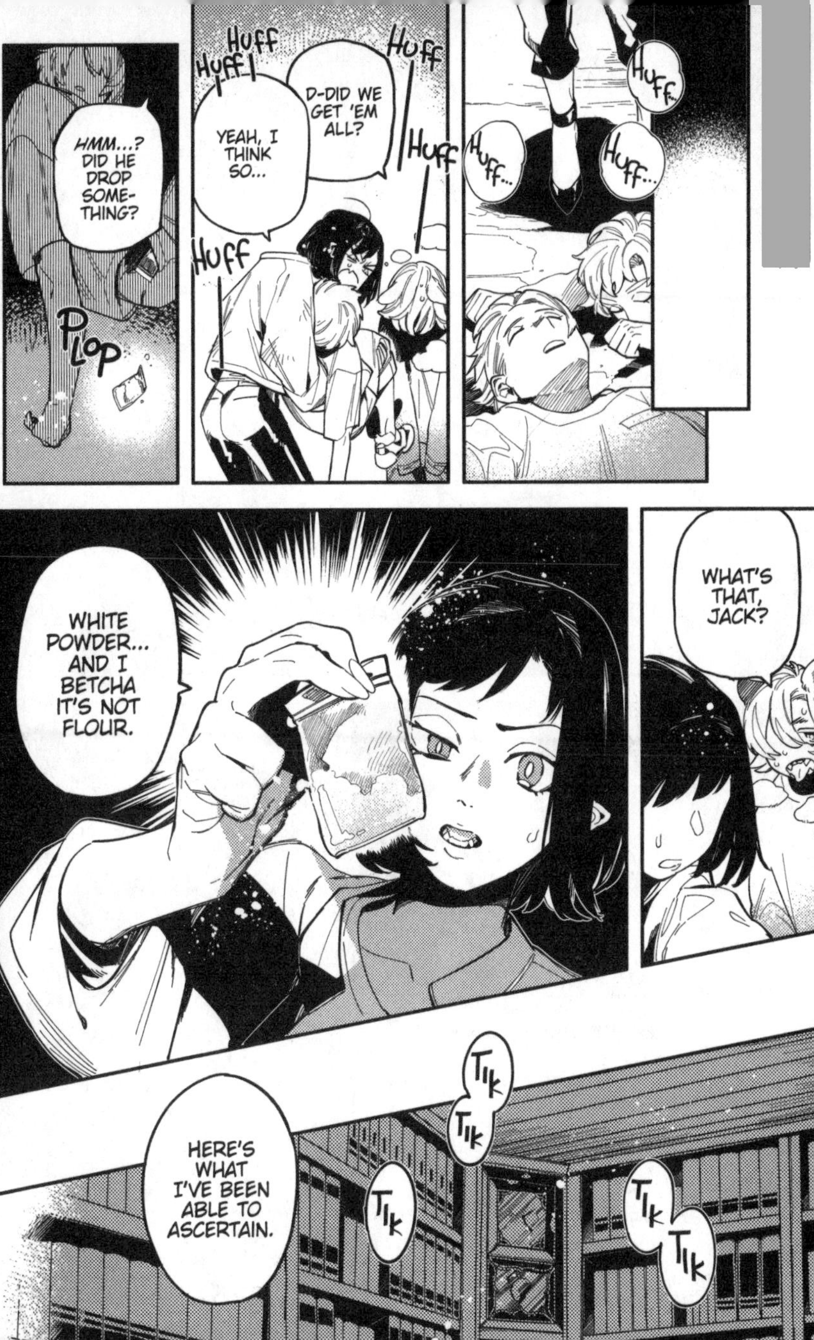
Huff...
Huff...
Huff...
Huff...
Huff
D-did we get 'em all?
Huff
Huff!
Yeah, I think so...
Huff
Hmm...? Did he drop something?
Plop
What's that, Jack?
White powder... and I betcha it's not flour.
Tik
Tik
Tik
Tik
Tik
Here's what I've been able to ascertain.

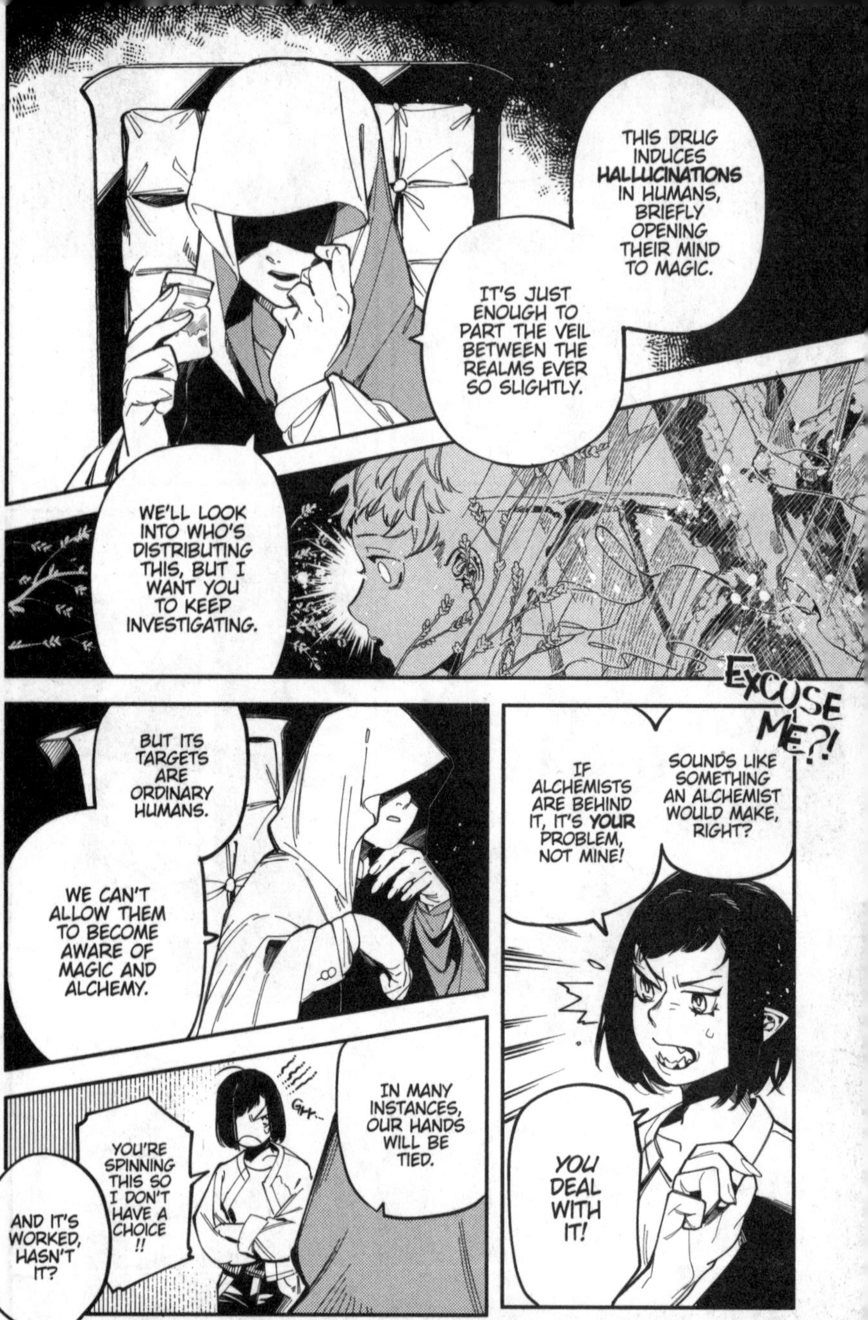
THIS DRUG INDUCES **HALLUCINATIONS** IN HUMANS, BRIEFLY OPENING THEIR MIND TO MAGIC.
IT'S JUST ENOUGH TO PART THE VEIL BETWEEN THE REALMS EVER SO SLIGHTLY.
WE'LL LOOK INTO WHO'S DISTRIBUTING THIS, BUT I WANT YOU TO KEEP INVESTIGATING.
EXCUSE ME?!
SOUNDS LIKE SOMETHING AN ALCHEMIST WOULD MAKE, RIGHT?
IF ALCHEMISTS ARE BEHIND IT, IT'S **YOUR** PROBLEM, NOT MINE!
YOU DEAL WITH IT!
BUT ITS TARGETS ARE ORDINARY HUMANS.
WE CAN'T ALLOW THEM TO BECOME AWARE OF MAGIC AND ALCHEMY.
IN MANY INSTANCES, OUR HANDS WILL BE TIED.
YOU'RE SPINNING THIS SO I DON'T HAVE A CHOICE!!
AND IT'S WORKED, HASN'T IT?

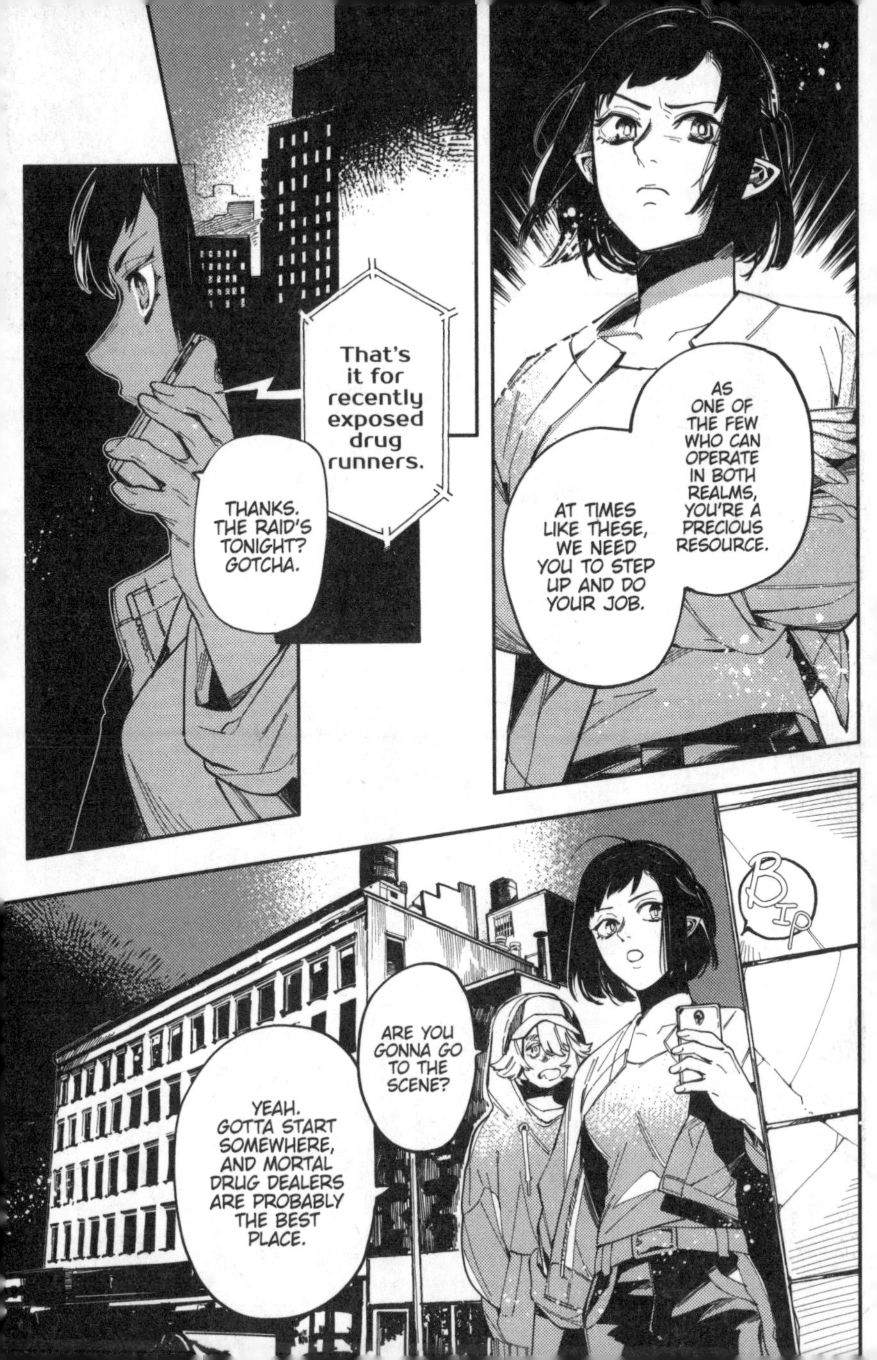
AS ONE OF THE FEW WHO CAN OPERATE IN BOTH REALMS, YOU'RE A PRECIOUS RESOURCE.
AT TIMES LIKE THESE, WE NEED YOU TO STEP UP AND DO YOUR JOB.
That's it for recently exposed drug runners.
THANKS. THE RAID'S TONIGHT? GOTCHA.
BIP
ARE YOU GONNA GO TO THE SCENE?
YEAH. GOTTA START SOMEWHERE, AND MORTAL DRUG DEALERS ARE PROBABLY THE BEST PLACE.

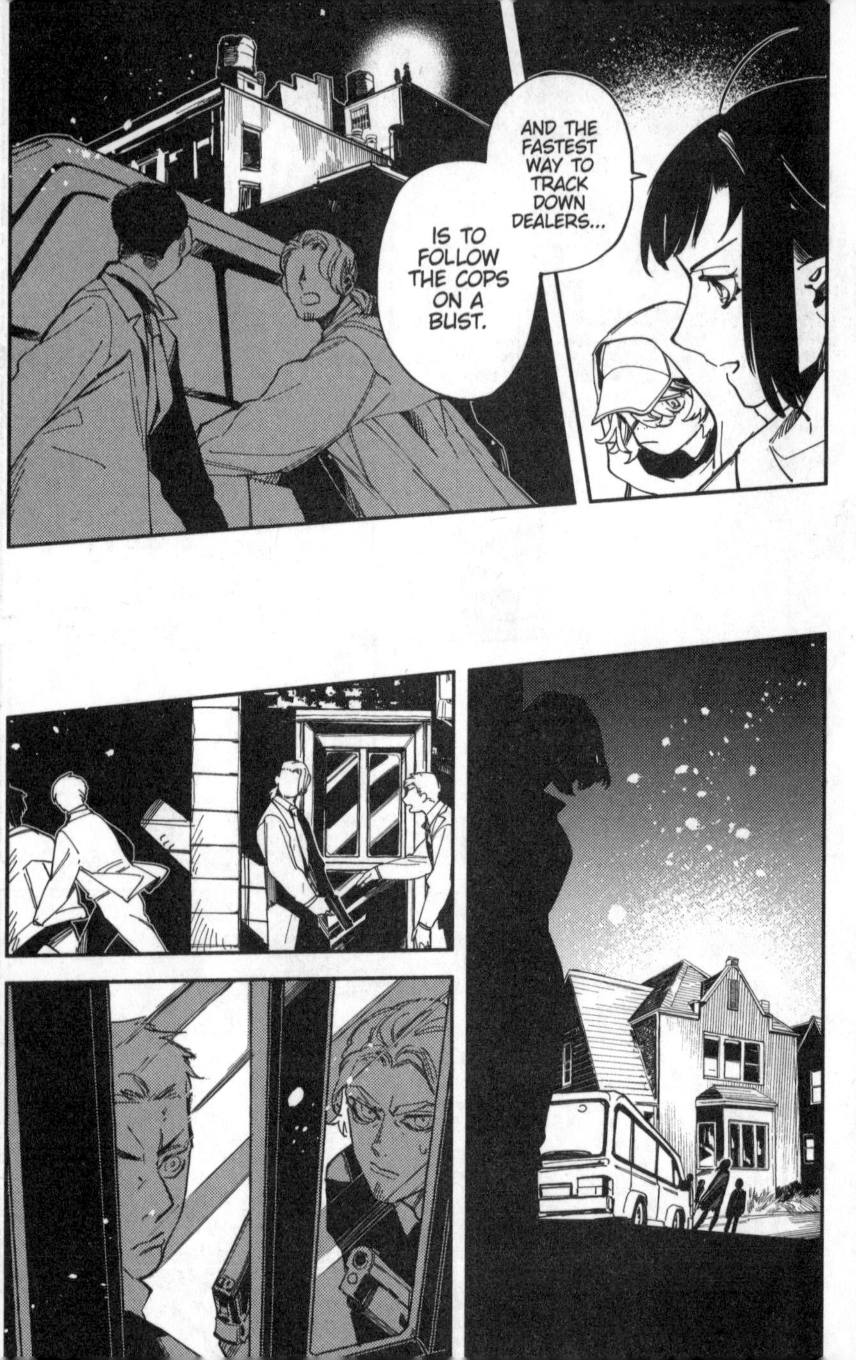
AND THE FASTEST WAY TO TRACK DOWN DEALERS...
IS TO FOLLOW THE COPS ON A BUST.

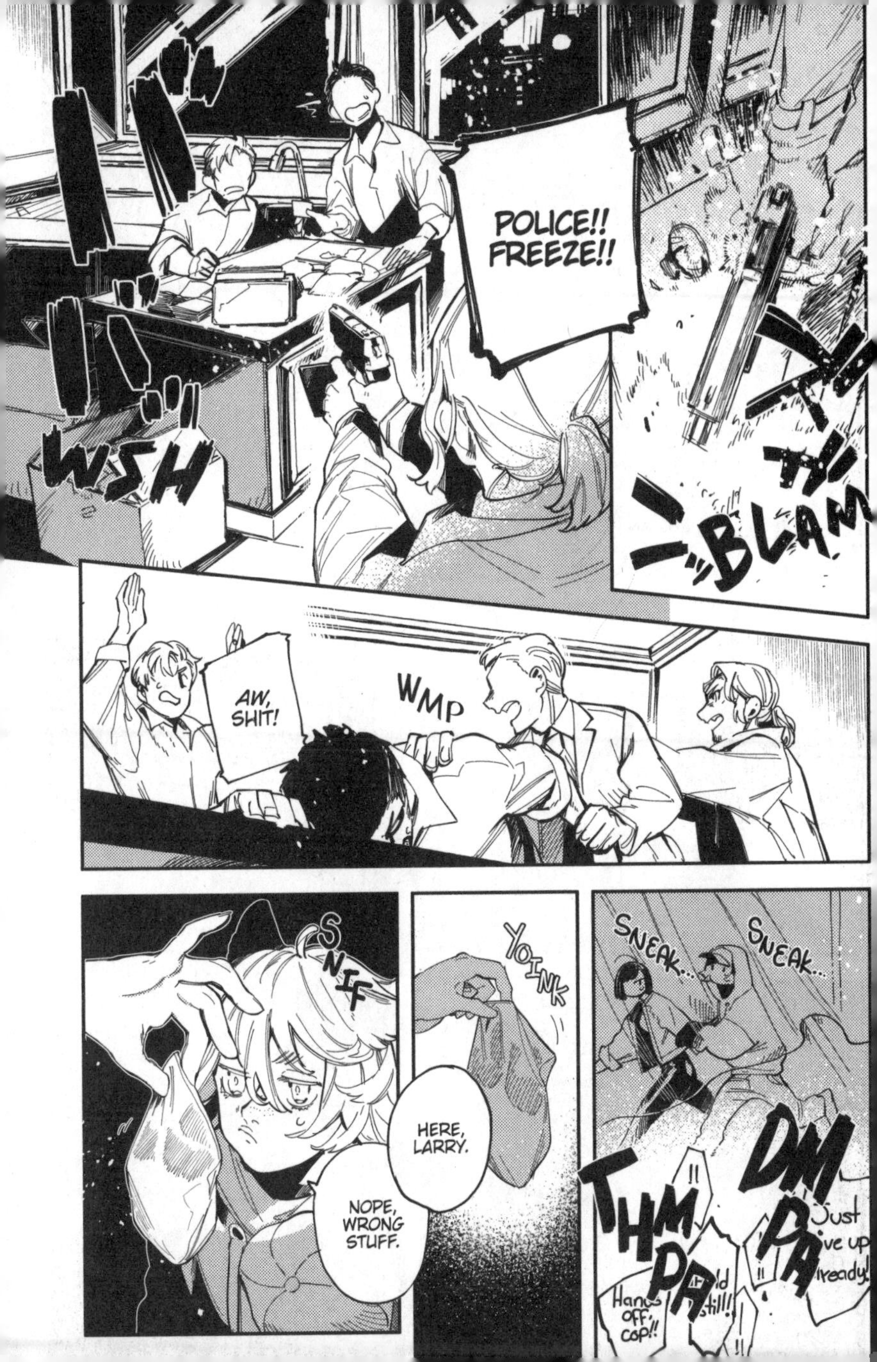
BLAM
POLICE!! FREEZE!!
WSH
AW, SHIT!
WMP
SNEAK...
SNEAK...
DM DA
!!
Just ive up lready!
THM PA
!!
!!
ld still!!
Hands off, cop!!
YOINK
HERE, LARRY.
NOPE, WRONG STUFF.
SNIF

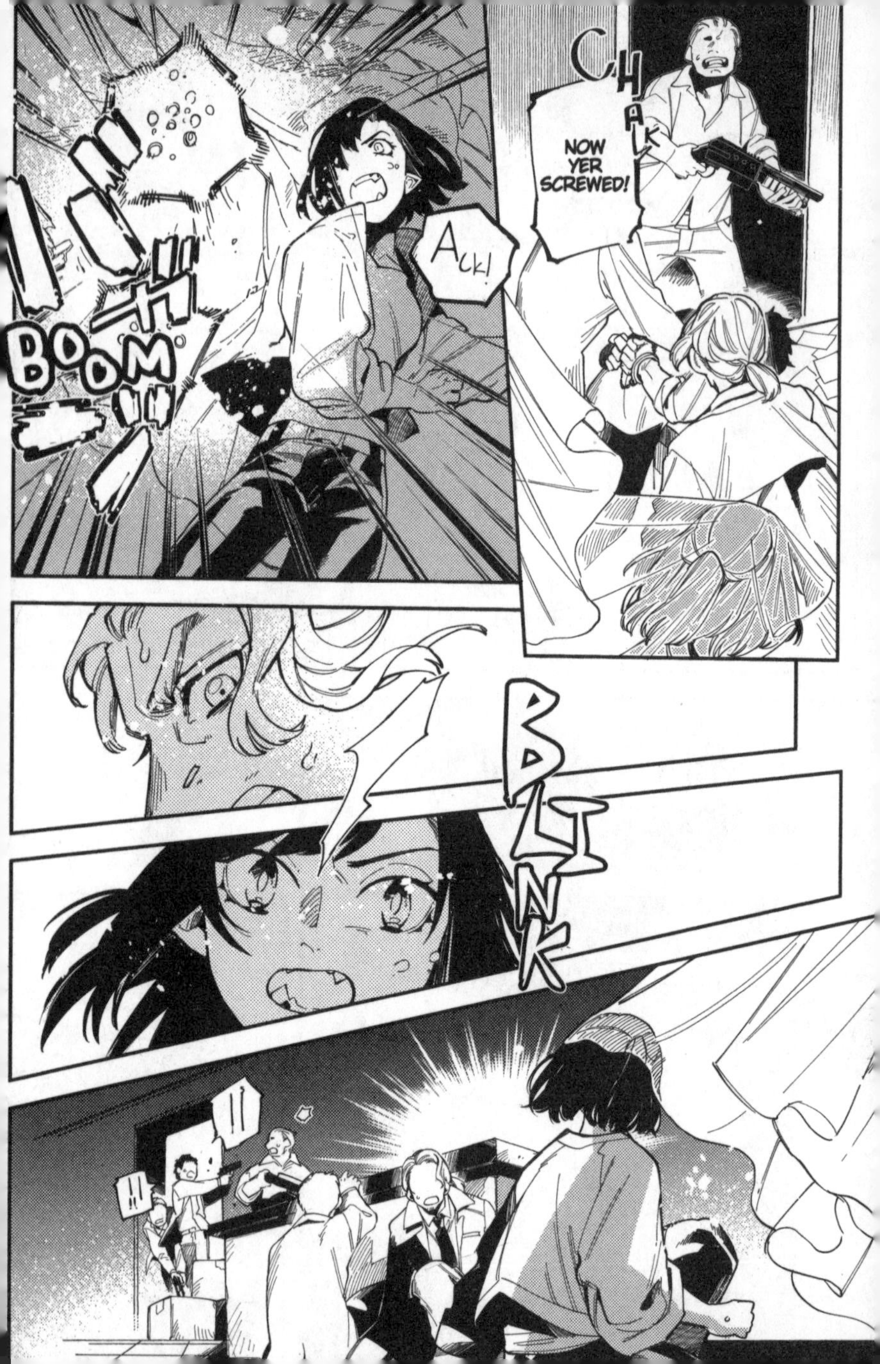
CHAK
NOW YER SCREWED!
Ack!
BOOM
BLINK
!!
!!

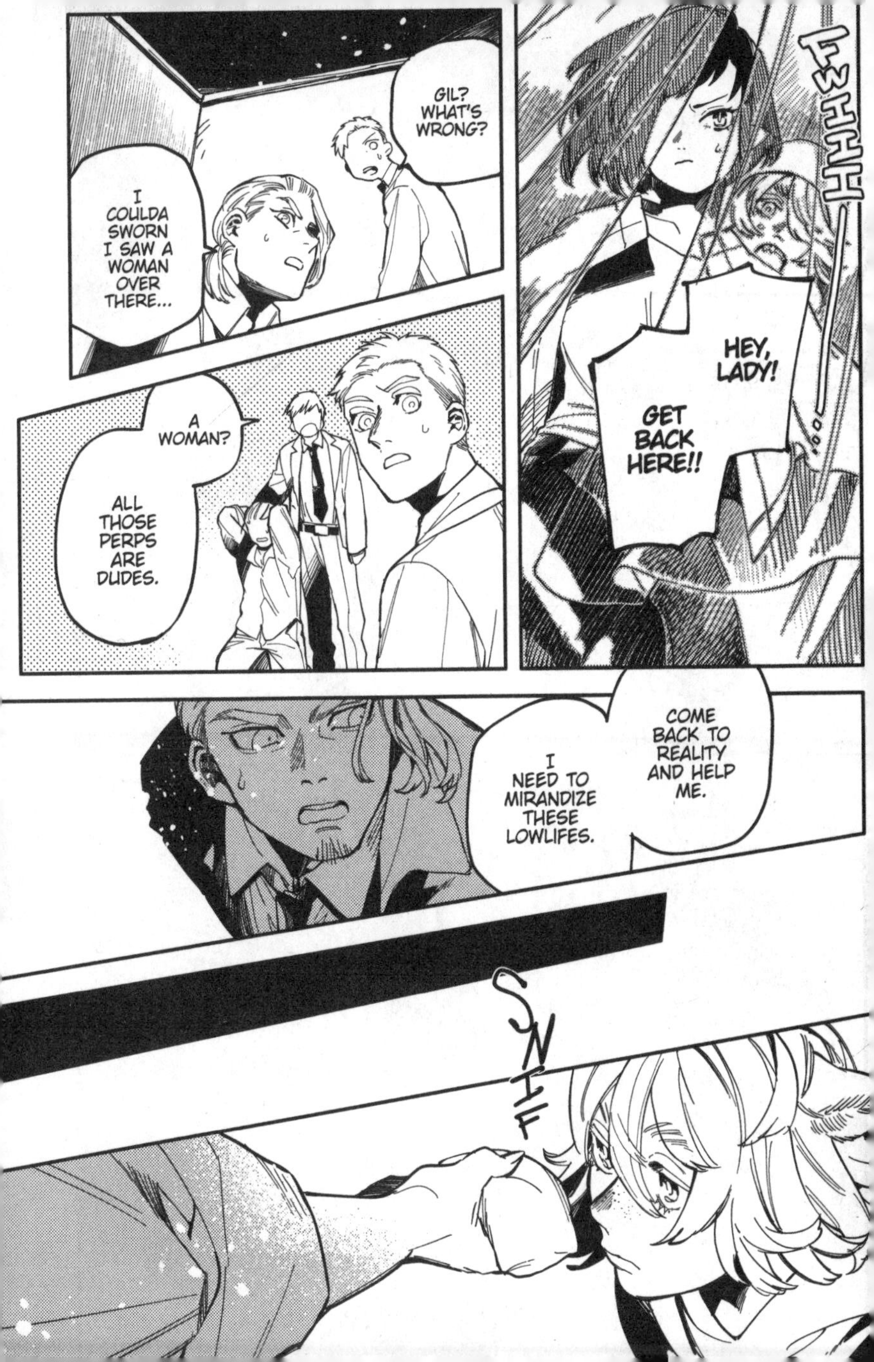
FWHHH—...
HEY, LADY!
GET BACK HERE!!
GIL? WHAT'S WRONG?
I COULDA SWORN I SAW A WOMAN OVER THERE...
A WOMAN?
ALL THOSE PERPS ARE DUDES.
COME BACK TO REALITY AND HELP ME.
I NEED TO MIRANDIZE THESE LOWLIFES.
SNIFF

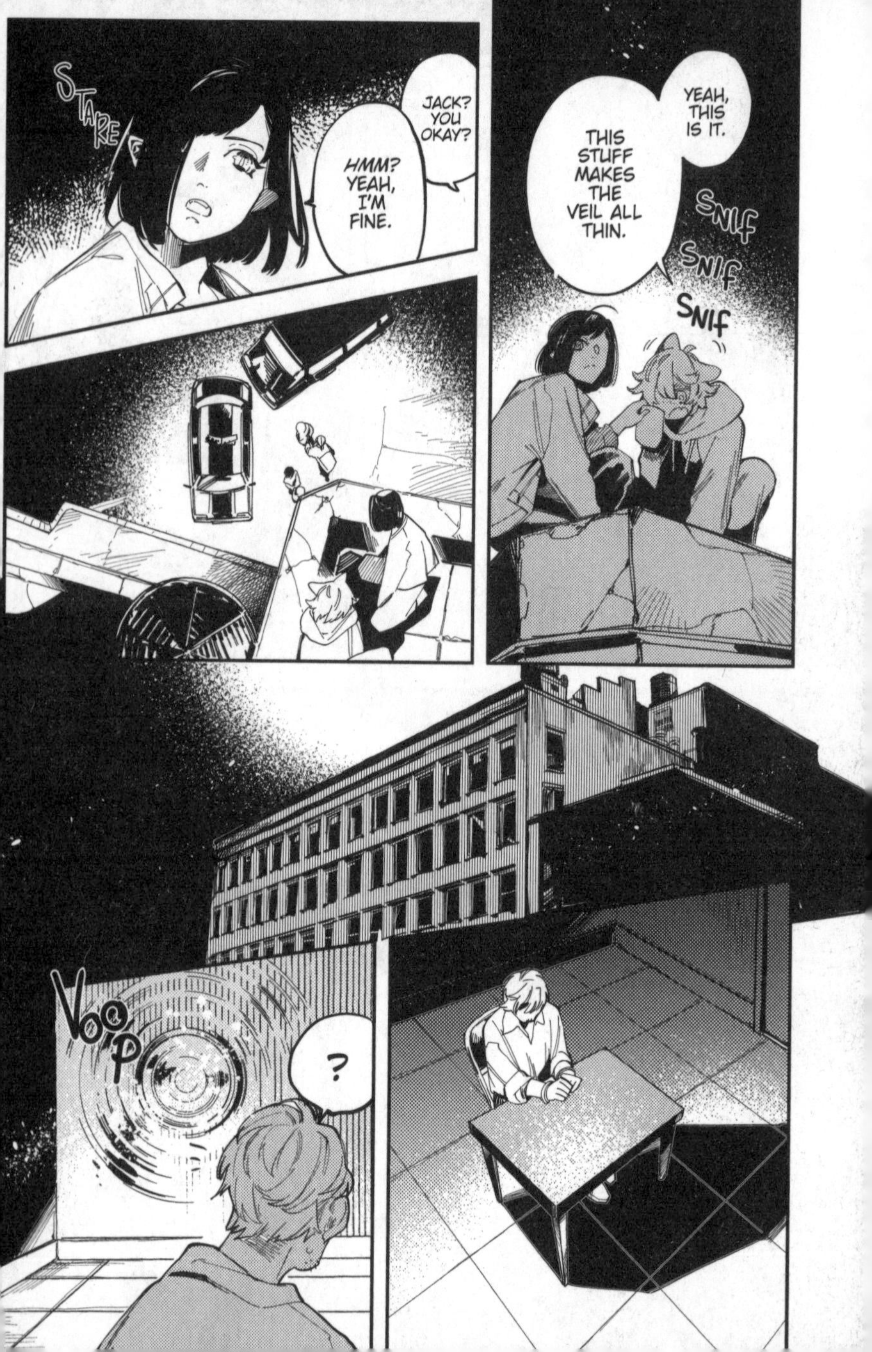
YEAH, THIS IS IT.
THIS STUFF MAKES THE VEIL ALL THIN.
SNIF
SNIF
SNIF
JACK? YOU OKAY?
HMM? YEAH, I'M FINE.
STARE
?
VOOP

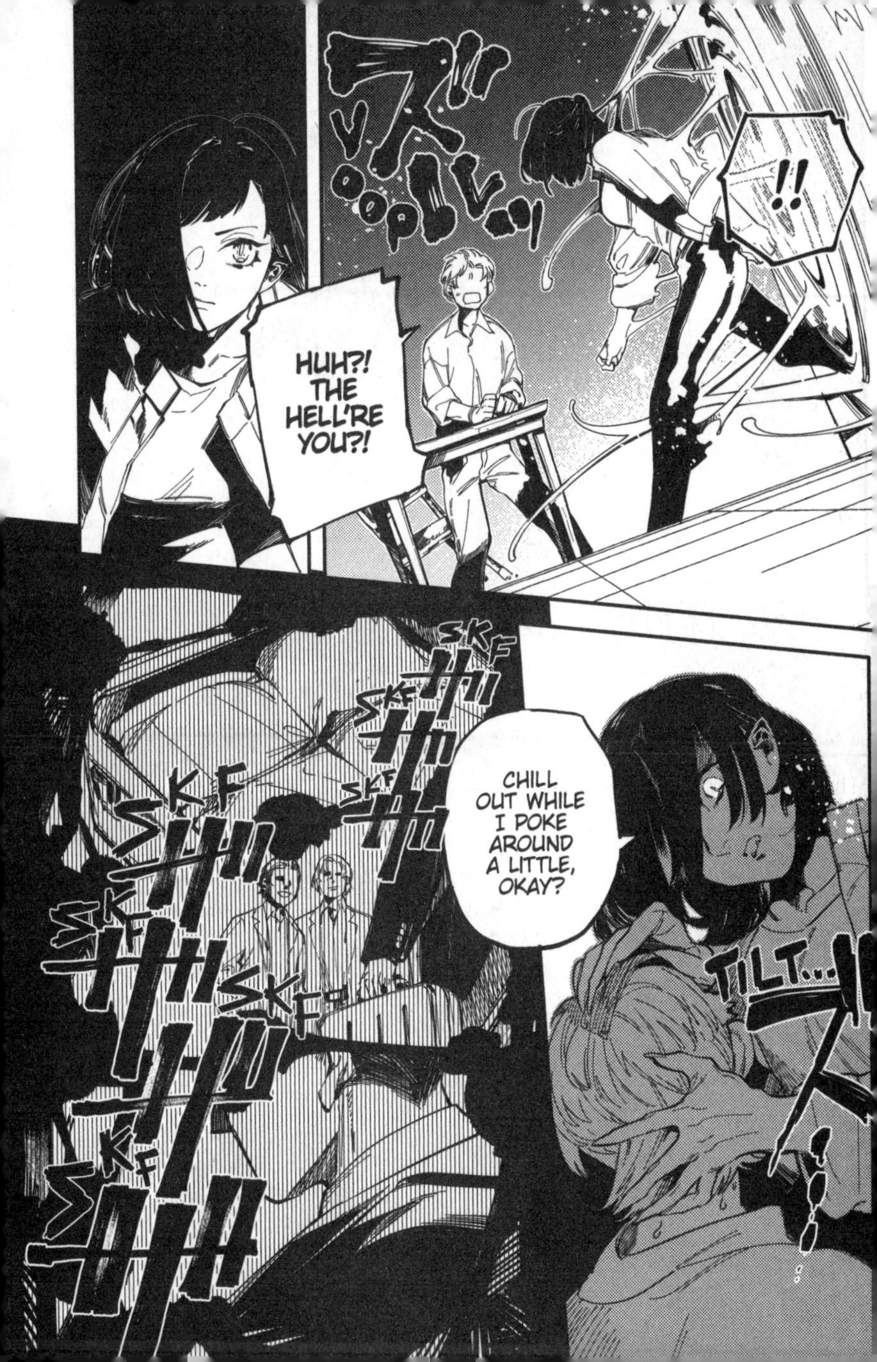
VOOP
!!
HUH?! THE HELL'RE YOU?!
TILT...
CHILL OUT WHILE I POKE AROUND A LITTLE, OKAY?
SKF
SKF
SKF
SKF
SKF
SKF
SKF

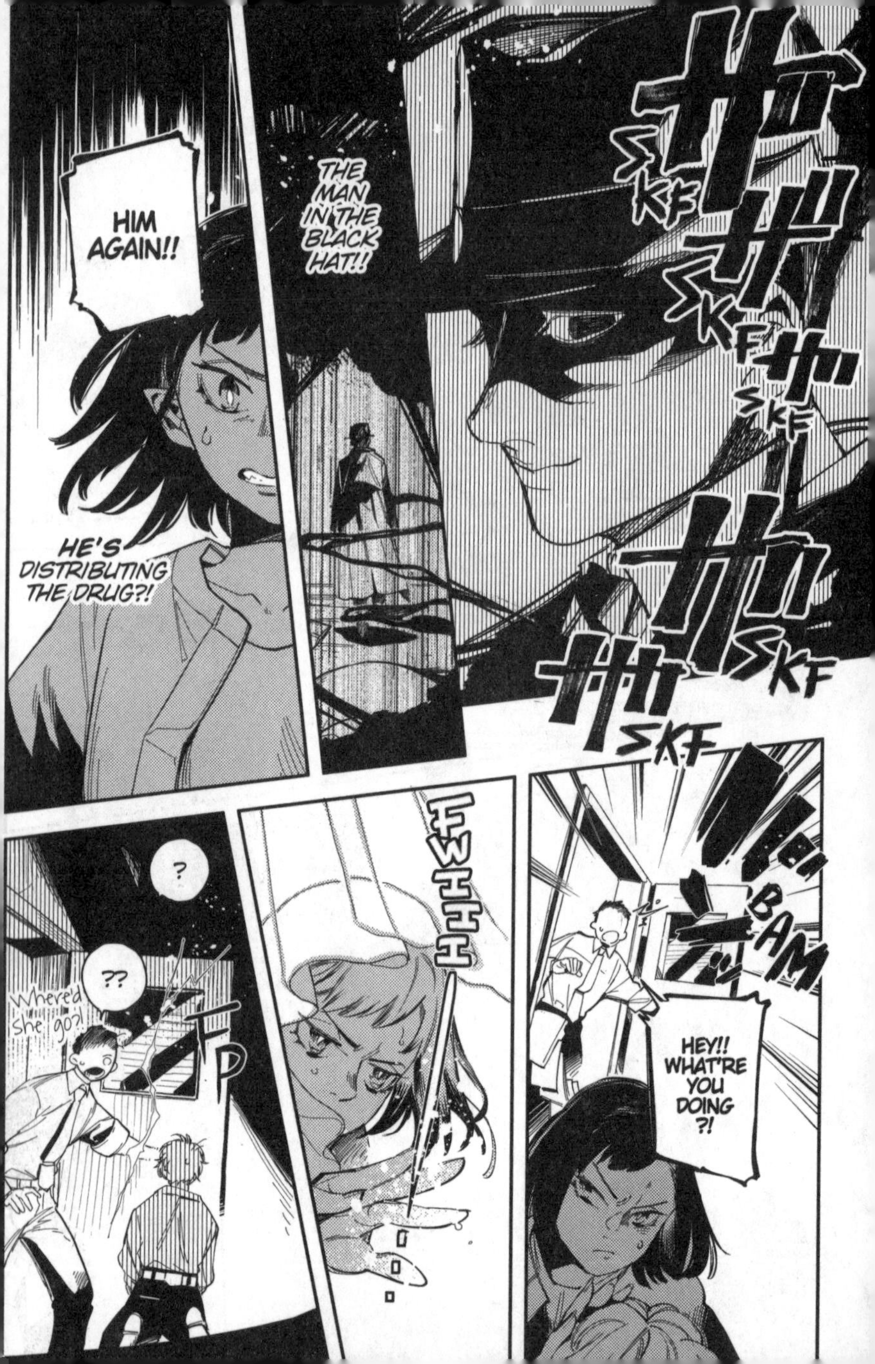
SKF
SKF
SKF
SKF
SKF
SKF
THE MAN IN THE BLACK HAT!!
HIM AGAIN!!
HE'S DISTRIBUTING THE DRUG?!
BAM
HEY!! WHAT'RE YOU DOING?!
FWIII
?
??
Where'd she go?!
TP

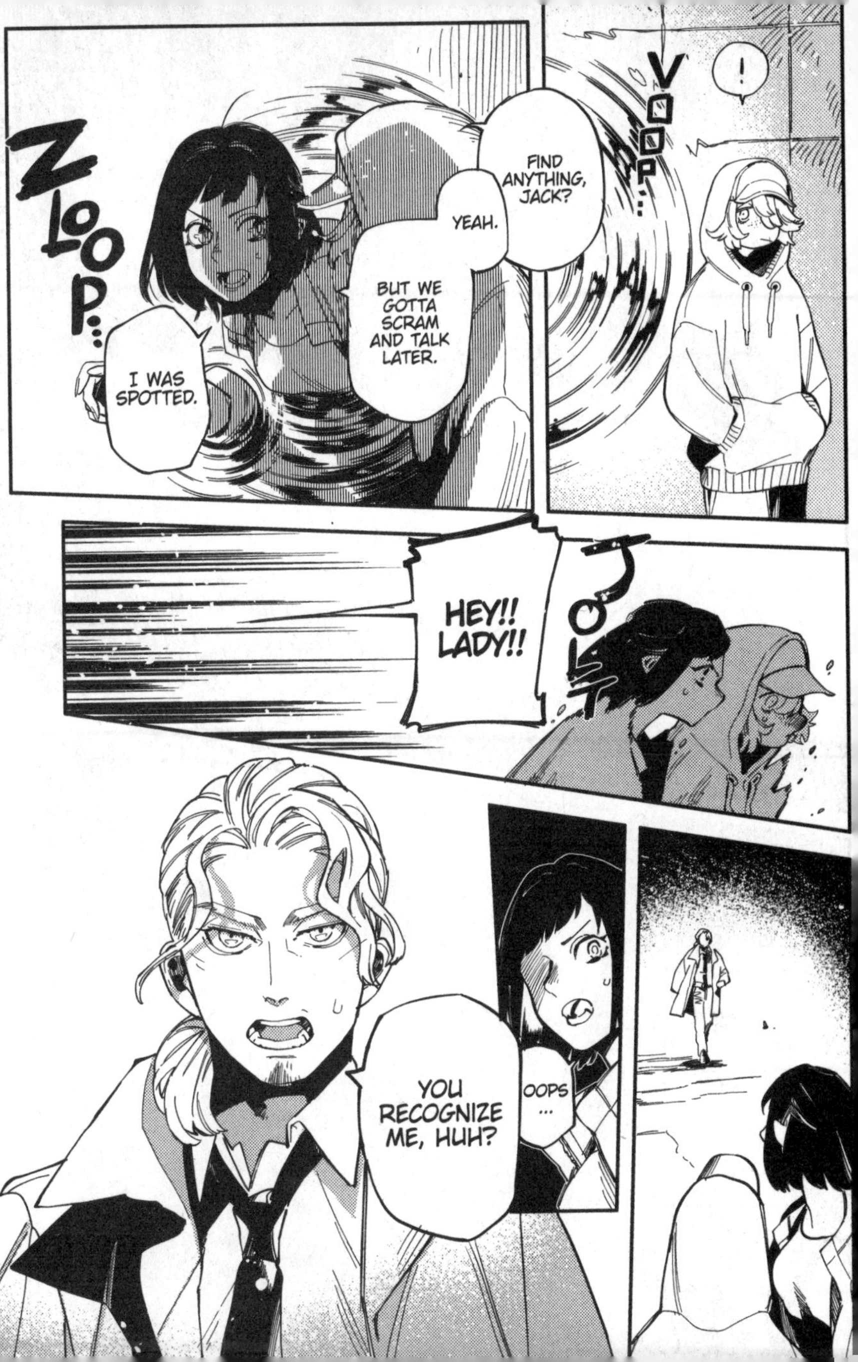
!
VOOP...
FIND ANYTHING, JACK?
YEAH.
BUT WE GOTTA SCRAM AND TALK LATER.
ZLOOP...
I WAS SPOTTED.
JOLT
HEY!! LADY!!
OOPS ...
YOU RECOGNIZE ME, HUH?

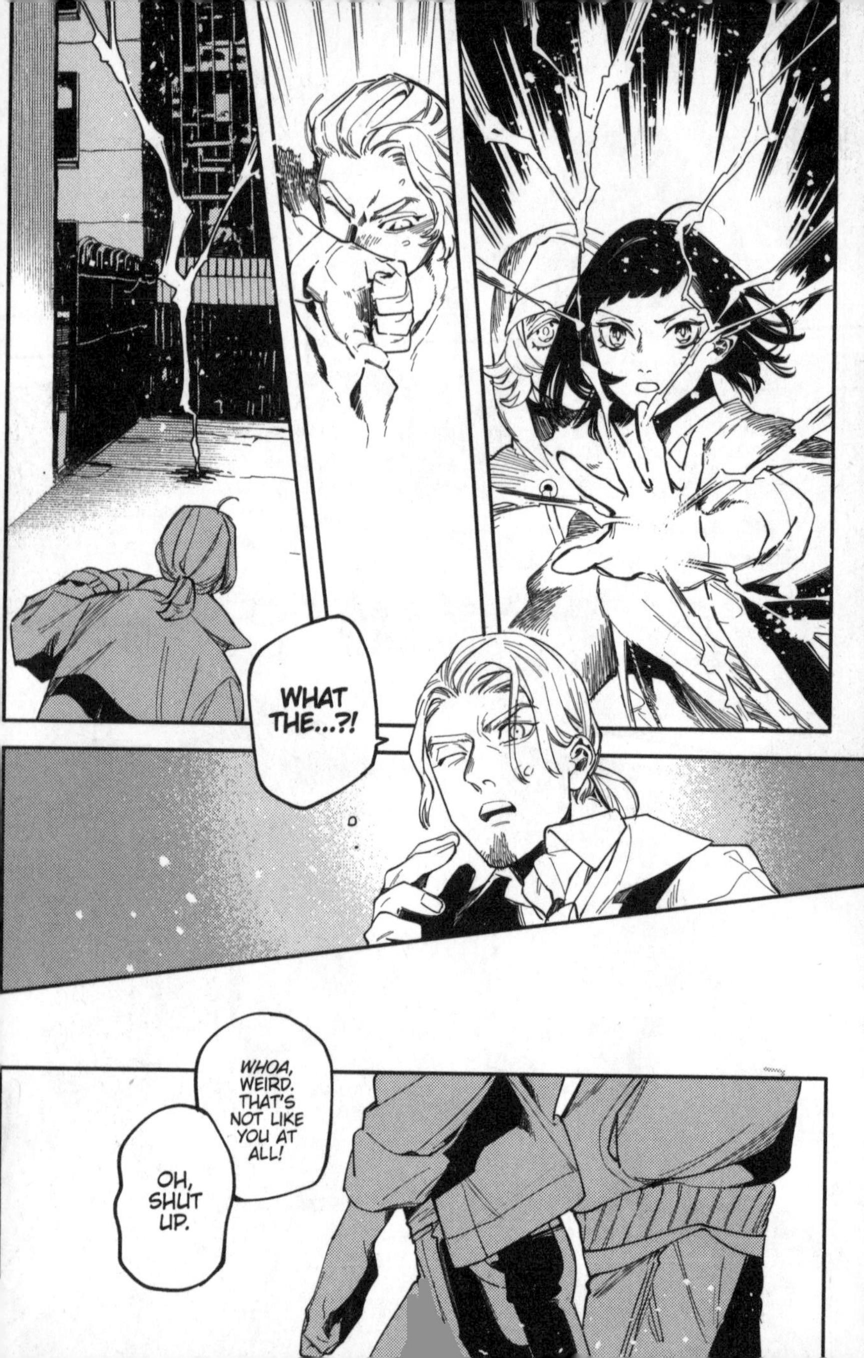
WHAT THE...?!
WHOA, WEIRD. THAT'S NOT LIKE YOU AT ALL!
OH, SHUT UP.

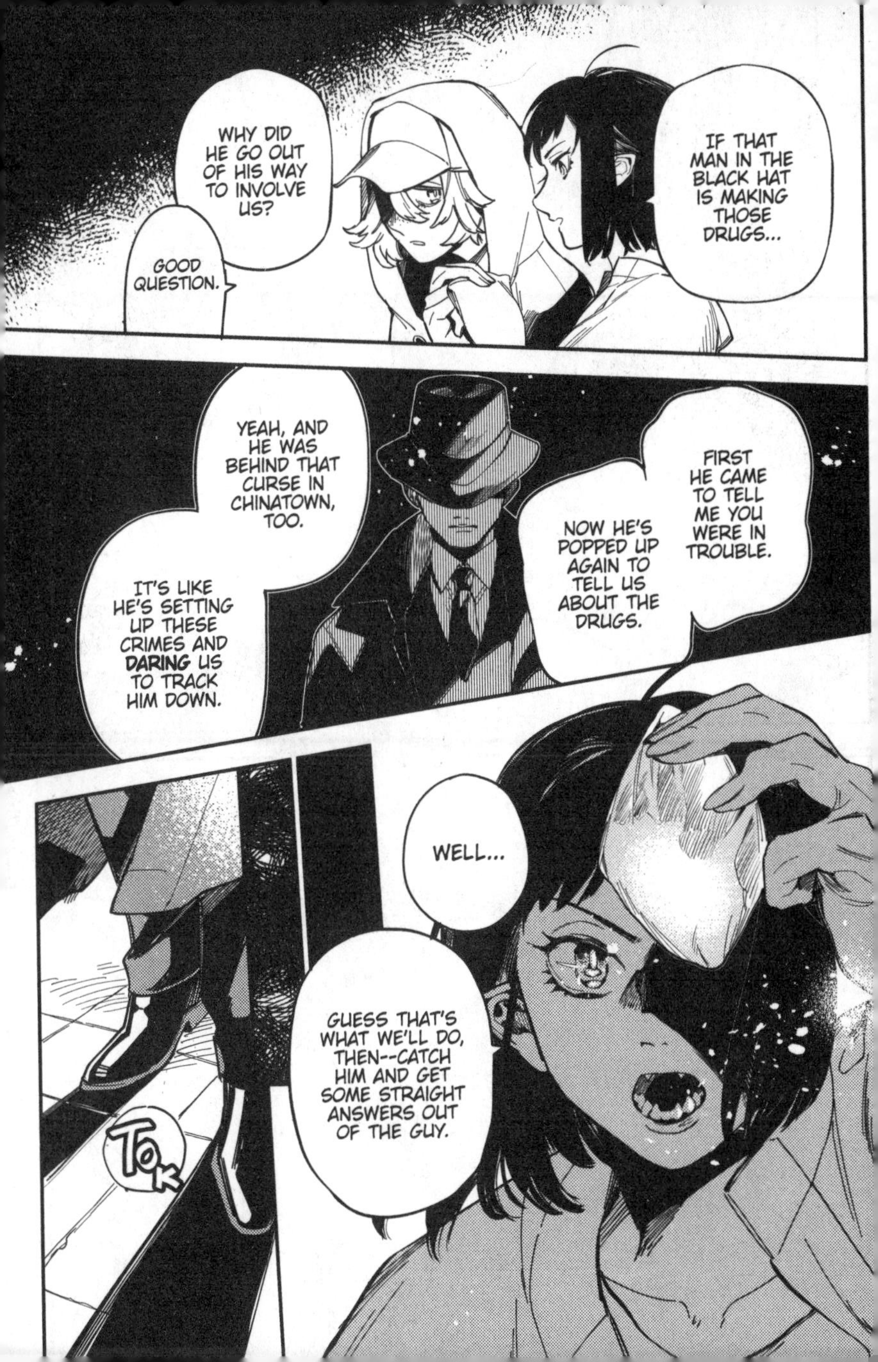
IF THAT MAN IN THE BLACK HAT IS MAKING THOSE DRUGS...
WHY DID HE GO OUT OF HIS WAY TO INVOLVE US?
GOOD QUESTION.
FIRST HE CAME TO TELL ME YOU WERE IN TROUBLE.
NOW HE'S POPPED UP AGAIN TO TELL US ABOUT THE DRUGS.
YEAH, AND HE WAS BEHIND THAT CURSE IN CHINATOWN, TOO.
IT'S LIKE HE'S SETTING UP THESE CRIMES AND **DARING** US TO TRACK HIM DOWN.
WELL...
GUESS THAT'S WHAT WE'LL DO, THEN--CATCH HIM AND GET SOME STRAIGHT ANSWERS OUT OF THE GUY.
TOK

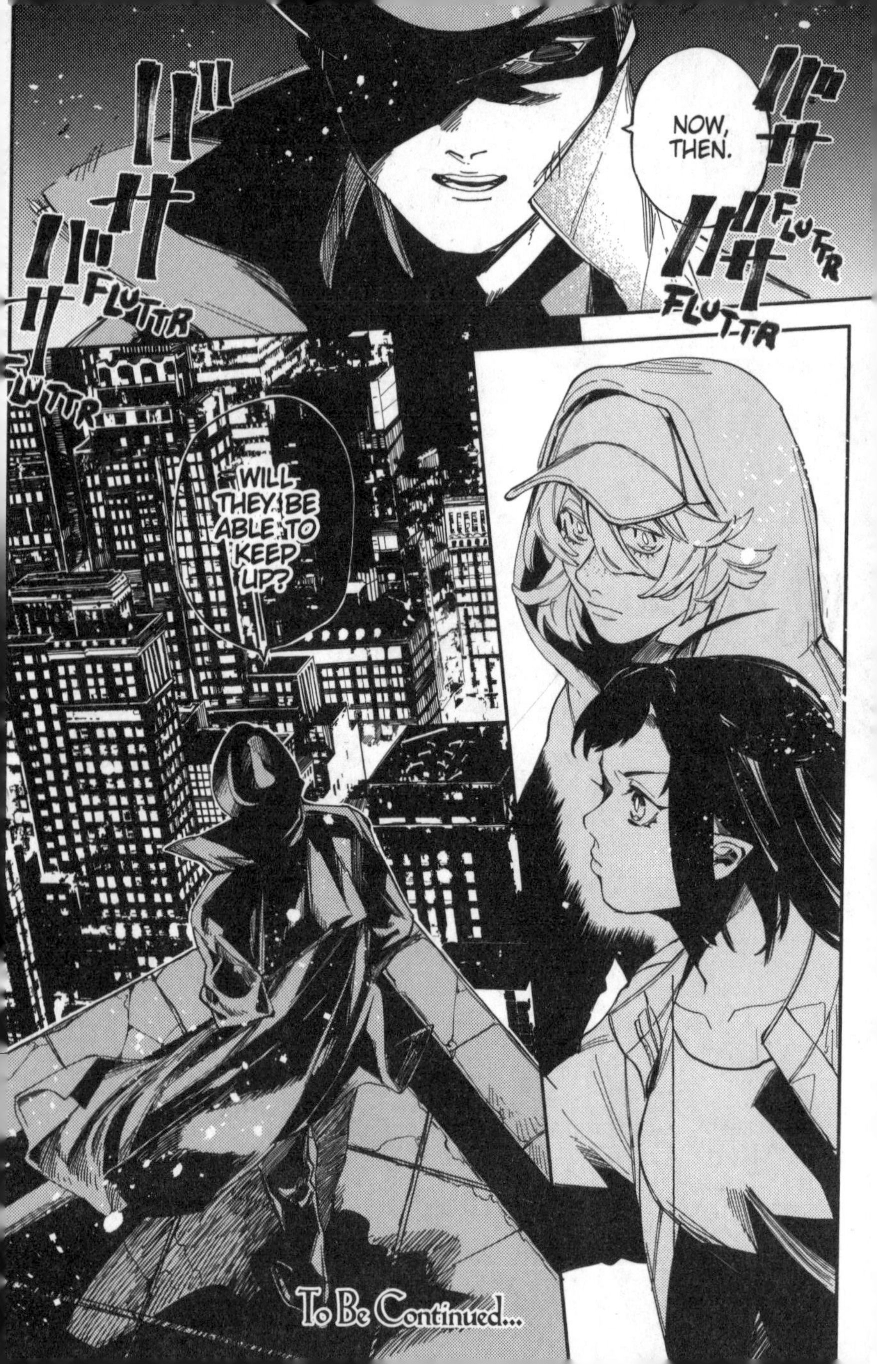
NOW, THEN.
FLUTTR
FL·U·T-TR
FLUTTR
WILL THEY BE ABLE TO KEEP UP?
To Be Continued...

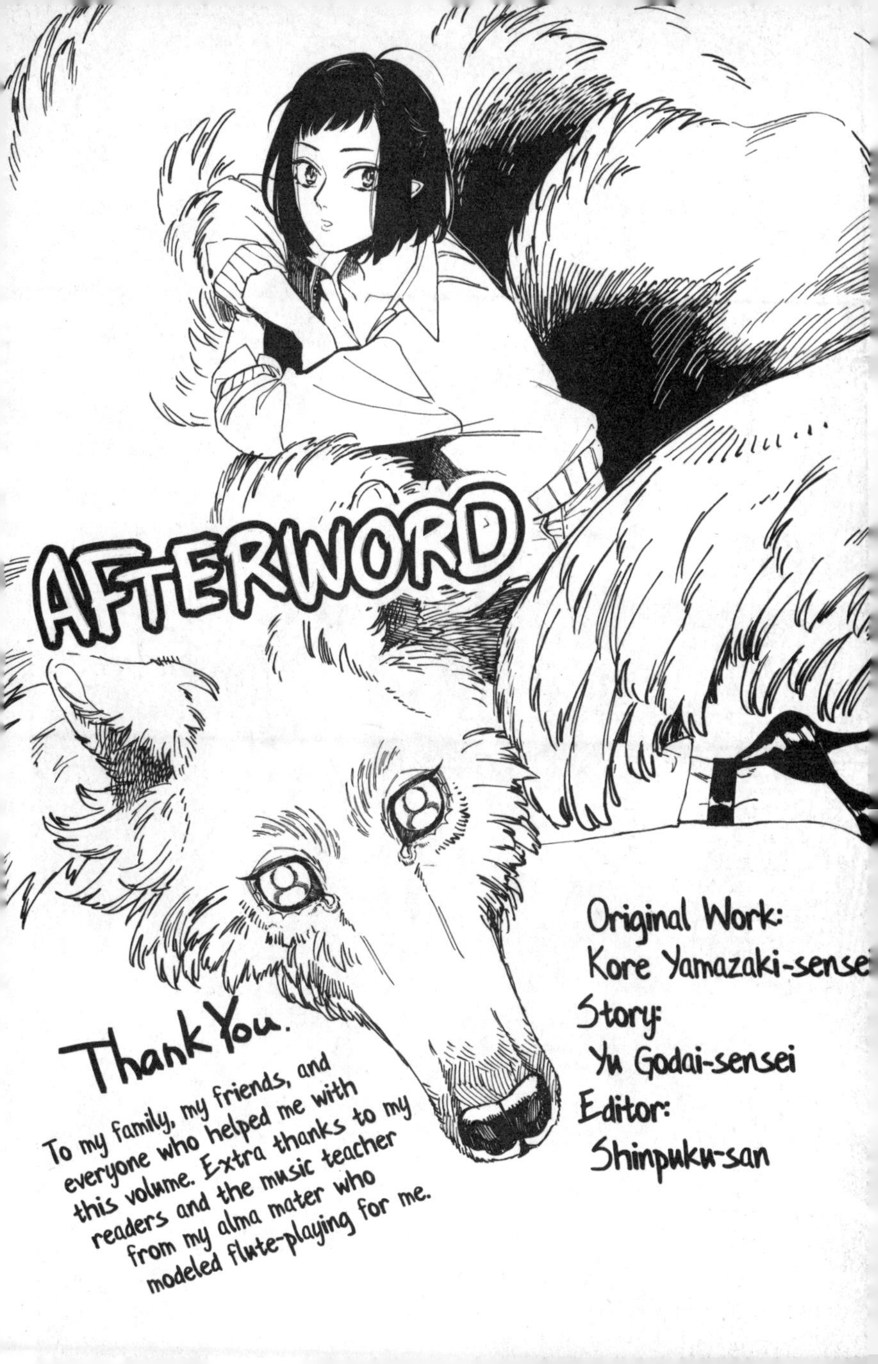
AFTERWORD
Original Work:
Kore Yamazaki-sensei
Story:
Yu Godai-sensei
Editor:
Shinpuku-san
Thank You.
To my family, my friends, and everyone who helped me with this volume. Extra thanks to my readers and the music teacher from my alma mater who modeled flute-playing for me.

The pieces are set in place, one by one...

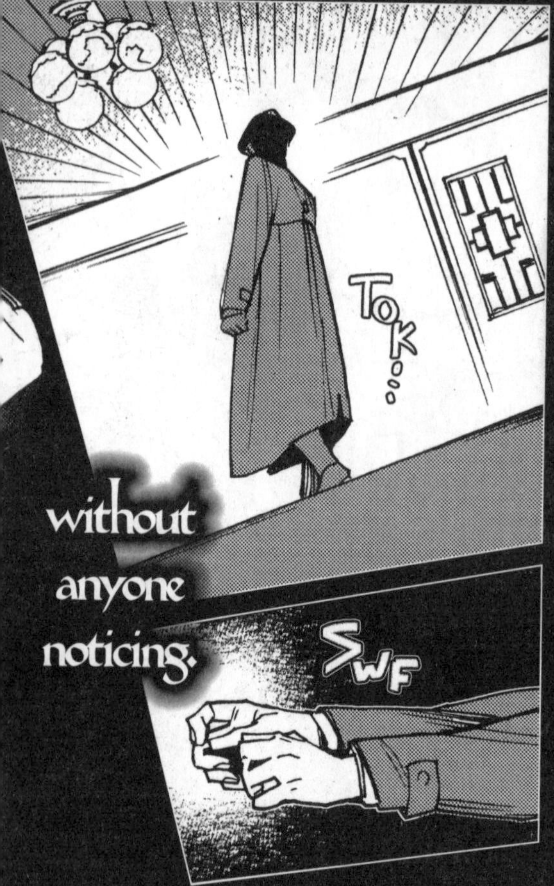
TOK...
SWF

without anyone noticing.

Things had gone back to normal for Jack and Larry in New York, with the usual local troubles keeping them busy. But when a drug that lets ordinary humans slip into the faerie realm starts turning up on the streets, Jack's new broker puts her on the case. Every step of the way, a mysterious, black-hatted man seems to be involved somehow. What does he want Jack and Larry to see...?

VOLUME 4 COMING SOON

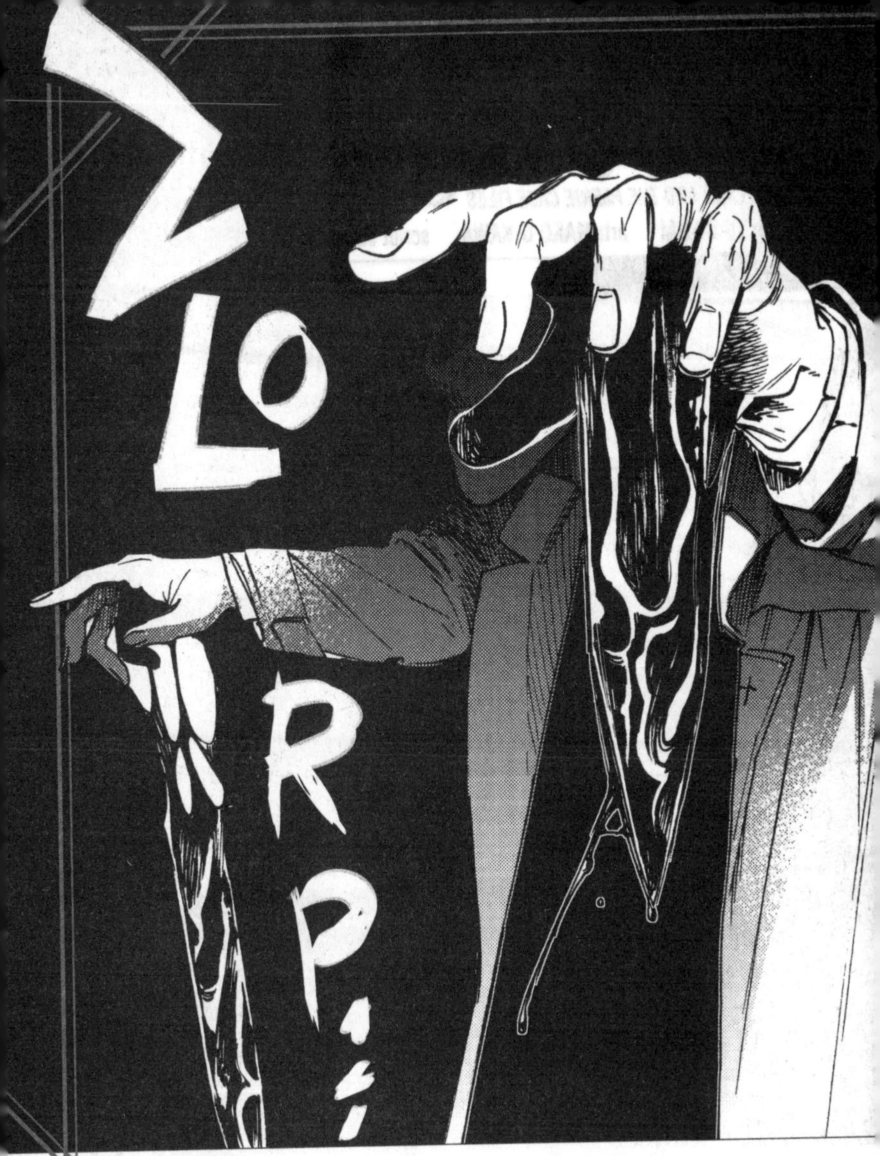
ZLORP!

Delve deeper into *The Ancient Magus' Bride* universe with *Jack Flash*'s fresh take on the relationships between the human and the inhuman!

SEVEN SEAS ENTERTAINMENT PRESENTS

Bride
VOLUME 3

visor: KORE YAMAZAKI

TRANSLATION
Adrienne Beck

ADAPTATION
Ysabet Reinhardt MacFarlane

LETTERING AND RETOUCH
Carolina Hernández Mendoza

COVER DESIGN
(LOGO) Kris Aubin   Nicky Lim

PROOFREADER
Janet Houck

EDITOR
Shanti Whitesides

PREPRESS TECHNICIAN
Rhiannon Rasmussen-Silverstein

PRODUCTION MANAGER
Lissa Pattillo

MANAGING EDITOR
Julie Davis

ASSOCIATE PUBLISHER
Adam Arnold

PUBLISHER
Jason DeAngelis

THE ANCIENT MAGUS' BRIDE PSA.75
JACK "THE FLASH" AND FAIRY INCIDENT VOL.3
©Kore Yamazaki ©Mako Oikawa ©Yu Godai 2020
Originally published in Japan in 2020 by MAG Garden Corporation, TOKYO.
English translation rights arranged through TOHAN CORPORATION, Tokyo.

Seven Seas press and purchase enquiries can be sent to Marketing Manager
Lianne Sentar at press@gomanga.com. Information regarding the distribution
and purchase of digital editions is available from Digital Manager CK Russell
at digital@gomanga.com.

Seven Seas and the Seven Seas logo are trademarks of
Seven Seas Entertainment. All rights reserved.

ISBN: 978-1-64827-273-8

Printed in Canada

First Printing: July 2021

10 9 8 7 6 5 4 3 2 1

FOLLOW US ONLINE: www.sevenseasentertainment.com

READING DIRECTIONS

This book reads from **right to left**, Japanese style.
If this is your first time reading manga, you start
reading from the top right panel on each page and
take it from there. If you get lost, just follow the
numbered diagram here. It may seem backwards at
first, but you'll get the hang of it! Have fun!!

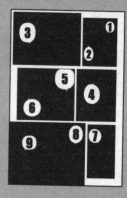